Think Tanks, Governance, and Development in Africa

NEW HORIZONS IN NONPROFIT RESEARCH

Series Editors: Bruce A. Seaman and Dennis R. Young, *Andrew Young School of Policy Studies, Georgia State University, USA*

The purpose of this series is to publish monographs and edited collections of original research that address previously understudied aspects of the social economy and civil society worldwide. The series will include theoretical and empirical research, with an emphasis on nonprofit organizations and social enterprises, including their internal management, governance and leadership challenges, and the changing economic, social, political and public policy environments in which they operate. The series will be interdisciplinary in character, with a particular emphasis on economics, management science and public policy analysis, but also embracing works based in other social science disciplines, including political science, sociology, psychology and anthropology. The series will also take a broad view of the social economy, to include the many service fields and industries in which nonprofit organizations, social purpose cooperatives, social purpose businesses, public–private partnerships and other forms of social purpose enterprise operate. Preference will be given to research with practical implications for management, governance and public policy, and to works which define new agendas for future research.

For a full list of Edward Elgar published titles, including the titles in this series, visit our website at www.e-elgar.com.

Think Tanks, Governance, and Development in Africa

Edited by

Frank L.K. Ohemeng

Assistant Professor, Department of Political Science, Concordia University, Montreal, Quebec, Canada

Joseph R.A. Ayee

Vice President of the Arts Section, Ghana Academy of Arts and Sciences, Ghana

NEW HORIZONS IN NONPROFIT RESEARCH

 Edward Elgar
PUBLISHING

Cheltenham, UK • Northampton, MA, USA

Published by
Edward Elgar Publishing Limited
The Lypiatts
15 Lansdown Road
Cheltenham
Glos GL50 2JA
UK

Edward Elgar Publishing, Inc.
William Pratt House
9 Dewey Court
Northampton
Massachusetts 01060
USA

A catalogue record for this book
is available from the British Library

Library of Congress Control Number: 2024933634

This book is available electronically in the **Elgar**online
Political Science and Public Policy subject collection
http://dx.doi.org/10.4337/9781800379879

ISBN 978 1 80037 986 2 (cased)
ISBN 978 1 80037 987 9 (eBook)

Printed and bound by CPI Group (UK) Ltd, Croydon, CR0 4YY

Contents

Figures

Tables

Contributors

Adigun A.B. Agbaje, Professor, Department of Political Science, University of Ibadan, Nigeria.

E. Remi Aiyede, Professor and Head, Department of Political Science, University of Ibadan, Nigeria.

Joseph R.A. Ayee, Professor, Department of Political Science, University of Ghana and Vice President of the Arts Section, Ghana Academy of Arts and Sciences.

Elias Ayuk, Director of Policy Advisory Services at Chaint Afrique Academy in Accra, Ghana.

Cheikh Oumar Ba, Executive Director, Initiative Prospective Agricole et Rurale (IPAR), Dakar, Senegal.

Emmanuel Botlhale, Professor, Department of Political and Administrative Studies, University of Botswana.

Denis A. Foretia, Co-Chair of the Denis & Lenora Foretia Foundation and Executive Chairman of the Nkafu Policy Institute, Cameroon.

Ibrahima Hathie, Distinguished Fellow, Initiative Prospective Agricole et Rurale (IPAR), Dakar, Senegal.

Eugenia Kayitesi, Executive Director of the Institute of Policy Analysis and Research (IPAR), Rwanda.

Jean Cedric Kouam, Director, Economics Affairs Division, Nkafu Policy Institute, Cameroon.

Bright Nkrumah, Assistant Professor, Department of Environmental Studies, Salisbury University, USA.

Frank L.K. Ohemeng, Assistant Professor, Department of Political Science, Concordia University, Montreal, Quebec, Canada.

Japheth O. Ondiek, Senior Associate-Research at Instream Consulting Group (ICG), Nairobi, Kenya.

Gedion Onyango, Lecturer of Public Policy and Administration in the

Department of Political Science and Public Administration, University of Nairobi, Kenya.

Omosefe Oyekanmi, Post Doctoral Research Fellow, Pan African Women Studies Unit, Institute of Pan African Thought and Conversation, University of Johannesburg, South Africa.

Radhamany Soorymoorthy, Professor, School of Social Sciences, University of KwaZulu-Natal, South Africa.

Francis Tazoacha, Director of Peace and Security Division, Nkafu Policy Institute, Cameroon.

Dhikru Adewale Yagboyaju, Professor, Department of Political Science, University of Ibadan, Nigeria.

1. Introduction and theoretical perspective on think tanks

Joseph R.A. Ayee and Frank L.K. Ohemeng

INTRODUCTION

What think tanks are, what they do, how they do what they do, and the effectiveness of what they do, are difficult and intricate questions with which scholars continue to grapple (Abelson and Rastrick, 2021). Clear and concise answers to these questions are yet to be provided by scholars who are interested not only in these institutions, but also in the general role of civil society organizations (CSOs) in policy development (Abelson and Rastrick, 2021).

This is despite their proliferation across the globe (McGann 2018, 2019; Menegazzi, 2018; Abelson and Rastrick, 2021: Pan, 2021; Jezierska, 2023) since the beginning of the 'third wave' of democratization (Haggard and Kaufman, 2016; Huntington, 1991), the idea of 'good' governance (Asefa and Huang, 2015; Fukuyama, 2013; Grindle, 2004, 2007), and the opening up of the policy and developmental spaces for non-state institutions (Brinkerhoff, 1999). Currently, there are more than 8000 think tanks operating across 169 countries, representing a range of organizations and interests (McGann, 2021).

In this chapter, we attempt to answer the call by Abelson (2021) for scholars to provide some answers that may help interested scholars, students and policy actors to understand these institutions and their influence in the policy-making process by developing a conceptual framework that will guide their future study and what they do. In doing so, we turn to institutional theory to provide a study guide. The *raison d'être* stems from the fact that although think tanks are classified as part of the larger notion of civil society (Stone, 2007), many see them as being quite different from other CSOs in terms of their interest in policy development and their limited role in policy implementation. As a result, think tanks have been considered as a 'civil society elite' (Jezierska, 2020; Landry, 2022; Rojansky and Shapiro, 2021), which therefore distinguishes them from other CSOs (Rojansky and Shapiro, 2021). This is because 'they hold relatively privileged positions, both [*sic*] in terms of wealth (on average bigger budgets and staff), political influence (their very raison d'être), knowledge (educational level of the staff), and social networks' (Jezierska, 2020: 152).

This privileged position emanates from the idea that, unlike other CSOs, think tanks are run by intellectual elites, which according to Bhatnagar (2021) enable them to introduce 'ideas into the policy frames as well as the creation of public opinion towards policy decisions'. Consequently, as organizations are conceived as the repository of policy ideas, the analysis of their role and importance in helping governments to develop better and effective policies to address wicked problems has become paramount and thus calls for a stronger understanding of these institutions (Abelson and Rastrick, 2021; Shaw et al., 2015). It is institutional differences that provide the platform for us to use institutional theory to analyse them.

Despite this, the best method by which to research these institutions – which seem to have much clout in public policy development across the globe – continues to elude scholars, even as think tanks as policy influencers are being increasingly studied as they continue to spread across the globe. Medvetz (2008) described think tanks as an emerging field, and he appears to be correct when one looks at the number of books, journals, newspapers and other publications that have addressed them in recent times (Pautz, 2020; Salas-Porras and Murray, 2017). Another issue affecting the discussion of think tanks is what Stone (2007: 259) describes as their 'fuzzy boundaries', which make a definition very difficult to arrive at, despite the ubiquitous nature of the concept in the political lexicon and its entrenchment in scholarly discussions of public policy, as well as in the 'policy wonk' of journalists, lobbyists and spin-doctors. How, then, can these institutions be studied to bring clarity to the academic literature?

We attempt to answer this question by focusing on institutional theory. Our choice of this theoretical position stems from the fact that the theory is broad enough to include institutions and the norms that guide them. Furthermore, as highlighted by Arshed (2017: 74), 'institutional theory provides a detailed theoretical understanding of the process, the environment, and the actors' in which these institutions operate. As noted by Keohane and Martin (1995: 42), institutions can provide information, reduce transaction costs, make commitments more credible, establish focal points for coordination, and in general facilitate the operation of reciprocity. By seeking to specify the conditions under which institutions can have an impact and cooperation can occur, institutionalist theory shows under what conditions realist propositions are valid. In addition, studying think tanks from the institutional perspective is essential in view of their role in the policy-making process. As noted by Hassel and Wegrich (2022: 253), 'if you want to solve a policy problem that requires a change in behaviour, it might not be enough to simply pick the right policy instrument. When addressing wicked problems, such as poverty, corruption, or economic development, policies need the support of the broader institutional context to be effective'. This institutional context includes organizations such as government and all its agencies, the private for-profit firms, and CSOs including think tanks, which must be understood in terms of their roles, ideas and the influence they may have over the policy-making process.

Thus, institutional theory helps to examine and explain these institutions. In addition, we agree with Arshed (2017: 74–75) that 'institutional theory allows us to understand how enterprise policy ideas originate in think tanks whereby institutionalisation (process), environment (political) and actors (relationships) are of importance', which seems to have been neglected in the quest to examine and understand these institutions. In addition, institutional theory allows for the understanding of a wide range of organizational and managerial problems, such as the maintenance of inefficient practices, and failures to introduce innovative practices and accomplish reforms (Aksom and Vakulenko, 2023: 2).

As already noted, in the context of developing countries, and particularly in Africa, institutional theory has the advantage of examining not only the process, but also the political relationships identified by Arshed (2017) within the environment they operate, and their continuous reliance on external largesse, especially from the Western world, and how this reliance continues to influence policy positions and analysis within the broader socio-economic and political environments. At the same time, the theory may help us to explain how think tanks, as policy institutions, help in designing and influencing public policy (Peters, 2020, 2022).

Against this backdrop, the chapter is organized as follows. First, there is a review of institutional theory and a discussion of how it can be applied to the study of think tanks, followed by an examination of how these institutions influence public policy at both national and regional levels. Thereafter, the effectiveness and ineffectiveness of these institutions are assessed in the policy-making process. The chapters of this book are then reviewed, followed by the conclusion, with future directions on these institutions in the policy-making process.

STUDYING THINK TANKS: INSTITUTIONAL THEORY PERSPECTIVE

One of the oldest theories used to explain how organizations and individuals behave in society is the institutional theory (Commons, 1934; Lawrence et al., 2011; Meyer, 2017; Hadler, 2015). As a result, scholarly discussion on the subject abounds. We do not systematically review this abundant literature here, but an important caveat is that over the years there has been a noteworthy advancement in examining and explaining institutions, which has led to significant refinements and the continuous growth of the concept, as it continues to be applied in different fields of study (Glynn and D'Aunno, 2022; Heugens and Lander, 2009). It is necessary to discuss institutions before proceeding to explain what institutional theory is about.

Various definitions abound in the literature, due to its ubiquitous nature (Lawrence et al. 2011). However, a common thread in all these is behaviour, which is shaped by norms and values, whether at the organizational or individual level (Meyer, 2017; Spohr, 2016; Voss, 2015). Thus, institutions can be seen at the organizational and individual levels (Clemens and Cook, 1999), and they can be formal or informal (Chavance, 2008). An explanation of institutions is instructive for the sake of clarity.

Earlier definitions of institutions focused on organizations. Commons (1934: 69), one of the earliest scholars to discuss the institution, perceived it as 'analogous to a building, a sort of framework of laws and regulations, within which individuals act like inmates. Sometimes it seems to mean the "behavior" of the inmates themselves'. Consequently, he defines an institution as 'collective action in restraint, liberation, and expansion of individual action' (Commons, 1934: 73). This definition establishes a relationship between the collective and the individual, which according to Chavance (2012: 30), 'is the foundation of growing concerns and their rules'.

Recent definitions, however, have focused on the regulation of social norms in the society, that is, at both the individual and organizational levels. For example, Jepperson (1991: 46), who accepts this view, defines institutions as regulated entities and 'socially constructed systems of roles or programs that produce routines'. On the other hand, the concept can be used in a dual way (Voss, 2015). First, it denotes rules, constraints or norms of human interaction. Second, it describes the resulting stable patterns of interaction. In Voss's view, 'institution' can be conceived to be the set of constraints or rules that determine the opportunities, beliefs and incentives of the relevant actors in each situation; and interactions within these rules generate equilibria, which may be stable over time if the situation is recurrent. Immergut (2011) refers to this as the degree of formalization of social behaviour, ranging from casual habits to formal arrangements, to the extent of the collective binding, ranging from traditions and folkways to sanctioned laws, and to the way they are sanctioned, ranging from being self-reinforced to coercion by other entities.

Since the interest of the authors is in organization, the focus is on institutional theory of organization (DiMaggio and Powell, 1991; Nadler, 2015), or what has been described as neo-institutionalism (Meyer, 2017). Neo-institutionalism considers institutions more broadly than the earlier scholars had perceived them, and thus rejects the rational actor model of institutions (DiMaggio and Powell, 1991; Peters, 2016). As a result, neo-institutionalists define the concept more broadly. From their perspective, institutions include those beliefs, rules, roles and symbolic elements which can affect organizational forms independently of resource flows and technical requirements (Scott, 1991: 165). In terms of organizations, an institution is defined as 'a rule-like, social fact quality of an organized pattern of action (exterior), and embedding in formal structures, such as formal aspects of organizations that are not tied to particular actors or situations (nonpersonal/objective)' (Zucker, 1987: 444). This is what some scholars have described as institutional work (Lawrence et al., 2009), which is 'the purposive action of individuals and organizations aimed at creating, maintaining and disrupting institutions' (Lawrence and Suddaby, 2006: 215). For these scholars, therefore, an institution can be defined as 'those (more or less) enduring elements of social life that affect the behavior and beliefs of individuals and collective actors by providing templates for action, cognition, and emotion nonconformity with which is associated with some kind of costs' (Lawrence et al., 2011: 53).

In his work, Scott (2014) is of the opinion that institutions, which consist of beliefs, rules, roles and symbolic elements, as defined by scholars, can be of different natures, depending on the environment in which such behaviours are being observed. This institutional environment consists of 'normative and regulatory pressures exerted on organizations by the state or society and the professions' (Swaminathan and Wade, 2016: 2). Consequently, Scott (2014) identifies three key institutional pillars in understanding how institutions work in organizations: these are the regulative, normative and cultural-cognitive. The regulative institution focuses on how institutions regulate and constrain behaviours. Such regulation is required or enforced by law and can be formal or informal within the prevailing environment. In normative institution, emphasis is placed on 'normative rules that introduce a prescriptive, evaluative, and obligatory dimension in social life' (Scott, 2014: 64). In this perspective, the emphasis is on values, routines and symbols that define the institutions. Peters (2016) has pointed out that values could be procedural or substantive, and can be transferred to the individuals who have become members of the institutions, and this enables the individuals to follow the guidelines and the values they have learned, and to act accordingly. Naturally, normative institutions are those shared beliefs of what is appropriate or not in each environment. Finally, an institution can be cultural-cognitive, which is deemed as the shared conceptions that constitute the nature of social reality and create the frames through which meaning is made (Peters, 2016: 67). This is what many consider as sociological institution. In cultural-cognitive institutions, the emphasis is on the existence of and the interaction between actors. In such an interaction, symbols (words, signs, gestures) shape the meaning that is attributed to objects and activities. The cognitive structures are constituted by the internalized understanding of each actor, based on the interpretation of their own social reality (Carvalho et al., 2017).

In all, the units of analysis of institutional theory as noted by Carvalho et al. (2017) are organizational fields and populations, with its basic assumptions being that reality is socially constructed, organizations are the concretization/ materialization of institutions, and organizations have similar structures and practices because they seek legitimacy. Indeed, it is within these basic assumptions that think tanks are situated, not only in developing countries but in the developed world as well, especially in the development of policies to address societal problems, the materials they produce to influence policy change, and above all, their legitimatization and what they do.

THINK TANKS: A SHORT REVIEW OF THE LITERATURE

As already noted, the world has seen a rise in think tanks, which will continue despite the challenges that these institutions face (McGann, 2021). Practically, their continued rise can be attributed to the recent emphasis on 'good' public governance, with the idea of bringing ownership of public service in the form of citizen participation to the process of policy development and implementation, rather than the idea of 'steering' and not 'rowing', as championed by neoliberals with the emergence of the political right since the late 1970s (Denhardt and Denhardt, 2000).

What, then, is a think tank? As noted throughout this book and in many other published works, defining the concept has become quite problematic (Abraham, 2019; McGann, 2019; Ohemeng, forthcoming). Part of this problem, as discussed earlier, stems from the difficulty in distinguishing these institutions from other CSOs. Another issue is the differentiation between publicly and privately funded think tanks, the latter being referred to as independent think tanks (Stone, 2015). Also, as discussed by Wellstead and Howlett (2022: 224–225):

> [a]lthough the role of these institutions in policymaking has been studied for decades, the emergence of organisations such as advocacy groups, policy innovation labs, policy institutes, national centres of excellence, policy and behavioural insight labs and the changing activities of think tanks themselves have led to discontent with the common taxonomies of such policy organisations used in the field. These concerns have to do with a nomenclature for policy research organisations which hides more than they reveal about the differences between types, and which leads to some confusion about, for example, whether policy labs are think tanks or vice versa.

It is this nomenclature for policy research organizations that forces us to define what think tanks are. How, then, are think tanks defined? One of the earliest works on think tanks is that of Dror (1980: 141). He defined think tanks as 'an island of excellence applying full-time interdisciplinary scientific thinking to the in-depth improvement of policymaking, or as a bridge between power and knowledge'. While this definition describes research as the fundamental work of these institutions, it ignores the fact that many of them are doing more than just producing scientific knowledge. In short, the scope of activities undertaken by these institutions has expanded to include policy advocacy and policy implementation, in addition to capacity-building initiatives such as the training of public officials and the empowering of local indigenes in many areas of development. Furthermore, as noted by Stone (1996), independent think tanks are not interdisciplinary units of the type that are found in universities, although they have been referred to as 'universities without students'. Thus, while we acknowledge that the main purpose of independent research institutions is policy research and analysis, they are not in any way connected to the vagaries of university life (Ohemeng, 2005).

On the other hand, Abelson and Brooks (2017) define them as 'organizations that carry out research and analysis of policy issues, whose primary function is to influence the ways those issues are thought about, and that produce policy advice and recommendations'. Here, we see the actual intent of think tanks, although this definition is more restricted to research. According to Stone (2015), they are 'policy research centers engaged in policy analysis and advocacy that are directed toward government but also undertaken for international organizations, the business and nonprofit sectors'. This definition is more expansive, as it includes other activities such as advocacy by these institutions.

Think tanks are institutions that undertake research on policy issues with the aim of influencing policy changes while at the same time engaging in advocacy work at both national and local levels. Their advocacy work has seen many forming networks as a collective voice to bring about policy changes, especially in developing countries.

Think tanks exhibit certain characteristics which differentiate them from other CSOs. In her study of think tanks, Ladi (2011) identified four common characteristics. First is the policy focus. The objective of these organizations, first and foremost, is to bring knowledge and policy-making together by informing and, if possible, influencing the policy process that generates policy advice on domestic and international issues, enabling policy-makers to make informed decisions, and bridging the gap between the government and the public at large. To Ladi, therefore, think tanks conduct and recycle research that aims to solve policy problems, not solely to advance the theoretical debate.

The second characteristic is public purpose, which refers to the reason for the existence of think tanks. Most think tanks claim that they conduct research to inform the public and the government on how to improve public policy. Their rhetoric often claims that their work is for the common good and to educate the public (Ladi, 2011). In fact, it is this common good that has made a number of them adopt advocacy as an instrument to influence public policy. According to James (1993: 492, 505), think tanks are 'idea brokers' and formally independent bodies that are 'engaged in multidisciplinary research intended to influence public policy'. Similarly, they are referred to as the 'progenitors of ideas and agenda setting' (Dorey, 2005: 19). This public purpose has enabled some of these organizations to extend their reach beyond the political arena. In the words of Stone (2015: 297):

> Outside the political sphere and state sector, think tanks have cultivated other audiences. Students and academics in colleges and universities regularly use think tank publications. Foundation officials, business executives, bureaucrats from various international organizations, university researchers, journalists, and, for want of a better term, the 'educated public' are often engaged by think tank pursuits ... Indeed, think tanks have become more accessible to a wider range of the public via blogs, YouTube, and other media ... As they do so, think tanks provide an organizational link and communication bridge between their different audiences. They connect disparate groups by providing a forum for the exchange of views, by translating academic or scientific research into policy-relevant 'sound bites,' and by spreading policy lessons internationally.

Third, the expertise and professionalism of their research staff are the key intellectual resources of think tanks, and a way of legitimizing their findings (Ladi, 2011). According to Pautz (2020), a characteristic of such organizations is the need to be perceived or portrayed as 'experts' and 'permanent persuaders', to provide expert opinions on policy matters to influence others. Drawing on this expertise and professionalism, they can influence policy development, especially at the agenda-setting stage. According to Rich (2005: 108):

> expertise is understood to play active ... roles in each stage of the policy process. During agenda setting, expertise is useful as a warning to policymakers of impending problems and as guidance to decision-makers on how to revise the policy. Expertise, at this point, can alter people to the extent [that] a given situation affects their interests or values.

The fourth characteristic, according to Ladi (2011), is that the key activities of think tanks are usually research analysis and advice, which come in the form of publications, conferences, seminars and workshops. As noted by Peetz, a common, but not universal, characteristic of permanent persuaders is that they produce 'reports: documents that purport to have investigated an issue, often using quantitative methods, and that reach some conclusion with implicit or explicit policy implications' (2017: 246). The essence of undertaking research is that it 'can have the purpose of informing late agenda-setting moments when interest among policymakers is building and ideas are being translated into legislative language ... In this form, studies provide general insight on how social, political, or economic problems might be addressed by policymakers' (Rich, 2005: 153). In addition, it has been noted that 'for researchers interested in policy impact, "do nothing" is not an option'; hence, the goal of the research is to contribute to policy outcomes (Stone et al., 2001). The research of these organizations focuses on agenda-setting, position papers, agenda-reinforcing reports and policy development programmes (Wells, 2012). Thus, through research, these organizations generate ideas or information for the purpose of persuading others of a particular view of the world or a particular policy approach (Pautz, 2012).

As a contribution to the debate, the ideological orientation of some think tanks has led to their classification into two broad types: (1) traditional, or politically neutral; and (2) advocacy, with a clear political or ideological orientation (Denham and Garnett, 1996, 1999). The traditional or politically neutral think tanks provide objective information and evidence on issues, which they hope will influence the ideas of policy-makers, irrespective of which political party is in government or which overarching set of ideas is prevalent at any given time (Dorey, 2005). On the other hand, the advocacy with a clear political orientation is to a large extent identified with a particular ideology, a specific political party, or even a particular strand within that party. These think tanks seek to influence policy-makers based on a particular ideological orientation or political perspective (Denham and Garnett, 2004; Dorey, 2005).

In Africa, think tanks are said to have contributed to the process of peace-building despite structural challenges such as inadequate funding, limited collaboration with the African Union (AU) and regional economic communities (RECs) and the shrinking policy space given to these institutions (Kinkoh and Tozoacha, 2023). This has been possible through their programmes and mechanisms such as conducting policy-relevant research, understanding the root causes of conflict, analysing conflict, mapping out solutions and making policy recommendations to policy-makers and the public on a broad range of issues around peace, security, governance and development (Kinkoh and Tazoacha, 2023). In fact, it has been pointed out that without the contribution of the right-functioning think tanks it may be difficult to attain the vision of the AU's Agenda 2063 for 'an integrated, prosperous and peaceful Africa driven by its own citizens and representing a dynamic force in the global arena'. This positive assessment seems to have been recognized by the AU in February 2023 when it officially launched the African Network of Think Tanks for Peace (NeTT4Peace) with the objective of driving the partnership between the African research community and the AU Department of Political Affairs Peace and Security (DPAPS) on governance, peace and security.

THE THINK TANKS AND INFLUENCE ON PUBLIC POLICY DEVELOPMENT[1]

One of the many problems affecting the study of think tanks is whether they really influence public policy, and how to measure this influence (Lindquist, 2021; Weidenbaum, 2010). This is because it is difficult to gauge influence in political science, due to the 'problem of identifying independent variables or determining the degree to which a particular variable has shaped a political event or policy outcome', in addition to some think tanks 'claiming credit for certain policies in order to enhance their credibility and attract new clients and funding' (Dorey, 2005: 19).

Yet, we know that an essential focus of think tanks is to provide reliable information to the policy-maker and attempt to influence or shape public policies. Indeed, as noted by McGann (2015):

> [p]olicymakers still require reliable, accessible, and useful information on the mechanics of current policies and on the costs and consequences of possible alternatives. These needs have long been central to government decision-making, but now, more than ever, the forces of globalization require analytical insight to bridge the gap between research and actually implementing policy solutions.

Yet, how do these institutions, seen as the repository of ideas, influence such policy-makers in the policy-making process, and how can one measure such influence? What kind of behaviour(s) do these institutions exhibit to enable them to influence public policies? In fact, these are old-age questions, which we cannot fully address here. This is because in an open environment or system, policy inputs may come from different sources including the political exigencies of the day, and not necessarily a carefully planned policy and different policy actors (Cairney, 2019; Quade, 1969; Stewart and Ayres, 2000; Heikkila and Cairney, 2018).

Scholars of public policy have indicated that such exigencies can be focusing events that immediately push a policy issue onto the government agenda (Birkland, 1998; Kingdon, 2011). In such a situation, policy-makers may not have the time and the resources to consult think tanks, and for such institutions to carefully develop policy proposals for the government to enact. Thus, whatever influence they may have in the policy-making process may happen in normal times, and this may also depend on the norms, values, and so on, of the think tanks involved in the process at a particular time.

How, then, can think tanks influence public policy? We first need to explain what 'influence' and 'policy influence' mean. The Merriam-Webster dictionary defines influence as both a noun and a verb. As a noun, it indicates the power or capacity of causing an effect in indirect or intangible ways; the act or power of producing an effect without apparent exertion of force or direct exercise of command; corrupt interference with authority for personal gain; one that exerts influence; an emanation of spiritual or moral force; an ethereal fluid held to flow from the stars and to affect the actions of humans; and an emanation of occult power held to derive from stars. As a verb, it denotes the ability to affect or alter by indirect or intangible means, or to influence the condition or development of something, such as productivity.

Both noun and verb definitions are applied in public policy discussions. From this perspective policy influence can be seen as involving the 'purposeful efforts of institutions and actors, by whatever means or mechanisms, to steer policy and behaviour' (Bernstein and Cashore, 2012: 586). Thus, policy influence stems from efforts steered by values, norms and behaviour to effect policy change. As noted by Diprose et al. (2019), policy influence aims to influence the beliefs or behaviour of authoritative policy-makers, whether through processes of ideational change, or shifts in the power or coalition structure of competing interest groups (ibid.: 225). Thus, policy influence can be conceived as the ability of an actor to get things done the way they want them done. In this circumstance, ideas and how to promote them are together fundamental and important means to change the contours of a policy (Ohemeng, 2015).

Public policy scholars believe that influence significantly shapes policy; but what do they mean by this? Its status as an essential prerequisite to knowing policy outcomes notwithstanding, it is difficult to define (Stone et al., 2001). According to Abelson (2010: 11), 'although the concept of influence is ambiguous and difficult to grasp, it is central to any discussion about politics and policymaking. It is also central to any discussion about think tanks and their efforts to become entrenched in the policymaking process'. Rich (2005: 153) defines influence as 'success by experts in making their work known among a set of policymakers so that it informs their thinking on or public articulation of policy-relevant information'. This definition moves beyond the more common one already mentioned, that focuses on implementation. As Rich (2005: 153) argues, 'whether this influence on individual policymakers carries over to affect final policy outcome is of interest'. We define policy influence as the ability to initiate or contribute ideas that affect a particular policy outcome or course of action being undertaken by the government. In this case, the approach or degree of influence may differ according to the nature of the policy.

To influence public policy, individuals and institutions must take a number of steps. These steps are geared towards regulating behaviours, especially that of policy-makers, in the policy-making process. Bernstein and Cashore (2012) have developed four steps which influence policy development at the international level, which can be adapted. The first step involves international rules. In the area of globalization, given the fact that the policy environment is open, international issues affect local policy-making. As noted by Bernstein and Cashore (2012: 589) 'the "international rules" pathway highlights the influence of issue-specific treaties and the policy prescriptions of powerful international organizations (e.g., the World Bank), whether perceived as resting on consent (what the diffusion literature refers to as "harmonization") or on coercion'. Indeed, international norms and rules impact upon how think tanks operate and attempt to influence policies that, although domestic, may have implications worldwide. For example, climate change policy may be a domestic issue, but has international consequences.

The second step may be considered as norms and discourse, which, 'whether embodied in institutions or constituted by broader socio-economic and political contexts, can define and regulate appropriate domestic behaviour' (Bernstein and Cashore, 2012: 591). In this scenario, the issue is about appropriateness, or what is acceptable behaviour in the environment. The third is step is the market, which:

> encompasses processes or tactics that attempt to manipulate, work with or leverage markets to create domestic policy change. It includes direct action such as boycott campaigns that target foreign export markets to put pressure on exporters, indirect action such as certification systems that attempt to regulate markets or otherwise embed them in social and environmental values or goals. (Bernstein and Cashore, 2012: 593)

Finally, there is direct access to domestic policy-making processes. In this perspective, influence 'can occur through direct funding, education, training, assistance and capacity-building, and possibly even through attempts at co-governance via partnerships between domestic and international public and private actors and authorities' (Bernstein and Cashore, 2012: 593).

In analysing the influence of think tanks on policies, one may have to consider which line of influence they may use. In addition, how these four steps affect these institutions and how they behave becomes important. In all, it is essential to examine in a more holistic manner how these institutions have affected their quest to change policies, as well as being able to identify independent variables, or determine the degree to which a particular variable has shaped a political event or policy outcome.

The influence any institutions have on policy outcomes or policy decision-making processes varies with the expertise, knowledge and technical proficiency available to the institutions, as well as their level of access to the decision-makers responsible for determining policy outcomes (Lowndes, 1996). For this reason, think tanks adopt a number of methods to achieve their objectives. These methods may differ according to the policy area and the size of the institution (Stone, 2007). The most common method is research. It is said that 'research can have the purpose of informing late agenda-setting moments when interest among policymakers is building and ideas are being translated into legislative language ... In this form, studies provide general insight on how social, political, or economic problems might be addressed by policymakers' (Rich, 2005: 153). The essence of research is that 'for researchers interested in policy impact, "do nothing" is not an option'; hence, the goal of research is to contribute to policy outcomes (Stone et al., 2001).

Peter Wells (2012) has identified four major types of research undertaken by think tanks: these are agenda-setting research, position papers, agenda-reinforcing reports and policy development programmes. Agenda-setting research deals with keynote reports, which are normally authored by senior figures in these institutions, and are launched as high-profile national events, with senior politicians invited as speakers. Position papers, on the other hand, seek to inform and influence debates, and are intended to send policy signals and give directions respecting forthcoming policy strategies of the government. Agenda-reinforcing research refers to sustaining and reinforcing the profile of either a government or a policy position on a particular issue; while policy development programmes may focus on research programmes around particular aspects of national development.

Other ways in which institutions can influence policy outcomes are through publicity campaigns and lobbying the government to make decisions consistent with their objectives. Such a *modus operandi* means that the behaviour and strategy of institutions are very similar to those of pressure groups (James, 1993). They also lobby governments, either in favour of or against policies they deem relevant to their interest or position, especially with ideologically inclined or issue-oriented think tanks.

Another important means by which think tanks can influence and change public outcomes is through the 'capturing of policy actors or elites in the society' (Schlesinger, 2009). Policy elites not only help to shape policy and institutional outcomes, but they also demonstrate how the options available to them are constrained by contextual factors. For such institutions to be heard in that quest, they need a strong hold on such elites, through either their research or their actors' personal relationships and networks. Policy elite capture is most likely to occur where close, even symbiotic, relationships have developed among bureaucratic actors, elected officials and regulated interests, and through the provision of vivid, compelling encounters and experiences that speak to their current policy discussion (Hart and Vromen, 2008: 138; Singleton, 2000: 7). Using their discursive leverage in the relevant policy subsystems, particularly (but not exclusively) among key policy-makers and stakeholder elites, for example, think tanks may produce frames and narratives capable of pervading the elite rhetoric and policy proposals that circulate in the policy subsystem (Hart and Vromen, 2008: 138). According to Abelson (2010: 26), 'the relationships and contacts that develop between think tanks and policymakers can often explain why some think tanks are able to enjoy considerable access to various stages of the policymaking process'.

Think tanks also use the media, both electronic and print, simply to acquire and maintain visibility, as well as to achieve their objectives (Abelson, 1992; Rich and Weaver, 2000), because 'the news media have direct contact with and influence upon elites' (Cook, 1998: 10). To this end, 'many think tanks have recognized this influence and have made securing media visibility a central feature of their missions' (Rich and Weaver, 2000: 100). Cummings (2005: 176) notes that:

> think tanks are more likely to influence the climate of opinion through the popular media than through their own publications ... The problem is that journalists tend to pick up on sound bites and eye-catching statistics rather than more substantial ideas and are unlikely to ask think tank researchers to write essays or to take part in television discussions lasting more than a minute or two.

Schlesinger (2009: 5) is of the view that 'because think tanks operate within a highly structured market place for ideas, marketing and promotion are central to their quest for influence over government. Consequently, their ability to achieve resonance within the media is of central importance; they are a major resource for journalists.'

In a nutshell, these four major types of research undertaken by think tanks have sought to reinforce the view that the influence of think tanks is 'greater in helping to shape the overall intellectual framework than indirectly and explicitly influencing specific policies' (Dorey, 2005: 22). Notwithstanding the strategies used by think tanks to influence public policies, their actual influence, as we have already pointed out, is methodologically difficult, largely because one does not know whether policy-makers would have adopted the relevant policies anyway, irrespective of the arguments of, or even the very existence of, certain policy think tanks (Dorey, 2005).

MEASURING THE EFFECTIVENESS OF THINK TANKS IN THE POLICY-MAKING PROCESS

Another perspective in examining think tanks in the policy-making process is their effectiveness, or lack of it. Unfortunately, this is one issue that the vast literature about them is silent on. Scholarly attention is more on the influence than on how effective these organizations are in the pursuit of their goals (Pautz, 2020). Understanding their effectiveness may help scholars to also comprehend the kind of challenges they face in the quest to influence policy.

Since we are interested in think tanks, which are organizations in the traditional sense, our focus is on organizational effectiveness. So, what is organizational effectiveness? Organizational effectiveness has become a fashionable idea both in academia and in society. Despite this, there is no consensus on what the concept means (Georgopoulos and Tannenbaum, 1957; Oghojafor et al., 2012). It has been said that a critical point to understand in defining effectiveness is that it is always situational. Hence, the concept's definition varies with different organizational environments, types and goals (Cohen, 1993: 48).

In general, organizational effectiveness is ordinarily used to refer to goal attainment (Georgopoulos and Tannenbaum, 1957); this is how many scholars see the concept. Consequently, Georgopoulos and Tannenbaum (1957: 534) are of the view that effectiveness as a concept is a functional rather than a structural idea. They therefore define the concept as 'the extent to which an organization as a social system, given certain resources and means, fulfils its objectives without incapacitating its means and resources and without placing undue strain upon its members' (Georgopoulos and Tannenbaum, 1957: 536–537). According to these authors, the conception of effectiveness subsumes the following general criteria: (1) organizational productivity; (2) organizational flexibility in the form of successful adjustment to internal organizational changes, and successful adaptation to externally induced change; and (3) absence of intra-organizational strain, or tension, and of conflict between organizational subgroups. In a nutshell, an organization that meets these criteria may be considered to be effective. Goal achievement is therefore the main criterion to measure an organization's effectiveness. A caveat, though, is defining organizational effectiveness based on industrial productivity, where it is easy to measure effectiveness.

If achieving organizational goals is the focus of organizational effectiveness, then how should the effectiveness of think tanks be measured? The literature is silent on this, but there are a series of questions that may help researchers in this direction. Since the main goal of think tanks is to influence public policy, should their effectiveness be measured based on how they interact with policy-makers? Should they be measured based on how well they are organized?

Chafuen (2013) has identified 15 ways to measure think tank policy outcomes. These include media appearances in major news outlets, TV, radio or newspapers; estimated advertising value of media appearances; text or language that was present in a research document by the think tank being used in bills and laws in the legislature; number of congressional testimonies; improvements in major indices, such as the economic freedom indices produced by the Fraser Institute and the Heritage Foundation, the Doing Business Index prepared by the World Bank and IFC, the Global Competitiveness Index, and others; economic impact generated through a public policy proposal made by an institute; increase in the number of donors and contributions; and other improvements in internal processes. Think tanks can be seen as a product in themselves; stopping a spending project in the legislature or a tax increase, or improving the cost-efficiency of a government; generating wasteful spending by the other side; number, quality and acceptance rate of applicants to attend programmes or to work for the institute; impact in social media; YouTube views and other certifiable measurements; judicial victories; number of think tank publications adopted in university and college courses; and scholarly citations of papers and books written by think tank researchers. Unfortunately, these are too vague to be used as a tool for measuring the effectiveness of think tanks and policy outcomes.

WHAT IS IN THIS BOOK?

This book contains 11 chapters, comprising this introduction and theoretical perspective on think tanks, a conclusion, a survey chapter on Africa, and eight country case study chapters covering Botswana, Cameroon, Ghana, Kenya, Nigeria, Rwanda, Senegal and South Africa. Even though these countries may not be considered representative of the 54 countries in Africa, the authors consider them as countries which have seen both gains and deficits in the operations of think tanks, and are therefore worthy of study. They have their unique history and circumstances, as well as the opportunities and challenges that they encountered in their politics, democratic governance experiments and economic reforms. In addition, the contribution of think tanks to politics, democratic governance and economic reform in these countries has not been adequately covered in the literature. Their selection was also based on the availability of researchers who were able to meet the deadlines in the midst of COVID-19, which some of the original contributors could not do.

Taken together, the chapters address the following questions:

1. What accounts for the proliferation of thinks tanks in sub-Saharan Africa since the 1990s, and what institutional forms do they take?
2. How and why do thinks tanks influence governance, policy formulation and implementation?
3. How are think tanks funded, and what are the implications for their operations?
4. What has been the contribution of think tanks, if any, to politics and the development process?
5. What challenges do think tanks face, and how have they been addressed?
6. What lessons can be learned from think tanks, and what are the implications for the literature on politics, public policy and administration, and civil society?

The chapters show special sensitivity to the concepts of institutionalism and think tanks, and how they have been able to expand the frontiers of knowledge in the case study countries. Moreover, they employ a combination of theoretical and empirical data to make a case for think tanks and how their activities can be improved despite their challenges.

The chapters have largely depended on secondary, documentary and internet sources, because of the volume of literature on think tanks. A few chapters, however, such as those on Botswana and Cameroon, combine both primary (fieldwork) and secondary sources. The historical-analytical approach was used to ensure some uniformity in the issues covered in the chapters from different countries, in addition to referring back to history to be able to give a good background and sometimes a more nuanced understanding of the logic behind the issues. Furthermore, the historical-analytical facilitates the tracking of the improvement of the think tanks over time, and enables future studies of these institutions as other scholars build on these chapters. The special focus on developments in the last decade of the Fourth Republic makes an original and significant contribution to the existing literature. In addition, some of the chapters have combined both theoretical and empirical material for more clarity and understanding. In a nutshell, the methodology aims to extend the literature empirically, analytically and ideationally. The analytical framework employed by the chapters is a review of the literature on think tanks, their evolution, categorization, the environment in which they operated, progress made, and challenges and how they were or could be addressed.

In Chapter 2 on the survey of think tanks in Africa, Aiyede and Agbaje provide a panoramic view of think tanks and their current state through a discussion of their rise, spread and contributions to policy-making, governance and development, as well as challenges and how they can be addressed. In this connection, the chapter addressed four key questions, namely: (1) What is the nature of the universe of think tanks in Africa today? (2) What role are they playing in governance and development in Africa? (3) What is their role in the effort to speak truth to power and infuse the policy process with evidence? (4) What are the challenges of African think tanks?

Botlhale, in Chapter 3 on Botswana, drawing on qualitative data collected through questionnaires and documentary analysis, examines the public policy space role of the Botswana Institute for Development Policy Analysis (BIDPA), which was established by the Government of Botswana as an independent trust, and started operation as a non-governmental policy research institute or think tank in 1995. Botlhale found that there is a legal institutional architecture that enables BIDPA to play in the public policy space in the country. This facilitated its capacity to largely execute its mandate according to its deed of trust, particularly 'to promote and conduct research, analysis and publication on development policy issues'. This notwithstanding, it faced key challenges such as skills capacity deficits; especially, at senior levels, a polit-icized public policy-making space; and a gap between research and policy.

In contrast to the Botswana chapter which focused on a single think tank, Chapter 4 by Kouam, Tazoacha and Foretia examines the evolution, catego-rization, influence and challenges of the several think tanks in Cameroon. The authors found that think tanks have very little influence on the prevailing socio-political and economic environment, largely due to the economic con-ditions in which they were created and which are evolving, and the political climate, which is not conducive to their development. Think tanks lack the capacity to make appropriate recommendations to decision-makers on current and obvious issues that divide the country (the socio-political crisis in the Anglophone regions of the country, insecurity in the Far North and East regions, poor governance, unemployment, public debt, and so on) and limited funding, a large chunk of it coming from abroad.

Ohemeng and Ayee discuss think tanks in Ghana in Chapter 5. They discuss the link between governance and development, and how think tanks have influenced these since the return to constitutional governance in the country in 1993 that created the policy space to enable them to function effectively for citizens' participation in policy formulation and implementation. The three questions addressed are: (1) How have think tanks influenced governance and development, and how do they continue to do so, in Ghana? (2) What are the major challenges they face in their quest to achieve their objectives? (3) How can these challenges be addressed?

In Chapter 6 on Kenya by Ondiek and Onyango, an effort is made to use institutional theory to understand the role of think tanks as social actors, and how they influence governance and policy visibility aspects, mainly policy communications, research, stakeholder engagements and training. The authors selected four think tanks which they consider 'outstanding', namely the Kenya Medical Research Institute (KEMRI) and Kenya Institute of Public Policy Research and Analysis (KIPPRA), which are government think tanks, and Amref Health Africa and Africa Population and Health Research Center (APHRC), which are non-governmental humanitarian and research organiza-tions, to explore their roles during the COVID-19 pandemic, the challenges, and remedies used to manoeuvre the public policy and research spaces.

Chapter 7 by Yagboyaju and Oyekanmi analyses the performance of Nigeria's leading think tanks, with a focus on their agenda-setting function. The authors show the interrelatedness between governance, development and think tanks and the pre-conditions for their effectiveness. Using public category think tanks such as the Nigerian Institute of Social and Economic Research (NISER), Nigerian Institute of International Affairs (NIIA) and National Institute for Policy and Strategic Studies (NIPSS), and the private category of research institutes and think tanks such as the Nigerian Economic

Summit Group (NESG), Centre for Democracy and Development (CDD) and Ibadan School of Government and Policy (ISGPP), they examine how and why the public and private think tanks are able to actualize, or not, the aspirations of governance and development goals in the country.

The Rwanda case is taken up in Chapter 8 by Kayitesi. Following the pattern set by the previous chapters, Kayitesi discusses the rationale for the proliferation of think tanks in Africa before focusing on their rise in Rwanda, the categorization of think tanks and their influence in the country's governance, development, legislation and socio-economic process. She also suggests some of the challenges facing them, and innovative ways that think tanks have employed to sustain themselves. The need to address the horrors of the 1994 Tutsi genocide and the country's chosen developmental and transformative path influenced the growth of think tanks. Some of the pioneer think tanks in Rwanda include the Institute of Policy Research and Analysis – Rwanda (IPAR-Rwanda), Never Again Rwanda, the Institute of Legal Practice and Development (ILPD) and Legal Aid Forum (LAF), which have fared reasonably well despite capacity constraints (including few researchers and limited participation by women) and funding constraints.

Ayuk, Hathie and Ba in Chapter 9 examine the contribution of think tanks in Senegal in informing and influencing public policy in Senegal. Using specific examples of public policies related to economic governance that have been informed by think tanks, they show how and why some of the think tanks have evolved, their categorization into independent think tanks, university-affiliated or university think tanks, and government-affiliated think tanks; how some of them influenced agriculture and economic public policy-making; their deficits and how they could be addressed. They include Initiative Prospective Agricole et Rurale (IPAR), which led the reform of the Senegalese agricultural subsistence system and informing rural youth employment policy; and the Consortium for Economic and Social Research (CRES), to provide evidence supporting fiscal policy reforms in the tobacco industry, which led to increases in existing tax rates in 2009 and 2014 and the adoption by the Parliament of a law in 2014 related to the manufacture, packaging, labelling, sale and use of tobacco.

Chapter 10 is devoted to the South Africa case. Nkrumah and Soorymoorthy briefly discuss the concept of think tanks and their evolution under the apartheid regime, and their subsequent proliferation since the 1990s. Thereafter, there is an examination of the different types of these institutes operating in their respective policy spaces, with specific reference to their ideological orientation, research and advocacy agendas, and the degree of their influence in agenda-setting and policy design and implementation. To these authors, think tanks are not merely founts of knowledge, but also shapers and implementers of policies. One of the interesting issues raised is the grouping of institutional ideologies of South Africa's contemporary think tanks under three headings. First, Pan-Africanism, which acknowledges that political stability on the African continent is a *sine qua non* for uplifting and unifying people of African descent. As a result, institutions that were originally launched in South Africa have extended their reach and provided policy recommendations to other African countries. Second, Evangelism, which engages in the dissemination of religious doctrines to shape the conduct of certain actors. Institutes in this category are often faith-based research centres that seek to foster religious tolerance and safeguard the vulnerable population from inhumane treatment. Third, Mandelaism, which was inspired by the ideals of Nelson Mandela. As an African nationalist, Mandela was a strong proponent of three ideals: non-racism, anti-poverty and accountable government.

Chapter 11 is the concluding chapter. In it, Ayee and Ohemeng summarize the findings on institutionalism, think tanks and the case studies, and their implications for the theoretical, comparative and empirical literature. Given the dynamic nature of scholarship and interest in think tanks, there is an agenda for future research especially in facing Africa's development challenges, which include new, complex problems and opportunities stemming from emerging technology and the Fourth Industrial Revolution. Managing them will require the building of smart partnerships between governments, regional organizations, the private sector and think tanks.

CONCLUSION

This chapter has discussed the institutional theory in the study of think tanks which shows that they are institutions with a set of rules and behaviour. Think tanks have not only shaped individual actors, but also influenced policies, governance and development in the case study countries and the other African countries. In fact, they have come to stay, and their contribution cannot be underestimated. Even though in some African countries think tanks fight for recognition, their expertise is generally respected, despite being considered by the political and security establishments as agents of some hidden powers. Behind this suspicion lies the interconnected issues related to independence and funding. The case studies also show that the effectiveness of think tanks depends on a number of factors such as contextual variables, legal framework, human and financial resources, leadership, organizational cohesion and culture. Finally, institutional theory continues to be attractive because of its importance in the study of public policy-making, governance and development. What criteria should be used when reforming or creating institutions: should these be efficiency norms or ethical principles, or a combination of both, relating to social justice, governance and development? Addressing this question lies at the heart of the scholarship to which this book has made a modest contribution, through an assessment of think tanks in eight African countries and a general chapter on Africa itself.

NOTE

1.   This section is based on Ohemeng (2015).

REFERENCES

Abelson, D.E. (1992) 'A new channel of influence: American think tanks and the news media', *Queens Quarterly*, 94(4), 849–872.

Abelson, D.E. (2010) *Do Think Tanks Matter? Assessing the Impact of Public Policy Institutes*, Kingston and Montreal: McGill-Queen's University Press.

Abelson, D.E. (2021) 'If it doesn't matter, why measure it? Reflections on think tank rankings and policy influence', in D.E. Abelson and C.J. Rastrick (eds), *Handbook on Think Tanks in Public Policy* (134–149), Cheltenham, UK and Northampton, MA, USA: Edward Elgar Publishing.

Abelson, D.E. and S. Brooks (2017) 'Struggling to be heard: the crowded and complex world of foreign-policy-oriented think tanks', in D.E. Abelson, S. Brooks and X. Hua (eds), *Think Tanks, Foreign Policy and Geo-Politics: Pathways to Influence* (1–19), London: Routledge.

Abelson, D.E. and C.J. Rastrick (2021) 'Introduction to the Handbook on Think Tanks in Public Policy', in D.E. Abelson and C.J. Rastrick (eds), *Handbook on Think Tanks in Public Policy* (xviii–xxv), Cheltenham, UK and Northampton, MA, USA: Edward Elgar Publishing.

Abraham, K.A.A. (2019) 'The role and activities of policy institutes for participatory governance in Ghana', in H.M. Grimm (ed.), *Public Policy Research in the Global South: A Cross-Country Perspective* (151–170), Cham: Springer.

Aksom, H. and V. Vakulenko (2023) 'Revisiting the scope and suggesting novel domains of institutional theory in the public administration research', *Teaching Public Administration*, Online First, 1–21. DOI: 10.1177/01447394231191935.

Arshed, N. (2017) 'The origins of policy ideas: the importance of think tanks in the enterprise policy process in the UK', *Journal of Business Research*, 71(2), 74–83.

Asefa, S. and W-C. Huang (eds) (2015) *The Political Economy of Good Governance*, Kalamazoo, MI: W.E. Upjohn Institute.

Bernstein, S. and B. Cashore (2012) 'Complex global governance and domestic policies: four pathways of influence', *International Affairs*, 88(3), 585–604.

Bhatnagar, S. (2021) *India's Pakistan Policy: How Think Tanks Are Shaping Foreign Relations*, New Delhi: Routledge.

Birkland, T.A. (1998) 'Focusing events, mobilization, and agenda setting', *Journal of Public Policy*, 18(1), 53–74.

Brinkerhoff, D.W. (1999) 'Exploring state–civil society collaboration: policy partnerships in developing Countries', *Nonprofit and Voluntary Sector Quarterly*, 28(1), 59–86.

Cairney, P. (2019) *Understanding Public Policy: Theories and Issues*, 2nd edn, New York: Bloomsbury.

Carvalho, A.D.P., S.K. da Cunha, L.F. de Lima and D.D. Carstens (2017) 'The role and contributions of sociological institutional theory to the socio-technical approach to innovation theory', *RAI Revista de Administração e Inovação*, 14(3), 250–259.

Chafuen, A. (2013) '15 ways of measuring think tank policy outcomes'. https://www .forbes.com/sites/alejandrochafuen/2013/04/24/15-ways-of-measuring-think-tank -policy-outcomes/?sh=474e9883357d (accessed: 28 August 2023).

Chavance, B. (2008) 'Formal and informal institutional change: the experience of post-socialist transformation', *European Journal of Comparative Economics*, 5(1), 57– 71.

Chavance, B. (2012) 'John Commons's organizational theory of institutions: a discussion', *Journal of Institutional Economics*, 8(1), 27–47.

Clemens, E.S. and J.M. Cook (1999) 'Politics and institutionalism: explaining durability and change', *Annual Review of Sociology*, 25, 441–466.

Cohen, S.A. (1993) 'Defining and measuring effectiveness in public management', *Public Productivity and Management Review*, 17(1), 45–57.

Commons, J.R. (1934) *Institutional Economics: Its Place in Political Economy*, New Brunswick, NJ: Transactions Publishers.

Cook, T.E. (1998) *Governing with the News: The News Media as a Political Institution*, Chicago, IL: Chicago University Press.

Cummings, D. (2005) 'Think tanks and intellectual authority outside the university: information technocracy or republic of letters?', in R. Finnegan (ed.) *Participating in the Knowledge Society: Research beyond University Walls* (166–179), New York: Palgrave.

Denham, A. and M. Garnett (1996) 'The nature and impact of think tanks in contemporary Britain', *Contemporary British History*, 10(1), 43–61.

Denham, A. and M. Garnett (1999) 'Influence without responsibility? Think tanks in Britain', *Parliamentary Affairs*, 52(1), 46–57.

Denham, A. and M. Garnett (2004) 'A "hollowed out" tradition? British think tanks in the twenty-first century', in D. Stone and A. Denham (eds), *Think Tank Traditions: Policy Research and the Politics of Ideas* (232–246), Manchester: Manchester University Press.

Denhardt, R.B and J.V. Denhardt (2000) 'The new public service, serving rather than steering', *Public Administration Review*, 60(6), 549–559.

DiMaggio, P.J. and W. Powell (1991) 'Introduction', in W. Powell and P.J. DiMaggio (eds), *The New Institutionalism in Organizational Analysis* (1–38), Chicago, IL: University of Chicago Press.

Diprose, R., N.I. Kurniawan and K. Macdonald (2019) 'Transnational policy influence and the politics of legitimation', *Governance*, 32, 223–240.

Dorey, P. (2005) *Policy Making in Britain: An Introduction*, London: SAGE Publications.

Dror, Y. (1980) 'Think tanks: a new invention in government', in C.H. Weiss and A.H. Barton (eds), *Making Bureaucracies Work* (139–152). Beverly Hills, CA: SAGE.

Fukuyama, F. (2013) 'What is governance?' Governance, 26(3), 347–368.

Georgopoulos, B.S. and A.S. Tannenbaum (1957) 'A study of organizational effectiveness', *American Sociological Review*, 22(5), 534–540.

Glynn, M.A. and T. D'Aunno (2022) 'An intellectual history of institutional theory: looking back to move forward', Academy of Management Annals, 17(1), 301–330.

Grindle, M.S. (2004) 'Good enough governance: poverty reduction and reform in developing countries', *Governance*, 17(4), 525–548.

Grindle, M.S. (2007) 'Good enough governance revisited', *Development Policy Review*, 25(5), 553–574.

Hadler, M. (2015) 'Institutionalism and neo-institutionalism: history of the concepts', *International Encyclopedia of the Social and Behavioral Sciences*, 2nd edn, Vol. 12 (186–189). http://dx.doi.org/10.1016/B978–0-08–097086–8.03187–1.

Haggard, S. and R.R. Kaufman (2016) 'Democratization during the third wave', *Annual Review of Political Science*, 19, 125–144.

Hart, P. and A. Vromen (2008) 'A new era for think tanks in public policy? International trends, Australian realities', *Australian Journal of Public Administration*, 67(2), 135–148.

Hassel, A. and K. Wegrich (2022) *How to do Public Policy*, Oxford: Oxford University Press.

Heikkila, T. and P. Cairney (2018) 'Comparison of theories of the policy process', in C.M. Weible and P.A. Sabatier (eds), *Theories of the Policy Process*, 4th edn, New York: Routledge.

Heugens, P.P. and M.W. Lander (2009) 'Structure! Agency! (and other quarrels): a meta-analysis of institutional theories of organization', *Academy of Management Journal*, 52(1), 61–85.

Huntington, S.P. (1991) *The Third Wave: Democratization in the Late Twentieth Century*, Norman, OK: University of Oklahoma Press.

Immergut, E.M. (2011) 'Institution/institutionalism', in B. Badie, D. Berg-Schlosser and L. Morlino (eds), *International Encyclopedia of Political Science*, London: SAGE. https://doi.org/10.4135/9781412994163.

James, S. (1993) 'The idea brokers: the impact of think tanks on British government', *Public Administration*, 71(4), 491–506.

Jepperson, R.D. (1991) 'Institutions, institutional effects, and institutionalism', in W.W. Powell and P.J. DiMaggio (eds), *The New Institutionalism in Organizational Analysis* (143–163), Chicago, IL: University of Chicago Press.

Jezierska, K. (2020) 'Three types of denial: think tanks as a reluctant civil society elite', *Politics and Governance*, 8(3), 152–161.

Jezierska, K. (2023) 'Coming out of the liberal closet. Think tanks and de-democratization in Poland', *Democratization*, 30(2), 259–277.

Keohane, R.O. and L.L. Martin (1995) 'The promise of institutionalist theory', *International Security*, 20(1), 39–51.

Kingdon, J.W. (2011) *Agendas, Alternatives and Public Policies*, 2nd edn, Boston, MA: Longman.

Kinkoh, M and F. Tazoacha (2023) 'Appraising the role of think tanks in peacebuilding in Africa'. https://onpolicy.org/appraising-the-role-of-think-tanks-in-peacebuilding-in-africa/ (accessed: 4 September 2023).

Ladi, S. (2011) 'Think tanks', in B. Badie, D. Berg-Schlosser and L. Morlino (eds), *International Encyclopedia of Political Science* (2608–2610), Thousand Oaks, CA: SAGE.

Landry, J. (2022) 'Do business-backed think tanks represent class interests? The co-evolution of policy learning and economic elites in the Canadian knowledge regime', *Administration and Society*, 54(7) 1305–1327.

Lawrence, T.B. and R. Suddaby (2006) 'Institutions and institutional work', in S.R. Clegg, C. Hardy, T.B. Lawrence and W.R. Nord (eds), *SAGE Handbook of Organization Studies*, 2nd edn (215–254). London: SAGE.

Lawrence, T.B., R. Suddaby and B. Leca (eds) (2009) *Institutional Work: Actors and Agency in Institutional Studies of Organizations*, Cambridge: Cambridge University Press.

Lawrence, T.B., R. Suddaby, and B. Leca (2011) 'Institutional work: refocusing institutional studies of organization', *Journal of Management Inquiry*, 20(1), 52–58.

Lindquist, E. (2021) 'Think tanks and policy communities: analysing policy influence and learning from the analogue to the digital era', in D.E. Abelson and C.J. Rastrick (eds), *Handbook on Think Tanks in Public Policy* (100–118), Cheltenham, UK and Northampton, MA, USA: Edward Elgar Publishing.

Lowndes, V. (1996) 'Varieties of new institutionalism: a critical appraisal', *Public Administration*, 74(2), 181–197.

McGann, J.G. (2015) 'For think tanks, it's either innovate or die', *Washington Post*. https://www.washingtonpost.com/news/in-theory/wp/2015/10/06/for-think-tanks-its-either-innovate-or-die/ (accessed: 25 August 2023).

McGann, J.G. (ed.) (2018) *Think Tanks and Emerging Power Policy Networks*, Cham: Palgrave Macmillan.

McGann, J.G. (2019) *Think Tanks: The New Knowledge and Policy Brokers in Asia*, Washington, DC: Brookings Institution Press and ADBI.

McGann, J.G. (2021) 2020 Global Go To Think Tank Index Report. https://www.bruegel.org/sites/default/files/wp-content/uploads/2021/03/2020-Global-Go-To-Think-Tank-Index-Report-Bruegel.pdf.

Medvetz, T. (2008) 'Think tanks as an emergent field', Social Science Research Council.

Menegazzi, S. (2018) *Rethinking Think Tanks in Contemporary China*, Cham: Palgrave Macmillan.

Meyer, J.W. (2017) 'Reflections on institutional theories of organizations', in R. Greenwood, C. Oliver, T.B. Lawrence and R.E. Meyer (eds), *The SAGE Handbook of Organizational Institutionalism* (831–852), London: SAGE.

Nadler, A. (2015) 'The other side of helping: seeking and receiving help', in David A. Schroeder and William G. Graziano (eds), *The Oxford Handbook of Prosocial Behavior* (307–328), Oxford: Oxford University Press.

Oghojafor, B.E.A., F.I. Muo and S.A. Aduloju (2012) 'Organisational effectiveness: whom and what do we believe?', *Advances in Management and Applied Economics*, 2(4), 81–108.

Ohemeng, F.L.K. (2005) 'Getting the state right: think tanks and the dissemination of New Public Management ideas in Ghana,' *Journal of Modern African Studies*, 43(3), 443–465.

Ohemeng, F.L.K. (2015) 'Civil society and policy making in developing countries: assessing the impact of think tanks on policy outcomes in Ghana', *Journal of Asian and African Studies*, 50(6) 667–682.

Ohemeng, F.L.K. (2024) 'Think tanks as collective policy entrepreneurs and the art of policy making in Ghana', in M. Kpessa-Whyte and J. Dzisah (eds), *Public Policy in Ghana: Conceptual and Practical Insights* (161–180), Cham: Palgrave Macmillan.

Pan, J. (2021) *DIIS Theory and Methodology in Think Tanks*, Singapore: Springer Nature.

Pautz, H. (2012) *Think-Tanks, Social Democracy and Social Policy*, London: Palgrave Macmillan.

Pautz, H. (2020) 'Think tanks and policymaking', *Oxford Research Encyclopedias*, https://doi.org/10.1093/acrefore/9780190228637.013.1420.

Peetz, D. (2017) 'Why establish non-representative organizations? Rethinking the role, form, and target of think tanks', in A. Salas-Porras and G. Murray (eds) *Think Tanks and Global Politics: Key Spaces in the Structure of Power* (245–263), New York, NY: Palgrave.

Peters, B.G. (2016) 'Institutionalism and public policy', in B.G. Peters and P. Zittoun (eds) *Contemporary Approaches to Public Policy: Theories, Controversies and Perspectives* (57–72), London: Palgrave Macmillan.

Peters, B.G. (2020) 'Designing institutions for designing policy', *Policy and Politics*, 48(1), 131–147.

Peters, B.G. (2022) 'Institutions, institutional theory and policy design', in B.G. Peter and G. Fontaine (eds), *Research Handbook of Policy Design* (54–71), Cheltenham, UK and Northampton, MA, USA: Edward Elgar Publishing.

Quade, E.S. (1969) The systems approach and public policy. https://www.rand.org/content/dam/rand/pubs/papers/2008/P4053.pdf.

Rich, A. (2005) *Think Tanks, Public Policy, and the Politics of Expertise*, New York: Cambridge University Press.

Rich, A. and R.K. Weaver (2000) 'Think tanks in the U.S. media', *Press/Politics*, 5(4), 81–103.

Rojansky, M. and J. Shapiro (2021) 'Why everyone hates think tanks: the world needs policy professionals. Respecting them is another matter', *Foreign Policy*. https://foreignpolicy.com/2021/05/28/why-everyone-hates-think-tanks/.

Salas-Porras, A. and G. Murray (eds) (2017) *Think Tanks and Global Politics: Key Spaces in the Structure of Power*, Basingstoke: Palgrave Macmillan.

Schlesinger, P. (2009) 'Creativity and the experts: New Labour, think tanks, and the policy process', *International Journal of Press/Politics*, 14(1), 3–20.

Scott, R.W. (1991) 'Unpacking institutional arguments', in W.W. Powell and P.J. DiMaggio (eds), *The New Institutionalism in Organizational Analysis* (164–183), Chicago, IL: University of Chicago Press.

Scott, W.R. (2014) *Institutions and Organisations: Ideas, Interests, and Identities*, 4th edn, Thousand Oaks, CA: SAGE.

Shaw, S.E., J. Russell, W. Parsons and T. Greenhalgh (2015) 'The view from nowhere? How think tanks work to shape health policy', *Critical Policy Studies*, 9(1), 58–77.

Singleton, J. (2000) *The American Dole: Unemployment Relief and the Welfare State in the Great Depression*, Westport, CT: Greenwood Press.

Spohr, F. (2016) 'Explaining path dependency and deviation by combining multiple streams framework and historical institutionalism: a comparative analysis of German and Swedish labor market policies', *Journal of Comparative Policy Analysis: Research and Practice*, 18(3), 257–272.

Stewart, J. and R. Ayres (2000) 'Systems theory and policy practice: an exploration', *Policy Sciences*, 34(1), 79–94.

Stone D. (1996). *Capturing the Political Imagination: Think Tanks and the Policy Process*, London: Portland.

Stone, D. (2007) 'Recycling bins, garbage cans, or think tanks: three myths regarding policy analysis institutes', *Public Administration*, 85(2), 259–278.

Stone, D. (2015) 'The Group of 20 transnational policy community: governance networks, policy analysis and think tanks', *International Review of Administrative Sciences*, 81(4), 793–811.

Stone, D., S. Maxwell and M. Keating (2001) 'Bridging research and policy', an international workshop funded by the UK Department for International Development, 16–17 July, Radcliffe House, Warwick University, UK.

Swaminathan, A. and J.B. Wade (2016) 'Institutional environment', in M. Augier and D.J. Teece (eds), *The Palgrave Encyclopedia of Strategic Management* (693–696), London: Palgrave Macmillan.

Voss, T.R. (2015) 'Institutions', in James D. Wright (ed.), *International Encyclopedia of the Social and Behavioral Sciences*, 2nd edn, Vol. 12 (186–189). http://dx.doi.org/ 10.1016/B978-0-08-097086-8.03187-1.

Weidenbaum, M. (2010) 'Measuring the influence of think tanks', *Society*, 47(2), 134–137.

Wells, P. (2012) 'Prescriptions for regional economic dilemmas: understanding the role of think tanks in the governance of regional policy', *Public Administration*, 90(1), 211–229.

Wellstead, A.M. and M. Howlett (2022) '(Re)thinking think tanks in the age of policy labs: the rise of knowledge-based policy influence organisations (KBPIO)', *Australian Journal of Public Administration*, 81, 224–232.

Zucker, L.G. (1987) 'Institutional theories of organization', *Annual Review of Sociology*, 13, 443–464.

2.   Survey of think tanks in Africa

E. Remi Aiyede and Adigun A.B. Agbaje

INTRODUCTION

We live in a world of rapid change with enormous implications for policy making. The COVID-19 pandemic and the effort to understand it, design interventions to stem its spread, and overcome it with utmost urgency, have demonstrated the importance of policy knowledge and evidence. The pandemic underscores the need to make scientific knowledge available to policy makers who must intervene to address life and welfare challenges in an increasingly uncertain environment. These call for translation of scientific or research outputs into forms that are accessible by those who are saddled with the responsibility of policy making and implementation. Indeed, the experience of the pandemic has further underscored a growing global concern for evidence-informed policy making. Think tanks play vital roles as knowledge brokers, contributing to the effort to translate scientific or research outputs into the policy process.

The importance of think tanks has been recognized globally. There is a growing interest in understanding their nature, as distinct from other civil society groups such as pressure groups; their role in knowledge production and knowledge brokerage for public policy; their organizational forms and management challenges; as well as the ways and means to make them more effective as independent means of speaking truth to power and for augmenting state capacity. The Think Tanks and Civil Societies Program of the Lauder Institute at the University of Pennsylvania has played a vital role in developing knowledge about think tanks and in underscoring their importance in policy making at the national, regional and global levels. Think tanks have been useful in critical policy areas such as international peace and security, governance and political reforms, human rights, international trade, environment and climate change issues, information and society, poverty alleviation, education and healthcare, and global health. The programme has been instrumental in promoting international collaborative efforts among think tanks to improve policy making around the world. It also provides the periodic Global Go To Think Tank Index Report that ranks think tanks globally (McGann 2009, 2012,

2015, 2017, 2019, 2021a, 2021b). A similar contribution has been made by the Think Tank Initiative (TTI) of the International Development Research Centre (IDRC).

Although the idea of think tanks is traced to the United States (US), such organizations have spread globally to all regions of the world. The Go To Think Tank rankings 2020 show that the US and United Kingdom (UK) continue to dominate the world of think tanks. The top think tank in the world for the year 2020 was the Japan Institute of International Affairs (JIIA). Africa has the lowest number of think tanks. Only South Africa, with 102, features in the 23 countries with the highest number of think tanks globally. In 2014, the first African think tank summit was held in Pretoria. The summit was titled 'The Rise of African Think Tanks' and addressed issues such as the organizational and policy challenges facing think tanks in the region, and how they might increase their sustainability, value and impact. Since then, six additional summits have been held; the last took place in February 2020, before the lockdown that followed the spread of the COVID-19 pandemic in Africa.

What is the nature of the universe of think tanks in Africa today? What role are they playing in the governance and development in Africa? What is their role in the effort to speak truth to power and infuse the policy process with evidence? What are the challenges of African think tanks? This chapter responds to these questions by exploring the nexus between think tanks, governance and development. Against this theoretical discourse, it examines the emergence, spread and contributions of think tanks to policy making, governance and development in Africa. It also analyses the current state of think tanks in terms of their relative number, distribution and types in Africa. Furthermore, it explores the challenges facing African think tanks and how they can be overcome.

THINK TANKS, GOVERNANCE AND DEVELOPMENT: A NEXUS

The think tank concept emerged in the US during the Second World War in reference to the environment in which military and civilian experts brainstormed to develop invasion plans and other military strategies. By the 1960s, the meaning was expanded to describe groups of experts who formulated various policy recommendations, including some research institutes concerned with the study of international relations and strategic questions (Dickinson 1972). By the 1970s, the term 'think tank' was expanded and also applied to institutions that focus on contemporary political, economic and social issues, as Western countries became increasingly receptive to advice coming from think tanks on domestic issues (McGann 2021b: 3).

Think tanks are institutions that provide ideas derived from the research and analysis of issues that are presented as policy advice to improve governance and public policy. This definition follows McGann's (2021b) approach to the definition of think tanks in terms of what they do. In his words, 'think tanks are institutions that provide public policy research, analysis, and advice'. They are 'engagement institutions that generate policy-oriented research, analysis, and advice on domestic and international issues which enable policymakers and the general public to make informed decisions about public policy issues'. Furthermore, think tanks 'act as a bridge between the academic and policymaking communities, providing a voice that translates applied and basic research into a language and form that is understandable, reliable, and accessible for policymakers and the public' (McGann 2021b: 2).

In other words, think tanks are a form of research organization. They are like universities in terms of the quality of research that they carry out, and the fact that they engage scholars and experts in their research activities. That is why Mirowski and Sent (2002: 18) describe think tanks as 'university campus[es] without students'. The main purpose of think tanks is to provide well-researched policy proposals that aim to solve public policy issues and provide governments with expert, non-partisan, disinterested advice (McGann and Sabatini 2010: 43).

Think tanks represent an alternative model of knowledge organization. Unlike in the universities, where knowledge for knowledge's sake or the pursuit of truth is considered a value, think tank research is driven by practical problems rather than disciplinary questions. Against the isolation of the ivory tower, think tanks are focused on responsiveness and accountability in research, and seek to impact on or gain uptake in policy circles (Asher and Guilhot 2010). Think tanks seek to bring scientific evidence to inform public policy making to improve the quality of decision making and service delivery in governance.

With regard to the role of think tanks in governance, there is a debate around issues of independence, advocacy roles, and partisan or ideological commitments. These relate to the varieties of think tanks in terms of their origin or affiliations. Some think tanks are government owned, or affiliated to institutions such as universities or corporations. To what extent does ownership or affiliation impact on the type, focus and orientation of the research conducted by such think tanks? Are their activities affected by partisan affiliation or informed by specific ideological commitments? What determines the issues investigated by think tanks, and to what extent should think tanks advocate for specific policy preferences in the marketplace of ideas on how specific public problems should be addressed? Should think tanks stay 'detached from the political process because of their commitment to preserve their intellectual and institutional independence and not influence policy decisions directly'? (Ahmad 2008: 532).

There are a variety of think tanks in Africa, as there are in the world today, with a differing orientation and focus. Some are national institutes owned by government to support decision making by providing analysis that can inform decisions. Some are issue driven and are focused on advocacy regarding specific issues. These issue-specific think tanks often establish sites outside the individual country of origin, foster formal relationships with international institutions, and draw on the ideas of specialists, advocacy experts and academics globally in addressing issues. Such think tanks have blurred the lines between the original concept of the think tank (which was academic) with that of an advocacy group (McGann and Sabatini 2010: 43). In general, think tanks have become indispensable in local, national and international development policy making globally. As a result, think tanks have become a major part of the evidence revolution, the global movement to promote evidence-informed policy making.

THE EMERGENCE AND SPREAD OF THINK TANKS IN AFRICA

There were a few institutes established during the colonial period in Africa to support research and development in specific sectors, such as health, education and agriculture. These institutes were designed to facilitate purposes of colonial exploitation, such as promoting agricultural production in the plantations for export. In the march to independence, several think tanks and research institutes were established to promote evidence for policy making. Laakso (2022: 25) identified the Nigerian Institute for Social and Economic Research and the Makerere Institute for Social Research as epitomizing the government intervention to promote development and policy research in the 1950s. The West African Institute of Social and Economic Research, which became the Nigerian Institute for Social and Economic Research (NISER), was founded in 1950 to provide information on economic and social ideas for development of British West African countries. It was affiliated with the University of Ibadan until 1977, when it became an autonomous body. Like NISER, some of these early institutes were attached to universities. In some cases, in the early 1960s, universities established their own institutes to conduct policy-oriented research to support the development initiatives of Africa's new governments. Furthermore, in some countries, the colleges earlier established for the training of public servants were upgraded, while in others new institutes were established by the government. These institutes were particularly active on the continent in the immediate post-independence years, which was also the time of central planning when government officials collaborated with academics in the universities and think tanks to address development challenges.

The popularity of think tanks was soon undermined by the increasing authoritarian political environment of the 1970s and 1980s. As governments became increasingly focused on consolidating power to extract economic gains, they became more repressive and intolerant of criticism. Under this environment, the collaborative relationship between intellectuals and the governments became strained. Suspicion, mistrust and antagonism, and a sterile lack of cooperation followed. Criticism of policy was taken as a challenge to the rule of leaders and intellectual freedom became constrained. The development of think tanks and similar research organizations by the government suffered setbacks. Many African states were not able to develop robust institutions to provide evidence for policy. There was a persistence of planning without facts in many countries before the onset of governance crisis of the 1980s. To address this crisis, African states had to implement structural adjustment programmes (Kimenyi and Datta 2011).

Severe fiscal pressures under crisis and adjustment forced governments to cut funds to the universities and research centres, constricting their ability to undertake independent research. The situation was worsened by 'brain drain', and the quality of policy making declined. Some university professors set up their own (donor-funded) research centres to take advantage of donor funds that were increasingly channelled towards civil society. They set up think tanks which returned them to the public policy arena. This represents the second phase in the evolution of think tanks in Africa. Such think tanks as the Development Policy Centre in Nigeria, the Economic and Social Research Foundation in Tanzania, and the Centre for Policy Studies in South Africa, emerged during this period (Kimenyi and Datta 2011). During the period, African intellectuals, who were largely under-utilized by their governments, turned to civil society, mostly foreign-funded non-governmental research institutes for policy research. They benefited from the research initiatives and funding from the Bretton Woods Institutions, the World Bank and the International Monetary Fund (IMF) and donor agencies attached to governments of the West, such as the UK's Department for International Development (DFID) and Germany's German Technical Cooperation (GTZ) (Mkandawire 2000).

The political liberalization and governance reforms of the 2000s was marked by the transfer to non-state actors of government functions, especially research, leading to the proliferation of independent think tanks. These think tanks have provided research and policy advice to governments and regional organizations on the continent. Political liberalization meant that politicians had to respond to their constituencies. They looked to the civil service, and public service reforms became a central element of political competition as the politicians sought for more effectiveness in policy making. Issues of account-ability and inclusivity in policy making led to the call for more participatory policy processes at the continental, regional and national levels, to improve coordination, mutual learning and the adoption of best practices. Kimenyi and Datta (2011) observed that under economic and political liberalization, the think tank landscape changed for the better. This period was characterized by the proliferation of new think tanks in response to increased donor funding and support for civil society in an expanding space for civic activism. Such think tanks initially focused on issues relating to political and economic liberaliza-tion. Many think tanks received funding support to monitor and help improve government policy implementation, from the donors lending to African governments as part of the effort to hold recipient governments accountable. Thus, African think tanks competed with governments for donor support, and competed with international institutions such as the World Bank and their research units for government influence.

The first and second African think tank summits were held in 2014 and 2015, respectively. The 2014 summit reflected on the transformation of think tanks, and the ways and means of making them more effective in playing effective roles in policy making and governance. A major preoccupation of the summit was to evolve strategies and programmes to engage private indigenous donors to support think tanks, establish a Pan African Think Tank network, strengthen, and fund the core operations of think tanks to help ensure the sustainability and independence of think tanks in Africa. A Pan African Think Tank network was subsequently established and hosted by the African Capacity Building Foundation (ACBF) in Harare. The second think tank summit was equally optimistic. The theme was 'The Rise of Africa's Think Tanks: Practical Solutions to Practical Problems', and the deliberations at the conference reflected the 'Africa Rising' discourse of the time, as many African countries recorded tangible progress in economic reform, political liberalization and governance reforms. A great deal of attention was focused on how African think tanks can be better positioned to support Africa's devel-opment priorities and initiatives, such as Agenda 2063 and the United Nations' Post-2015 Development Agenda. However, the democratic space soon began to shrink as African states descended into authoritarian practices, and faced severe challenges with the global recession of 2016. The rise of illiberal prac-tices meant that government was increasingly hostile to dissent, criticism and alternative policy options. As the democratic space shrank, patronage of think tanks dwindled. The situation has been worsened by the preference of donors for short-term and project-specific funding, accountability and evidence of impact (Okeke-Uzodike 2021: 35).

Table 2.1   *Global distribution of think tanks*

Region	Number of Think Tanks
Europe	2932
North America	2397
Asia	3389
South and Central America	1179
Sub-Saharan Africa	679
Middle East and North Africa	599
Total	11 175

Source: McGann (2021a: 43).

NUMBER, DISTRIBUTION AND TYPES OF THINK TANKS IN AFRICA

According to the Go To Think Tank Index Report 2020, there are 679 think tanks in Sub-Saharan Africa, representing an increase from the 554 recorded in 2012. Relative to other regions covered in the report, Sub-Saharan Africa has the lowest number of think tanks, apart from the Middle East/North Africa. Although Africa recorded an increase in the number and types of think tanks between 2011 and 2020, as shown in Table 2.1, Africa accounts for only 6 per cent of the 11 175 think tanks in the world as of 2020. In the 2011 report, Africa accounted for 8.4 per cent, that is, 555 of 6545. This shows that the relative growth of African think tanks is below the global growth level. Only South Africa has appeared in the list of countries with the highest number of think tanks. It occupies the 15th position in the list of 23 countries in 2020. The US occupies the top position with 2203 think tanks, while Belgium, the Netherlands and Canada occupied the bottom position with 85 think tanks each.

In terms of spread, think tanks are unevenly spread across the continent, with South Africa – which has the oldest think tank on the continent – having 102 think tanks. Kenya takes second place with 64 think tanks; while Nigeria comes third place with 52 (see Figure 2.1). Guinea Bissau has only one think tank. According to the report, many think tanks in these regions continue to be dependent on government funding, along with gifts, grants and contracts from international public and private donors. The think tank summit in 2017 raised the alarm about the threat to the survival of think tanks in Africa.

There are several frameworks for classifying think tanks, even though it is generally accepted that each think tank is unique. Anheier (2010) identified three basic types: (1) those that are like universities without students, scholastic organizations, with individual scholarship and academic independence

Source: Based on data from McGann (2021a).

Figure 2.1   *Distribution of think tanks in Sub-Saharan Africa*

shielded from the wider political and economic systems; (2) advocacy groups that pursue ideological or political goals; and (3) those that produce knowledge on demand for third parties. McGann (2021b) classified think tanks in terms of their geographic scope, thematic focus and institutional structure. McGann's scheme is used by the Go To Think Tank Project. In terms of geographic scope of think tanks, many in Africa primarily operate on a domestic, national level. There are few regional or international-level think tanks. Most of the government think tanks are domestic, and often restrict their research to subjects pertaining to the specific country. Examples of such institutions include the Kenya Institute for Public Policy Research and Analysis (KIPPRA) (Kenya) and the Nigerian Institute for Social and Economic Research (NISER).

Regional think tanks offer knowledge on issues at the regional level. Their research work is focused on a region. They are interested in regional-level policy initiatives and are too geographically specific to be relevant to global research. Examples are the Partnership for African Social and Governance Research (PASGR) and African Economic Research Consortium (AERC) based in Kenya. The AERC was established in 1988 as a capacity-building institution to inform economic policies in Sub-Saharan Africa, while PASGR was established in 2011 to support the production and dissemination of policy-relevant research to improve governance and policy making for the overall wellbeing of Africans. The African Centre for the Constructive Resolution of Disputes (ACCORD) founded in 1992, and based in South Africa it works throughout Africa to bring creative African solutions to the challenges posed by conflict. It generates and shares knowledge on conflict prevention, management and resolution, and develops the capacity of individuals and institutions for conflict management, towards building sustainable peace, security and development.

Global think tanks are international think tanks that focus on a particular family of issues on a global scale: issues that transcend borders, such as climate change, education and economic stability (Wihardja 2014; Winthrop 2014). Many of the global think tanks in the US, UK and developed world establish operational centres, field offices or outreach centres outside the country of their headquarters or establish a network of think tanks to aid their global reach (McGann 2021a: 25). These include the Brookings Institution, International Institute for Sustainable Development, Friedrich-Ebert-Stiftung (FES), the Overseas Development Institute and Konrad-Adenauer-Stiftung. Some of these think tanks operate in Africa or work with African think tanks.

Think tanks are also classified according to their independence, or according to their mode of organization. McGann and Weaver (2000) categorized think tanks into four types: academic/university without students, contract researcher, advocacy think tank and party think tank. McGann (2021a) also tries to classify think tanks in terms of their focus on 15 core issues: transparency and good governance; defence and national security; foreign and defence policy; domestic economic policy; energy and resource policy; foreign policy and international affairs; environment; education policy; domestic health policy; international development; international economic policy; science and technology; social policy; water security; and food security. Think tanks may also be classified in terms of affiliation: government-affiliated, university-affiliated or foundation. These classes of think tanks exist in Africa. While many of the think tanks in Africa focus on broad social-economic development issues, a few address specific issues or sectors such as foreign policy, conflict and security, health or social policy.

THE ROLE OF AFRICAN THINK TANKS

In recent times, there has been an increasing investment of African governments in policy evaluation. Evaluation is central to evidence generation and use, and for infusing evidence into the policy making process. Policy evaluation on a national scale is beginning to take root in many countries in Africa (Aiyede and Quadri 2022). This environment would have been fertile ground for the development and consolidation of think tanks, but for the entrance of the COVID-19 pandemic. The first African Evidence Week was held in September 2019 as a virtual event design for think tanks to showcase their activities regarding the use of evidence in policy making. Participants at the event showcased how they have promoted the use of evidence in decision making, such as the use of blogs, evidence synthesis, systematic reviews and networking. Sensitization meetings were held in Ghana with parliamentary leadership; a stakeholder forum on evidence use in the sanitation sector in Ghana; multi-stakeholder consultations in Benin; West African Health Organization's (WAHO) use of evidence in moving maternal, new-born and child evidence into policy in West Africa, in Burkina Faso; and so on. The second Evidence Week was held in Uganda in September 2023. The event marks ten years of the anniversary of the Africa Evidence Network to support evidence-informed decision making (EIDM) in Africa.

COVID-19 has further underscored the need for evidence-informed policy making and the importance of think tanks in Africa. Policy think tanks have always been a major influence on food and agricultural policy systems in Africa. In the policy process, think tanks play critical roles at several stages and in multiple policy issues such as urbanization, industrialization, poverty alleviation, education, health, freedom, regional integration and international terrorism. These roles include setting the policy agenda, designing policy interventions, advocating for adoption of certain policies, monitoring the implementation of policies, and evaluating the policies and programmes for their impact and refinements. Some think tanks, such the Anap Foundation in

Nigeria, were established to help respond to the COVID-19 pandemic on the continent. Others have responded by exploring how the pandemic affected the field of activities. For instance, ACCORD has focused attention on COVID-19 and peace-building initiatives in Africa (Gounden and de Coning 2021; Acquah 2021).

Diawara (2020) noted that think tanks played a central role in the continental, regional and national COVID-19 response strategies in Africa. In countries such as Kenya, Nigeria, Rwanda, Senegal, South Africa, Tanzania, Uganda, Zimbabwe, they provided research, policy analysis and dialogues. For instance, the Cameroon Policy Analysis and Research Centre (CAMERCAP-PARC) supported the government with evidence-informed analysis and policy options to inform its COVID-19 response and recovery. African think tanks reviewed their research strategies for the year to ensure their relevance to COVID-19 and the attendant crisis. Many have already produced various knowledge products (such as policy briefs, blogs, think pieces, case studies) and organized online training and workshops on COVID-19 to support government efforts. Thus, while COVID-19 has come as a major disruption to the policy process in Africa, it has also presented challenges that demonstrated the relevance of think tanks and their continued contribution and existence. While the pandemic has created a new vision of policy making that emphasized the need to build national capabilities in policy making and state intervention to address welfare in the uncertain and risky environment of the COVID-19 pandemic, the continuation and institutional development of policy think tanks remains challenging in Africa, as several of them struggle to survive in the face of chronic funding challenges. Diawara (2020) noted that the COVID-19 environment negatively affected think tanks in several ways: staff were overwhelmed and stressed, funding commitments did not materialize, civic space was compromised, and development partners' priorities changed to a short-term focus in response to COVID-19. Despite these challenges, think tanks remain important to evolving homegrown policy solutions to COVID-19 and other challenges facing African countries.

Think tanks in Africa have played vital roles in governance. They provide evidence-based research and advice on specific socio-economic problems. They promote high-level stakeholder dialogues, publish articles and draft legislation used by governments or private entities to achieve their goals. They hold events focused on dismantling the pillars of corruption and encouraging sustainable growth and development. Some of them, such as the Nigeria Economic Summit Group, produce radio programmes. NESG Radio, a weekly syndicated podcast, helps to communicate critical information to a cross-section of Nigerians on economic policies, ideas, health, trends and interventions. The Kenya Institute for Public Policy Research and Analysis (KIPPRA) provides quality public policy advice to the Government of

Kenya through objective research, analysis and capacity building, towards the achievement of national development goals. The Centre for Democracy and Development (CDD) in Nigeria contributes to shape global opinion, and provides resources to address challenges hampering democratic development in West Africa (Musa 2021).

Ngugi (2021: 49) notes that African think tanks played a 'critical role in supporting African countries to address development challenges through evidence-based policy design, implementation and monitoring, capacity development for state and non- state actors, and provision of platforms for stakeholder engagement, dialogue, and advocacy'. She also noted, however, that there is need for collaboration, for coordination of efforts, through networking, communities of practice and coordination of activities to pool skills and capacities, remove duplication of efforts and enhance bargaining power, improve the quality of products and create impact.

RELATIVE PERFORMANCE OF AFRICAN THINK TANKS

In the world ranking of think tanks, the African Centre for the Constructive Resolution of Disputes (ACCORD) (South Africa) occupies the 23rd position in a list of 174 think tanks. The African Economic Research Consortium (AERC) (Kenya) occupies the 69th position and the Food, Agriculture and Natural Resources Policy Analysis Network (FANRPAN) (South Africa) the 72nd position. The South African Institute of International Affairs (SAIIA) (South Africa) is 85th, the Centre for Conflict Resolution (CCR) (South Africa) 87th, and the Kenya Institute for Public Policy Research and Analysis (KIPPRA) (Kenya) is in 100th position.

Within the African continent, think tanks were ranked for performance in terms of quality of research, analysis and public engagement on a wide range of policy issues. These are based on think tank aims of advancing debate, facilitating cooperation between relevant actors, maintaining public support, and funding, and improving the overall quality of life in the relevant country and region. On these bases, the Botswana Institute for Development Policy Analysis (BIDPA) (Botswana) was the Sub-Saharan Africa Centre of Excellence for 2017–2019.

Table 2.2 shows the ranking of think tanks in terms of performance in Africa in 2020. In this ranking ACCORD remains at the top, and South African think tanks remained dominant with six of the best think tanks. Think tanks from nine countries appeared in the first 20. These are South Africa, Kenya, Ghana, Tanzania, Senegal, Côte d'Ivoire, Ethiopia, Nigeria and Uganda.

Table 2.2   *Top 20 think tanks in Sub-Saharan Africa 2020*

1. African Centre for the Constructive Resolution of Disputes (ACCORD) (South Africa)

2. Kenya Institute for Public Policy Research and Analysis (KIPPRA) (Kenya)

3. African Centre for Economic Transformation (ACET) (Ghana)

4. REPOA, FKA Research on Poverty Alleviation (Tanzania)

5. Council for the Development of Social Science Research in Africa (CODESRIA) (Senegal)

6. South African Institute of International Affairs (SAIIA) (South Africa)

7. Institute of Economic Affairs (IEA) (Kenya)

8. IMANI Centre for Policy and Education (Ghana)

9. Ethiopia Policy Studies Institute (PSI) FNA Ethiopia Development Research Centre (Ethiopia)

10. African Economic Research Consortium (AERC) (Kenya)

11. Centre for Democracy and Development (CDD) (Nigeria)

12. Centre Ivoirien de Recherches Economiques et Sociales (CIRES) (Côte d'Ivoire)

13. Food, Agriculture and Natural Resources Policy Analysis Network (FANRPAN) (South Africa)

14. Centre for Development and Enterprise (CDE) (South Africa)

15. Institute for Security Studies (ISS) (South Africa)

16. Institute of Economic Affairs (IEA) (Ghana)

17. Ethiopian Economics Association (EEA) (Ethiopia)

18. Advocates Coalition for Development and Environment (ACODE) (Uganda)

19. Centre for Conflict Resolution (CCR) (South Africa)

20. Africa Heritage Institution (Afri-Heritage) (Nigeria)

Source: McGann (2021a: 45).

CHALLENGES FACING AFRICAN THINK TANKS

During the first African Think Tank Summit, Dr Frannie Leautier, former Executive Secretary of the ACBF, had reported that 30 per cent of Africa's think tanks may close or be in crisis. During the sixth African Think Tank Summit, the African think tanks were described as an 'opportunity in crisis'. According to the summit report, African think tanks were beset by the following challenges:

- Fleeing funds, most notably the departure of donor funds following a massive increase in research support, leaving behind inflated budgets and new, large gaps in funding.
- A lack of core funding (instead, project specialized), leading to a lack of core infrastructure and long-term planning.
- A legacy of colonialism that manifests in distrust between Northern and Southern think tanks (McGann 2018: 4).

African think tanks continue to face enormous challenges. Writing about the crisis of African think tanks (McGann et al. 2017) identify four major challenges facing African think tanks: funding; independence and autonomy; quality and capacity; and impact and effective engagement with policy makers. They perceived these challenges as constituting a serious threat to the survival of independent think tanks in Africa.

In addition, drawing from data collected on African think tanks, the Think Tanks and Civil Society Program has estimated that 60 percent (that is, 30 percent, plus an additional 25–30 extremely fragile organizations) of think tanks are highly vulnerable with a serious risk of disappearing, given unstable funding, staff turnover and brain drain. The nature and the scope of the think tank crisis constitute a big risk to sustained African transformation. Arguing that the shift of perception, over the past two decades, from an Africa facing permanent crisis to 'Africa Rising' is partly attributed to the work of African think tanks who provide stronger and more nuanced knowledge and options for improving policy and governance, it calls for intervention to address the issues. It considered funding to be one of the biggest challenges faced by African think tanks, posing a threat to them. Funding is often 'uncertain, irregular, insufficient, and unequally distributed in the think tank space exacerbated by the fact that African think tanks are overly dependent on international funding'. African think tanks are locked in competition with diverse government and non-government actors for international financial resources, and there is a dearth of private sector funding.

With regard to independence and autonomy, African think tanks face myriad challenges, including the risk of co-optation by government agencies or the political opposition. They also face the risk of becoming promoters of special interests. They are particularly vulnerable to promoting the interest and policy agenda of specific donors. Some think tanks face the risk of becoming consultancy firms, as the requirements of survival push them into more consultancy activities, shrinking the space for an independent research agenda.

In terms of quality and capacity, some African think tanks perform below recognized global standards; they struggle with producing quality work that meets global standards for quality because they have too few well-trained scholars, communication and development professionals, and think tank leaders and administrators. Where they have such staff, they are unable to retain them. A few years after training, professional staff often get better-paid positions at other organizations such as international institutions, foundations and in the private sector.

African think tanks are also not able to ensure tangible impacts. They lack effective engagement of policy makers and the public because of insufficient ability to communicate, limited media exposure and networks, low interest of and access to policy makers, misaligned priorities, limited responsiveness to immediate demands, and a lack of trust. Other challenges, which are not particular to African think tanks, include:

- Failure to understand and respond to non-traditional sources of competition.
- Failure to adopt new technologies and marketing and communications strategies.
- A political and regulatory environment that is increasingly hostile to think tanks, experts and policy advice.
- Decreasing funding for policy research by public and private donors.
- Public and private donor tendency toward short-term, project-specific funding instead of investing in ideas and institutions.
- Underdeveloped institutional capacity and the inability to adapt to change.
- Increased competition from advocacy organizations, for-profit consulting firms, law firms and 24/7 electronic media.
- Institutions having served their purpose and discontinued their operations (McGann 2021a: 16).

CONCLUSIONS

African think tanks have been a major factor in the development of a more responsive and engaged social science community. They have served and continue to serve as knowledge brokers between the social community in higher education, and the policy world. However, many of these think tanks rely on donor agencies for funding, and therefore are sometimes promoters of the research agenda of such agencies by advancing the preferences and priorities of such bodies.

For think tanks to be able to provide independent capacity-building, research, policy analysis and advocacy services to governments and key stakeholders, they must be able to source funds from domestic foundations and wealthy individuals. They must acknowledge that knowledge is contextual, and create a platform for the conversation around the public use of knowledge and be able to provide a critical reflection on the relationship between research and policy making on the continent.

They must be strategic in fund raising such that they are able to fund independent studies. Flexible funding can guarantee a context-specific research agenda addressed using practical and home-grown solutions to African problems. They should build or strengthen strategic partnerships and seek long-term contracts for sustainability. This means that they must diversify their sources of funding. While staying true to their missions, think tanks should strive for a better understanding of evolving philanthropy in the think tank space, and seek to define synergies and value propositions that attract the private sector. African think tanks need to develop and strengthen national and regional think tank networks, and develop collective responses to address common problems. Donors should seek long-term relationships with think tanks to help institutional strengthening, and help in building their fundraising capacity to develop streams of revenues. African think tanks still require institutional development support to strengthen virtual operations and reach, to engage experts in areas that have become critical in the rapidly changing environment with its uncertainties.

McGann et al. (2017) suggest rightly that think tanks must be 'data and fact-driven, bold and consistent in seeking to make a policy difference', and 'produce actionable solutions relevant for society'. They also suggest that 'in order to achieve a sustainable future, think tanks should develop a unified voice and act collectively, including for funding'. Think tanks should build partnerships with similar think tanks in the developed world for mutual benefit, sharing ideas on best practices in research and outreach, the training of qualified leaders, and in strategic planning, networking with highly skilled scholars, building trust and engagement with policy makers and the public.

Think tank leaders must recognize that they operate in a competitive environment and must strive to produce quality work to achieve high impact with policy makers and the public. Their outputs, such as briefs, reports, social media engagements, public debates, policy conferences, roundtables, forums, and so on, must be of the highest standard. Think tanks must clearly state in their mission whether their organization is partisan or non-partisan, to ensure a high level of integrity. They must implement accountability practices and reporting mechanisms.

REFERENCES

Acquah, E. (2021). The Future of African Think Tanks, in J.G. McGann (ed.), *The Future of Think Tanks and Policy Advice Around the World*, Cham: Springer Nature/ Palgrave Macmillan, 27–40.

Ahmad, Mahmood (2008). US Think Tanks and the Politics of Expertise: Role, Value and Impact, *Political Quarterly* 79 (4): 529–555.

Aiyede, E.R. and M. Quadri (2022). Policy Evaluation in Africa, in Gedion Onyango (ed.), *Routledge Handbook of Public Policy in Africa*, London: Routledge Taylor & Francis, 164–176.

Anheier, H. (2010). Social Science Research Outside the Ivory Tower: The Role of Think-Tanks and Civil Society, in UNESCO and International Social Science Council (eds), *World Social Science Report: Knowledge Divides*, 338–340.

Asher, T. and N. Guilhot (2010). The Collapsing Space between Universities and Think-Tanks, in UNESCO (ed.), *World Social Science Report: Knowledge Divides*, 341–345.

Diawara, B. (2020). Covid-19 and African Think Tanks: Challenges, Needs and Solutions on Think Tanks (OTT), Covid-19 Survey Report on the Impact of COVID-19 on Think Tanks, 7 April – 25 May 2020. https://onthinktanks.org/wp -content/uploads/2020/07/COVID-19_SurveyReport_1.pdf.

Dickinson, Paul (1972). *Think Tanks*, New York: Atheneum.

Gounden, V. and C. de Coning (2021). The Future of Think Tanks in Africa, in J.G. McGann (ed.), *The Future of Think Tanks and Policy Advice Around the World*, Cham: Springer Nature/Palgrave Macmillan, 21 26.

Hassan, I. (2021). Bringing Think Tanks into the Digital Era, in J.G. McGann (ed.), *The Future of Think Tanks and Policy Advice Around the World*, Cham: Springer Nature/Palgrave Macmillan, 41–44.

Kimenyi, M.S. and A. Datta (2011). Think Tanks in sub-Saharan Africa: How the Political Landscape has Influenced Their Origins, London: Overseas Development Institute. https://cdn.odi.org/media/documents/7527.pdf.

Laakso, L. (2022). The Social Science Foundations of Public Policy in Africa, in Gedion Onyango (ed.), *Routledge Handbook of Public Policy in Africa*, London: Routledge Taylor & Francis, 23–31.

McGann, J.G. (2009). 2009 Global Go To Think Tanks Index Report, Philadelphia, PA: University of Pennsylvania. https://repository.upenn.edu/cgi/viewcontent.cgi?article=1001&context=think_tanks.

McGann, J.G. (2012). 2011 Global Go To Think Tanks Index Report, TTCSP Global Go To Think Tank Index Reports, 6. https://repository.upenn.edu/think_tanks/6.

McGann, J.G. (2015) 2015 Africa Think Tank Summit Report: The Rise of Africa's Think Tanks: Practical Solutions to Practical Problems, TTCSP Global and Regional Think Tank Summit Reports, 12. http://repository.upenn.edu/ttcsp_summitreports/12.

McGann, J.G. (2017). 2017 Africa Think Tank Summit Report: Fit for the Future: Enhancing the Capacity, Quality, and Sustainability of Africa's Think Tanks, TTCSP Global and Regional Think Tank Summit Reports, 20. https://repository.upenn.edu/ttcsp_summitreports/20.

McGann, J.G. (2018), 2018 Africa Think Tank Summit Report: Deepening Expertise and Enhancing Sustainability: Insights into Contemporary Challenges Facing African Think Tanks (2018), TTCSP Global and Regional Think Tank Summit Reports, 23. https://repository.upenn.edu/ttcsp_summitreports/23.

McGann, J.G. (2019). 2018 Global Go To Think Tank Index Report, TTCSP Global Go To Think Tank Index Reports. 16. https://repository.upenn.edu/think_tanks/16.

McGann, J.G. (2021a). 2020 Global Go To Think Tank Index Report, TTCSP Global Go To Think Tank Index Reports, 18. https://repository.upenn.edu/think_tanks/18.

McGann, J.G. (2021b). Introduction and Background, in J.G. McGann (ed.), *The Future of Think Tanks and Policy Advice Around the World*, Cham: Springer Nature/Palgrave Macmillan, 1–20.

McGann, James and Richard Sabatini (2010). *Global Think Tanks: Policy Networks and Governance*, New York: Taylor & Francis.

McGann, J., L. Signe and M. Muyangwa (2017). The Crisis of African Think Tanks: Challenges and Solutions, *Africa in Focus*, 13 December. https://www.brookings.edu/blog/africa-in-focus/2017/12/13/the-crisis-of-african-think-tanks-challenges-and-solutions/.

McGann, James G. and R. Kent Weaver (2000). *Think Tanks and Civil Society: Catalysts for Ideas and Action*, New York: Routledge Taylor & Francis.

Mirowski, P. and E.-M. Sent (2002) *Science Bought and Sold: Essays in the Economics of Science*. https://api.semanticscholar.org/CorpusID:15952210

Mkandawire, T. (2000). *Non-Organic Intellectuals and Learning. In Policy-making Africa*. Stockholm: Learning in Development Co-operation EGDI Publication.

Musa, B. (2021). Top 10 Think Tanks Telling Sub-Saharan Africa's New Story, *The Guardian*, 19 September. https://guardian.ng/features/focus/top-10-think-tanks -telling-sub-saharan-africas-new-story/.

Ngugi, R. (2021). Think Tanks in the Context of Africa's Development, in J.G. MacGann (ed.), *The Future of Think Tanks and Policy Advice Around the World*, Cham: Springer Nature/Palgrave Macmillan, 45–50.

Okeke-Uzodike, U. (2021). The Future of Think Tanks and Policy Advice: An African Perspective, in J.G. MacGann (ed.), *The Future of Think Tanks and Policy Advice Around the World*, Cham: Springer Nature/Palgrave Macmillan, 33–39.

Wihardja, M.M. (2014). Center for Strategic and International Studies (CSIS): Shaping Development Policy in a Globalized World, in J.G. McGann, A. Viden and J. Rafferty (eds), *How Think Tanks Shape Social Development Policies*, Philadelphia, PA: University of Pennsylvania Press, 185–199.

Winthrop, R. (2014). Brookings Institution: The Case for Global Education, in J.G. McGann, A. Viden and J. Rafferty (eds), *How Think Tanks Shape Social Development Policies*, Philadelphia, PA: University of Pennsylvania Press, 65–75.

3. Think tanks and public policy-making: the case of Botswana

Emmanuel Botlhale

INTRODUCTION

For expository clarity and to delineate the universe of the discourse, the term 'think tank' must be defined. While the term 'think tank' is modern, it can be traced to the humanist academies and scholarly networks of the 16th and 17th centuries (Soll, 2017). However, modern-day think tanks began in the United States in the 19th and early 20th centuries (McGann and Weaver, 2009; Stone, 2006). Forerunners are the Brookings Institution (founded 1916), the Carnegie Endowment for International Peace (1914), the Kiel Institute of World Economics (1914) and the Royal Institute for International Affairs (Chatham House) (1920). There has been remarkable growth in the number of think tanks over the past century (Chatham House, 2021). In the 1920s, there were a few think tanks, and 'in the 1950s, there were a hundred or so mainly clustered in Western cities' (ibid.). Today, there are nearly 800 think tanks scattered all over the world (ibid.). Originally, they were study groups comprising academics and government officials that discussed policy issues in confidential settings, using the Chatham House Rule (ibid.). In addition, they hosted lectures and reviewed research papers and reports. Their work was purposed to influence specific individuals and communities, not the wider public as is the case today, and they used a 'rifle, not a shotgun approach' (ibid.). The term 'think tank' was first used in military jargon during World War II to describe a safe place where plans and strategies could be discussed, but its meaning began to change during the 1960s when it came to be used in the United States to describe private non-profit policy research organizations (Ladi, 2015). Notably, there are definitional difficulties with the concept of think tanks (e.g., see Abelson and Lindquist, 2009). In this regard, Abelson and Lindquist (2009, p. 38) argue that 'defining typical think tanks can be extraordinarily difficult, since their policy interests, intended audiences, and organisational structures vary enormously'.

Despite definitional difficulties, a working definition of the term 'think tank' is needed. For the purpose of this chapter, we use Ladi's (2015) and Stone's (2006), because they capture the essence of the term. A think tank is an institute, corporation or group organized for interdisciplinary research with the objective of providing advice on a diverse range of policy issues and products through the use of specialized knowledge and the activation of networks (Ladi, 2015). On a related note, Stone (2006, p. 149) states that think tanks are 'policy research institutes involved in the research and analysis of a particular policy area or a broad range of policy issues, seeking to advise policymakers or inform public debate on policy issues'. They are non-state actors, but their work services both governmental entities and commercial clients.

Think tanks come in different shapes and sizes, that is, they present different characteristics. Despite the heterogeneity, they share common characteristics. Ladi (2015) identifies four: (1) policy focus (their objective is to bring knowledge and policy-making together by informing and, if possible, influencing the policy process); (2) public purpose (the reason for the existence is to serve the public purpose); (3) expertise and professionalism (the two are the key intellectual resources of think tanks and they ztheir findings); and (4) Research analysis and advice (these are typically presented in papers, workshops, conferences and seminars). Regarding their role, 'the key activities of think tanks are usually research analysis and advice, which come in the form of publications, conferences, seminars, and workshops' (Ladi, 2015, p. 2).

On the whole, think tanks bring expert knowledge to bear on public decision-making (McGann and Weaver, 2009). This is a very important undertaking, because 'government and individual policy-makers throughout the world face the common problem of bringing expert knowledge to bear in governmental decision-making' (McGann and Weaver, 2009, p. 1). The situation is more acute in sub-Saharan Africa (SSA) due to the unavailability of reliable data. Data – not any kind of data, but data of good quality – is imperatively critical in the age of data-driven policy-making, but SSA has grave data and statistical deficits (e.g., see Bédécarrats et al., 2016; Kinyondo and Pelizzo, 2018). Data and statistical deficits detract from SSA's ability to make the right policy decisions, hence the uniquely difficult terrain that SSA-based think tanks have to contend with. Kinyondo and Pelizzo (2018, p. 851) put it concretely, decrying that 'one of the problems that scholars encounter when conducting research is that data from Africa are poor', and that 'indeed, they either do not exist in a complete sense or they are not of good quality in the sense of lacking validity and reliability'. Hence, they argue that the lack of quality data detracts from the 'continent's ability to generate a pertinent body of knowledge' and 'prevents analysts from generating the evidence that policymakers need to make proper decisions'.

EVIDENCE-BASED PUBLIC POLICY-MAKING

In conformity with standard economic theory, this chapter models the government as a rational and utility-maximizing economic agent (*Homo economicus*). The underlying assumptions are the ability to: (1) always maximize economic self-interest; and (2) assess the economic costs and benefits among different and competing alternative decision choices. Hence, the government prefers more rather than less of a given good or service, *ceteris paribus*. For instance, given a choice between US$100 billion worth of goods and/or services and US$50 billion worth of goods and/or services, it should prefer the former over the latter, all things remaining equal. Due to the *Homo economicus* assumption, the government practises economic decision-making. This is the equivalent of rational decision-making, and it primarily entails the collection and processing of information (Day, 1971). Being the opposite of intuitive decision-making, the rational model of decision-making is a model where individuals use facts and information, analysis, and a step-by-step procedure to come to a decision (Uzonwanne, 2016, p. 78). The rational model of decision-making is an advanced type of decision-making model. Amongst others, rational decision-making is actualized through the PACED decision-making guide. PACED includes the following steps: state the problem, list alternatives, identify criteria, evaluate alternatives, and make a decision. Clearly, the foregoing is in clear contrast to other models, these being the collegial model, the political model, the bureaucratic model, and organized anarchy.

The PACED model is anchored in three key assumptions: (1) availability of time; (2) availability of data; and (3) sufficient cognitive abilities to process data. These factors are not always present; consequently leading to the assailing of the model by behaviourists, notably Simon (1955, 1979). Despite the criticism, the rational man model helps us to model the behaviour of economic agents such as governments when they engage in rational or economic decision-making.

The general proposition that reliable knowledge is a powerful instrument for advising decision-makers and for achieving political success is a very old doctrine, linked to the exercise of effective statecraft and efficient governance in early modern Europe (Head, 2010, p. 78). In this regard, both researchers and policy-makers are in agreement regarding the benefits that science confers on the policy-making process (Ruggeri et al., 2020). Thus, evidence matters in public policy-making (see Parkhurst, 2017), and this is done through evidence-based decision-making (EBDM). EBDM is a process for making the best decisions possible using the evidence available (Heathfield, 2021). Thus, this model 'avoids decision making that is based on gut feeling, intuition, or instinct and instead relies on data and facts' (Heathfield, 2021, p. 1).

The term 'evidence-based' originated in the field of medicine in the 1990s; however, today it is used in many and varied disciplines such as education, criminology, public policy, social work and, latterly, management (Center for Evidence-Based Decision Making, 2021). Where does evidence come from? It comes from many sources, including: (1) scientific evidence (findings from published scientific research); (2) organizational evidence (data, facts and figures gathered from the organization); (3) experiential evidence (the professional experience and judgement of practitioners; and (4) stakeholder evidence (the values and concerns of people who may be affected by the decision (Barends and Rousseau, 2014). According to Rousseau, 'evidence-based management ... derives principles from research evidence and translates them into practices that solve organizational problems' (Rousseau, 2006, p. 256). It does this by incorporating principles based on the best available evidence into organizational practice. There are many works on evidence-based management (EBM/EBMgt), for example, Barends and Rousseau (2014, 2018), Holloway (2007), Pfeffer and Sutton (2006), Reid and Spinks (2007), Rousseau (2006) and Vishwanath and Hakem (2012). Notably, Rousseau (2006) is the foremost proponent of EBM. In essence, EBM aims to bridge the research–practice divide (Rousseau, 2006).

EBM has been renamed as evidence-based decision-making (EBDM) in the public policy field. Although EBDM was formally introduced by the United Kingdom's Blair government in 1997, it is not new because it has roots in antiquity (de Marchi et al., 2016). To illustrate, Aristotle (350 BC) counselled that decisions should be informed by knowledge. Evidence-based policy-making has become increasingly popular in many areas, as can be seen by the proliferation of think tanks and initiatives supporting and advocating for evidence-based policy-making (Leuz, 2018, p. 582). Evidence-based policy-making uses the best available research and information on programme results to guide decisions at all stages of the policy process, and in each branch of government (Pew Charitable Trusts, 2014, p. 2). Thus, evidence-based policy-making places a very high premium on rigorous research findings (Urban Institute, 2016). The practice takes many forms; for example, using research findings to inform new policies or improve the effectiveness of existing programmes, supporting data collection and analysis for research, and so on (Urban Institute, 2016, p. 2). Evidence-based policy-making (EBPM) helps policy-makers and providers of services make better decisions, and achieve better outcomes, by drawing upon the best available evidence from research and evaluation and other sources (Department of Planning, Monitoring and Evaluation (South Africa), 2014, p. 1). Thus, it is different from opinion-based policy-making (OBPM).

There are many benefits and/or advantages that attach to EBPM. In this regard, the Pew Charitable Trusts (2014, p. 2) states that by taking this approach, governments can:

Reduce wasteful spending; by using evidence on program outcomes to inform budget choices, policymakers can identify and eliminate ineffective programs, freeing up dollars for other uses.

Expand innovative programs; requiring that new and untested programs undergo rigorous evaluation helps determine whether they work and identifies opportunities to target funding to innovative initiatives that deliver better outcomes to residents or reduce costs.

Strengthen accountability; collecting and reporting data on program operations and outcomes makes it easier to hold agencies, managers, and providers accountable for results.

Admittedly, EBPM is not the fabled silver bullet, for there are challenges in the research–policy channel. Some argue that research findings do not effortlessly translate into policies. Examples are Head (2010), National Academies of Sciences (2017) and Saltelli and Giampietro (2017). In this regard, Head (2010, p. 77) cautions that while there is a rational expectation that research will engender improved policy analysis, things are different in the real world of public policy-making. He thus argues that 'key issues for consideration include the forms of evidence that are of greatest relevance or utility for decision-makers, and the most productive forms of interaction between the producers and the users of research and evaluation findings'. In a similar vein, Leuz (2018) discusses the challenges of evidence-based public policy-making. Leuz asserts that it is far easier to demand it, as opposed to doing it. Leuz lists its challenges as: 'it faces many challenges related to the difficulty of providing relevant causal evidence, lack of data, the reliability of published research and the transmission of research findings' (ibid., p. 582). On a related note, Florin (2014) asserts that evidence-based public policy-making is challenged when it comes to making decisions in situations of uncertainty and emergency. This is so because the 'collection and provision of scientific information for policy and decision-making is particularly important during emergencies or when uncertainty and ambiguity creates situation[s] of fear and anxiety' (Florin, 2014, p. 303). Sutcliffe and Court (2005, p. iv) describe the challenges as:

(i)   *What evidence is used in the policymaking process?* What is clear from the literature is that policy should be informed by a wide breadth of evidence, not just hard research. Key issues include the quality, credibility, relevance and the cost of the policy.
(ii)   *How evidence is incorporated into policymaking.* Policy processes ideally involve different stages, from agenda-setting to formulation to implemen-

tation. Evidence therefore has the potential to influence the policymaking process at each stage. However different evidence and different mechanisms may be required at each of the policy stages.

(iii) *Evidence is not the only factor which influences policymaking.* It is important to acknowledge that at each stage of the policy cycle, a number of different factors will also affect policy. This occurs at an individual level – for example, a policymaker's own experience, expertise and judgement – and at an institutional level, for example in terms of institutional capacity.

Despite the foregoing challenges, EBPM is believed to be superior to OBPM on the balance of probabilities. However, it is notable that EBPM does not mean 'EBPM at any cost'. So there is a need for an appreciation of the fact that EBPM is a costly exercise. Thus, it entails opportunity costs, hence cost–benefit analysis (CBA) is key. CBA can be performed through marginal analysis. This is the examination of the additional benefits of an activity compared to the additional costs incurred by that same activity (Hutchinson et al., 2017). Thus, this chapter uses marginal analysis as a theoretical model to discuss the government's utilization of EBPM.

MARGINAL ANALYSIS AS A THEORETICAL MODEL FOR USING EBPM

This chapter models the government as a utility maximizer; it maximizes utility from EBPM 9 (Table 3.1). Thus, it thinks at the margin by maximizing benefits and minimizing costs. We further assume that the market (*Demand* = *Benefit* and *Supply* = *Cost*) situation is as given in Figure 3.1.

Table 3.1   Demand and supply of EBPM

Units of EBPM (millions)	Cost (US$) (millions)	Marginal Cost	Benefit (US$) (millions)	Marginal Benefit
1	10	0	20	0
2	15	5	60	40
3	30	15	90	30
4	47	17	110	20
5	65	18	128	18
6	86	21	140	12
7	110	24	145	5
8	140	30	146	1
9	175	35	146.5	0.5
10	215	40	146.8	0.3

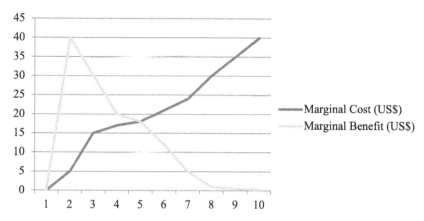

Figure 3.1   Marginal benefit versus marginal cost of EBPM

Using laws of diminishing marginal returns and increasing marginal costs, marginal returns are increasing at an increasing rate and then at a decreasing rate and marginal costs are increasing at an increasing rate. Equilibrium is reached when *Marginal Benefit = Marginal Cost* where equilibrium quantity and price are 5 million units and US$18 million, respectively. At this point, the optimum quantity of EBPM is attained. Any quantity below 5 million units of EBPM is suboptimal because *Marginal Benefit > Marginal Cost*. Contrariwise, any quantity above 5 million units of EBPM is suboptimal because *Marginal Benefit < Marginal Cost* as shown in Figure 3.1.

Using marginal analysis, the government uses EBPM until the point of equilibrium. Admittedly, in the real world, there are limits to the rational man model due to time, informational and cognitive limitations, hence leading to satisficing (as opposed to maximizing behaviour; see Simon, 1947, 1955). Thus the government, subject to informational and cognitive limitations, will satisfice by using the socially optimum quantity of EBPM. To do so, the government outsources this chore to think tanks, or policy institutes. The think tanks and government sit on the demand and supply sides of the policy research market. Assuming perfect, or near perfect, conditions in the policy research market, an equilibrium will be reached which will ensure that the policy research demanded by the government (demand) is equal to the quantity of research supplied (supply) by think tanks.

There are many works on the role of think tanks in the policy-making space (e.g., see Abelson, 2018; Abelson and Rastrick, 2021; CIPE, 2021; Fraussen and Halpin, 2017; McGann, 2006, 2015, 2016; McGann et al., 2014). CIPE (2021) puts it cogently, stating that 'think tanks act as brokers of policy knowledge, centres of research, and incubators of new ideas'. In line with CIPE

(2021), the Botswana Institute for Development Policy Analysis does this in Botswana.

RESEARCH METHODOLOGY

Research methodology is the strategy or architectural design by which the researcher maps out an approach to problem-finding or problem-solving (Buckley et al., 1976). In essence, it answers the following questions: (1) What data must be collected? (2) Who/where is the data to be collected from (sampling design)? (3) How is the sought-after data to be collected (data collection methods)? and (4) How is the data to be analysed (data analysis methods)?. Given the nature of the enquiry, the study is based on interpretivism. Interpretivist research 'is conceptualized as having a relativist ontology with a subjectivist epistemology and is aligned with postmodern thought' (Levers, 2013, p. 3). It is guided by the researcher's set of beliefs and feelings about the world, and how it should be understood and studied (Denzin and Lincoln, 2005, p. 22). The study adopted a qualitative case study approach, and data collection consisted of both primary and secondary data collection sources. Data analysis was in the form of questionnaire and document analysis.

FINDINGS AND DISCUSSIONS

The Botswana Institute for Development Policy Analysis (BIDPA) was established by the Government of Botswana as an independent trust, and started operation as a non-governmental policy research institute or think tank in 1995 (BIDPA, 2019a). According to BIDPA's deed of trust, it pursues many objectives, including:

> To promote and conduct research, analysis and publication on development policy issues, which are of relevance to Botswana and the Southern African region.
> To monitor the performance of the Botswana economy and the management of public policy implementation, especially with regard to the implications for economic and social development.
> To provide technical and financial assistance, directly and indirectly, to individuals and organizations in Botswana as deemed desirable for purposes of facilitating policy analysis.
> To assist professional training and public education of Botswana citizens in matters relating to policy analysis and encourage collaboration between expatriates and local professionals in these matters in ways which build, or augment, national capacities for performance and understanding of policy analysis. (BIDPA, 2019a)

BIDPA's core activities are research, consultancy and capacity-building. Research involves the following: (1) macroeconomics and development; (2) trade, industry and private sector development; and (3) human and social development. Macroeconomics and development research focuses on transitioning the economy to diversified, export-led growth. This covers fiscal policy, monetary and exchange rate policy, infrastructure and development of the financial sector. These areas are grouped under three research themes: macroeconomic policy, finance, and infrastructure development (BIDPA, 2019a). Trade, industry and private sector development research focuses on development issues from the perspective of the firms and industries that will be integral to the transformation of the economy. This focus area has three research themes: trade and regional integration; economic sectors; and productivity, competitiveness and innovation (BIDPA, 2019a). Human and social development research focuses on education and health policies, employment, unemployment, poverty, inequality and the nature of social protection policies (BIDPA, 2019a).

Environment, agriculture and natural resources research focuses on the exploitation of mineral resources and resource governance and land use. This research focus area has three research themes: environmental sustainability, agriculture and natural resources (BIDPA, 2019a). Lastly, governance and administration research focuses on public sector reforms and effective public sector project management. There are two research themes in this area, namely: public sector service delivery, and political economy of development (BIDPA, 2019a).

Regarding research and consultancy, BIDPA conducts research, analysis and publication on developmental policy issues which are relevant to Botswana and the Southern African region (BIDPA, 2019a). It conducts two types of research: supply-driven and demand-driven. Some supply-driven projects undertaken to date are: Financial Inclusion and its impact on Employment Creation in Botswana; Education and Labour Market Activity of Women in Botswana; challenges of Project Implementation in Local Government – The case of the Francistown City Council and Kweneng District Councils; and the impact of Macroeconomic Variables on Capital Market Development in Botswana's Economy. Under demand-driven research, BIDPA provides consultancy and advisory services to government ministries, departments, parastatals and other clients by tendering for research projects. To date, it has undertaken several projects: Assessment of the Investment Opportunities within the Manufacturing Sector in Botswana (in 2019); Revision of Existing National Poverty Eradication Policy Framework (2019); and Study on the Contribution of Copyright Industries to the National Economy of Botswana (2018). Lastly, regarding capacity-building within the areas of economic and social development, BIDPA provides formal training in the form of Masters and Doctoral degrees, together with short courses, attachments, seminars and workshops (BIDPA, 2019a).

BIDPA has an extensive library of publications that comes in many and varied forms: newsletters, annual reports, policy briefs, journal articles and working papers. Annual reports provide a window into the organization's operational performance, as illustrated next. The year 2019/2020 was productive in the area of research. The Institute produced nine working papers, two policy briefs and eight journal articles, two conference papers and one book chapter (BIDPA, 2020, p. 16). In terms of demand-driven research, four projects were completed, while four are ongoing. Regarding client satisfaction on consultancy projects, it scored above the target: 80 per cent against the target of 70 per cent (BIDPA, 2020). In terms of rankings, BIDPA is highly ranked, as instanced by the Think Tanks and Civil Societies Program (TTCSP) of the Lauder Institute at the University of Pennsylvania. The TTCSP conducts research on the roles that policy institutes play in governments and civil societies around the world (TTCSP, 2021). It is often referred to as 'the think tank of think tanks'. In this regard, in 2019/2020, the TTCSP ranked BIDPA the top think tank in sub-Saharan Africa for 2019 (BIDPA, 2020). Notably, the 2019 ranking was a repeat of previous top rankings in 2017 and 2018.

Regarding supply-driven research during 2019/2020, the following were produced: eight working papers, two policy briefs, and four peer-reviewed journal articles. As for demand-driven research during 2019/2020, four completed works and six ongoing were produced (BIDPA, 2020). It is notable that alongside the foregoing successes, there were challenges. The key ones are skills capacity challenges, especially at senior levels, and COVID-19. COVID-19 meant restricted travel to undertake research regarding a great number of commissioned studies, hence delaying the process. To mitigate the challenge, virtual platforms were used. Notably, the pandemic gave impetus to BIDPA's digitization drive, so engendering operational efficiencies and effectiveness.

To triangulate data collection sources by using both primary and secondary data, the author sent a questionnaire (see Box 3.1) to BIDPA as the main respondent. In response, the BIDPA sent the author a PowerPoint presentation. In addition, the same questionnaire was emailed to two other respondents, but only one responded.

BOX 3.1   GENERAL QS

i.   What accounts for the proliferation of think tanks in sub-Saharan Africa since the 1990s?
ii. How and why do think tanks influence governance, policy formulation and implementation?

Specific to BIDPA:

iii. Why was BIDPA established?

iv. What is BIDPA's general contribution to development policy-making in Botswana?

v. What are major milestones that BIDPA has achieved in the development policy arena? Any major examples where it has significantly influenced development policy in Botswana?

vi. What major activities/programs does it embark on that influence development policy in Botswana?

vii. How do policy briefs and related activities influence development policy in Botswana?

viii. How does BIDPA navigate the not-so-linear path between research and policy?

ix. How does BIDPA ensure the effective communication of policy research to the government?

x. What major challenges/issues does BIDPA face and how have they been addressed?

xi. How do you see the role of BIDPA evolving in the face of COVID-19 fiscal challenges?

xii. What Africa-wide lessons can be learned from BIDPA's work and what are the implications for the literature on public policy?

A summary of the responses is presented next. In general, the proliferation of think tanks in sub-Saharan Africa since the 1990s is attributable to the expanded use of evidence-based public policy-making. That is, SSA governments would want to ensure that policy follows the evidence. On the whole, think tanks influence governance, policy formulation and implementation, particularly formulation, in service of the ethic of evidence-based public policy-making. It is notable that according to BIDPA's deed of trust, one of its objectives is 'to promote and conduct research, analysis and publication on development policy issues, which are of relevance to Botswana and the Southern African region' (BIDPA, 2019a). Hence, BIDPA, like other think tanks in Africa – for example the Institute for Democratic Government (Ghana), Centre Mauritanien d'Analyse de Politique (Mauritania), Ethiopian Development Research Institute, and so on – is pushing the evidence-based public policy-making agenda.

Specific to BIDPA, the deed of trust provides reasons behind its establishment. Its strategic foundation is to 'provide evidence-based socio-economic policy advice and related capacity-building' (BIDPA, 2019b, p. 4). It is notable that since its inception, BIDPA has made a substantial contribution to development policy-making in Botswana. BIDPA is a major player in the national policy formulation landscape, and its mandate is defined by the following five elements: economic research and policy analysis; institutional capacity-building; professional training; networking; and public education (BIDPA, 2019b, p. 2). Regarding milestones that BIDPA has achieved in the development policy arena, there are many, but a few notable ones were mentioned. Since its inception, BIDPA has undertaken much demand- and supply-driven research, in accordance with its mandate of policy formulation and policy analysis (BIDPA, 2019b, p. 15). Some of the policy-impactful projects include: (1) consultancy for the development of a Long-Term Vision for Botswana;[1] (2) the state of governance in Botswana; (3) consultancy for the development of a new Long-Term Vision for Botswana;[2] and (4) evaluation of the Effectiveness of the Citizen Empowerment Policy (BIDPA, 2019b, p. 15). These have significantly influenced development policy in Botswana, hence answering the question about specific examples where BIDPA has significantly influenced development policy in Botswana. In addition, BIDPA occasionally produces policy briefs meant to influence development policy, hence answering the question about how policy briefs and related activities influence development policy in Botswana. Notably, the presentation did not provide answers to questions *viii* to *xii*, leading to data gaps.

From Respondent 2, who responded to the questionnaire via a WhatsApp message, it is deducible that BIDPA does not navigate the not-so-linear path between research and policy. It was stated that 'it [BIDPA] produces policy advice which the recipient (mostly the government) receives, analyses and uses as it deems fit'. Thus, it can be concluded that BIDPA produces policy advice, but does not perform follow-ups to check whether or not it translates into policy. Relatedly, research findings are said to be clearly communicated to the government, and in this regard BIDPA ensures the effective communication of policy research to the government. Thus:

> When government seeks BIDPA's advice – BIDPA delivers only to the paying department/ministry. Research reports normally carry a recommendations section as well as an Executive Summary which captures the essence of the matter. Prior to finalizing the reports, BIDPA presents to steering committees which gives BIDPA an insider's view of the policy matters in question and provide a quality control process. (WhatsApp communication, 28 June 2021)

Regarding major challenges/issues, these were highlighted as: (1) BIDPA currently appears to fail to attract senior researchers (financial rewards versus burden of the job); (2) BIDPA also seems unable to retain many of its middle-level researchers; and (3) BIDPA fails to optimize policy advice

(WhatsApp communication, 28 June 2021). On a related note, it was pointed out that the government often interferes with policy advice:

> They simply receive the results, including recommendations and if they do not like them, they simply pay you and ignore what you gave them. But there is also the Cabinet memo process; the results and recommendations are taken by technocrats and processed internally to speak to implementability. This means that once a cab memo is written, it is then circulated for comment in the government enclave and later sent for comment at the Directorate of Public Service Management (DPSM) and later at cabinet meetings. What comes out would normally have little resemblance to the initial research. (WhatsApp communication, 28 June 2021)

The scenario depicted in the foregoing is in accord with what Mikesell (2003, p. 252) said about public policy-making. He stated that 'what characterizes the public decision process is political bargaining, not an exercise in rational consideration by non-political administrators'.

Lastly, regarding the question of what Africa-wide lessons can be learned from BIDPA's work and what the implications are for the literature on public policy, it was stated that 'the government of Botswana has been supportive of BIDPA by funding the institution and refraining from interfering in its running' (WhatsApp communication, 28 June 2021). Furthermore, it was stated that 'the government funds up to 75% (if not more) of the BIDPA budget, including formal training which provides the basis for capacity building' (ibid.).

While the main respondent, BIDPA, did not directly address the questionnaire, and therefore did not address questions *viii* to *xii*, the PowerPoint presentation covered some of the questions. Respondent 2's input was comprehensive in terms of shedding light on issues that were not covered by the presentation, consequently giving a near complete picture. Ideally, the author would have liked to explore all the issues with all the respondents, particularly the main one, BIDPA. Hence, the foregoing is the data gap challenge that pertained to this study.

What can be concluded from the foregoing? Firstly, that there is a legal-institutional architecture which enables BIDPA to play in the public policy space in Botswana. Secondly, that BIDPA has largely executed its mandate according to the deed of trust, particularly 'to promote and conduct research, analysis and publication on development policy issues'. Despite the successes described above, there are challenges: for example, skills capacity challenges, especially at senior levels. Thus, these challenges detract from BIDPA's operational efficiency and effectiveness. BIDPA's story is typical. Hence, it is an African story with lessons for the continent.

POLICY IMPLICATIONS EMANATING FROM THE CASE STUDY

Even though this study was based on one case study, Botswana, there are many policy implications that ensue from it. For brevity, only a few issues, with possible solutions, are discussed here.

The Necessity of Evidence-Based Public Policy-Making

Clearly, there is no substitute for evidence-based public policy-making; hence, there is an imperative need to found and nurture African think tanks. The quest for evidence-based public policy-making has been given impetus by the COVID-19 pandemic. The pandemic means reduced revenue, particularly for mono-cultural economies that depend on a single export commodity (for example, Botswana is dependent on diamonds). In the face of chronic budget deficits that are mainly attributable to reduced demand for primary products in the international commodity markets, resource scarcity is being heightened. Therefore, there is a need for evidence-based public policy-making to ensure allocative efficiency.

In addition, SSA countries have inaugurated various COVID-19 economic recovery plans. To illustrate, in the face of COVID-19 challenges, Botswana formulated the 2020/21–2022/2023 Economic Recovery and Transformation Plan; Sustainable and Resilient Recovery Towards High-Income Status (ERTP) in 2020. The plan is meant to support the restoration of economic activity and incomes, facilitate economic growth, accelerate economic trans-formation, and build the resilience of the economy (Matsheka, 2020; Ministry of Finance and Economic Development, 2020). In this regard, the World Bank loaned the government $250 million through the Programmatic Economic Resilience and Green Recovery Development Policy Loan (DPL) in June 2020 to support the implementation of the ERTP (World Bank, 2020). Other SSA countries have similar COVID-19 economic recovery plans. An example is the South African Economic Reconstruction and Recovery Plan 'that is aimed at stimulating equitable and inclusive growth' (Republic of South Africa, 2020). Namibia has the COVID-19 Socio-Economic Recovery Plan (SERP). Its pillars include economic recovery (United Nations Namibia, 2020). Zimbabwe has a COVID-19 Economic Recovery and Stimulus Package priced at ZWL$18 billion (Ministry of Finance and Economic Development (Zimbabwe), 2020). One of its objectives, as a result of COVID-19, is to reinvigorate the economy. To get feasibly maximum benefit from these initiatives, evidence-based public policy-making is key; thus, think tanks in Botswana, Namibia, South Africa and Zimbabwe should aid economic recovery.

Funding

One of the biggest challenges faced by African think tanks is funding availability and sustainability (McGann et al., 2017). It is notable that this observation was made in 2017, two years before the outbreak of the COVID-19 pandemic. Given fiscal strictures that are majorly attributable to COVID-19, funding for African-based think tanks is problematic. Thus, there is a need for innovative funding initiatives by self-funding think tanks. Even those that are funded by the state, for example Botswana's BIDPA, are facing chronic financing challenges during the COVID-19 era. Hence, the need for innovative funding initiatives is equally applicable to them.

Capacity Issues

It emerged from the study that 'BIDPA also seems unable to retain many of its middle-level researchers' (WhatsApp communication, 28 June 2021). This has negative implications for both capacity and the quality of research. It is vital to note that this is an Africa-wide problem. In a confirmatory note, McGann et al. (2017) opine that 'the quality of outputs from some African think tanks is sometimes below recognized global standards, thus threatening sustainability'. Thus, there is a need to attend to capacity issues, so that African think tanks produce good-quality research that will have a meaningful policy impact.

Data Challenges

The successful operation of think tanks is heavily contingent on data. Notably, good-quality data is imperative for data-driven policy-making. Unfortunately, SSA has data deficits (e.g., see Bédécarrats et al., 2016; Kinyondo and Pelizzo, 2018). Hence, this issue must be resolved. Also, data gatekeeping must be resolved, because some are overly distrustful of researchers.

De-politicization of Public Policy-Making

Public policy-making is highly political (e.g., see Zittoun, 2014), discrediting the *Homo economicus* model (a point raised by, amongst others, Herbert Simon, Charles Lindblom, Aaron Wildavsky and Giandomenico Majone). Thus, politics lays to waste the rational model; and in a related vein, Mikesell (2003, p. 252) asserts that 'what characterizes the public decision process is political bargaining, not an exercise in rational consideration by non-political administrators'. Despite the truthfulness of what Mikesell says, public policy-making needs to be partially de-politicized by using work from think tanks.

Other Issues

Other issues are effective engagement with policy-makers, and independence and autonomy (McGann et al., 2017). Often, researchers and policy-makers have conversations across each other, not with each other. Therefore, the researcher must effectively engage with the policy-maker. Lastly, independence and autonomy are key, so think tanks must stay true to science. While honest mistakes can be made due to limitations of a rational man model, time and information constraints, and cognitive limitations, leading to bad science, think tanks must maintain their autonomy and independence. Accordingly, they must tell the client what it needs to hear.

CONCLUSION

Public decision-making is not a perfect science; in fact, it is more art than science. Therefore, the science substantially helps the actualization of evidence-based public decision-making. Resource scarcity necessitates evidence-based public decision-making. Latterly, COVID-19-related resource scarcities are increasing the use of evidence-based policy-making. Thus, think tanks are very favourably positioned to help governments engage in evidence-based policy-making, because they possess the skills to do so and, theoretically, enjoy autonomy and independence from their clients (mostly, governments). There are many think tanks in sub-Saharan Africa, but this chapter has discussed the role of BIDPA in the public policy space in Botswana. It concludes that although BIDPA plays a meaningful role in the development policy-making space, there are challenges. Some are: the not-so-straight path from research to policy; capacity constraints; and a politicized public policy-making space.

Finally, there are many policy implications for SSA that ensue from this study, including: (1) the need to appreciate the research–policy link; (2) capacity building for think tanks; (3) ensuring that policy research seamlessly translates into policy relevance; and (4) dealing with data deficits and data gatekeeping. Attending to these challenges will enhance the operational efficiencies and effectiveness of think tanks in SSA. Operational efficiencies and effectiveness will greatly favour the ability of think tanks to improve the policy impact of research. Ultimately, with evidence-based public policy-making in place, this will help SSA countries to deliver Agenda 2063 and Agenda 2030 commitments. On a related note, they will be able to deliver national aspirations such as National Development Plans and National Visions to facilitate economic growth and development. Finally, and importantly, evidence-based public policy-making is an important tool to deliver COVID-19 economic recovery programmes.

NOTES

1.   Vision 2016 (1996–2016).
2.   Vision 2036 (2016–2036).

REFERENCES

Abelson, D.E. 2018. *Do Think Tanks Matter? Assessing the Impact of Public Policy Institutes*. Montreal, Kingston: McGill-Queen's University Press.

Abelson, D.E., and Lindquist, E.A. 2009. Think Tanks in North America. In J.G. McGann and R.K. Weaver (eds), *Think Tanks and Civil Societies: Catalysts for Ideas and Action* (pp. 37–66). New Brunswick, NJ: Transaction Publishers.

Abelson, D.E., and Rastrick, C.J. 2021. *Handbook on Think Tanks in Public Policy*. Cheltenham, UK and Northampton, MA, USA: Edward Elgar Publishing.

Aristotle. 350 BC. *Nicomachean Ethics*. Oxford: Oxford University Press, 1990. English edition by I. Bywate.

Barends, E., and Rousseau. D.M. 2014. *Evidence-Based Practice: The Basic Principles*. Amsterdam: Center for Evidence-Based Management.

Barends, E., and Rousseau. D.M. 2018. *Evidence-Based Management: How to Use Evidence to Make Better Organizational Decisions*. London: Kogan Page.

Bédécarrats, F., Cling, J., and Roubaud, F. 2016. The data revolution and statistical challenges in Africa: introduction to the special report. *Afrique contemporaine*, 2(2), 9–23.

BIDPA (Botswana Institute for Development Policy Analysis). 2019a. BIDPA background. https://bidpa.Botswana/about-us/ (accessed 28 June 2021).

BIDPA. 2019b. BIDPA presentation (September 2019). Gaborone: BIDPA.

BIDPA. 2020. *2019/2020 Annual Report*. Gaborone: BIDPA.

Buckley, J.W., Buckley, M.H., and Chiang, Hung-Fu. 1976. *Research Methodology and Business Decisions*. Ontario: National Association of Accountants.

Center for Evidence-Based Decision Making. 2021. *What Is Evidence-Based Management?* https://cebma.org/faq/evidence-based-management (accessed 21 June 2021).

Chatham House. 2021. *A History of Think-Tanks: 12 Things You Should Know*. https://medium.com/chatham-house/a-history-of-think-tanks-12-things-you-should-know-4283b76b2da3 (accessed 18 June 2021).

CIPE (Center for International Private Enterprise). 2021. *The Role of Think Tanks*. https://www.cipe.org/reports/how-to-guide-for-economic-think-tanks/the-role-of-think-tanks/ (accessed 28 June 2021).

Day, R.H. 1971. Rational choice and economic behavior. *Theory and Decision*, 1, 229–251. doi.org/10.1007/BF00139569.

De Marchi, G., Lucertini, G., and Tsoukiàs, A. 2016. From evidence-based policy making to policy analytics. *Annals of Operations Research*, 236(1), 15–38.

Denzin, N.K., and Lincoln, Y.S. 2005. Introduction: the discipline and practice of qualitative research. In N. Denzin and Y. Lincoln (eds), *The SAGE Handbook of Qualitative Research*, 3rd edn (pp. 1–32). Thousand Oaks, CA: SAGE.

Department of Planning, Monitoring and Evaluation (South Africa). 2014. *What is Evidence-Based Policy-Making and Implementation?* https://www.dpme.gov.za/keyfocusareas/evaluationsSite/Evaluations/What%20is%20EBPM%2014%2010%2013_mp.pdf (accessed 21 June 2021).

Florin, M. 2014. Dealing with the challenge of evidence-based decision-making in situations of uncertainty and emergency. *European Journal of Risk Regulation*, 5(3), 303–308.

Fraussen, B., and Halpin, D. 2017. Think tanks and strategic policy-making: the contribution of think tanks to policy advisory systems. *Policy Science*, 50, 105–124.

Head, B.W. 2010. Reconsidering evidence-based policy: key issues and challenges. *Policy and Society*, 29(2), 77–94. doi:10.1016/j.polsoc.2010.03.001.

Heathfield, S. 2021. *What Is Evidence-Based Decision Making?* https://www.thebalancecareers.com/evidence-based-decision-making-for-hr-4799980 (accessed 18 June 2021).

Holloway, J. 2007. *Where's the Evidence for Evidence-Based Management?* Paper presented at the ESRC Seminar Series 'Advancing Research in the Business and Management Field', Oxford Brookes Business School, Oxford, 18 May.

Hutchinson, E., Nicholson, M., Lukenchuk, B., and Taylor, T. 2017. *Principles of Microeconomics*. Victoria: University of Victoria.

Kinyondo, A., and Pelizzo, R. 2018. Poor quality of data in Africa: what are the issues? *Politics and Policy*, 46(6), 851–877. 10.1111/polp.12277.

Ladi, S. 2015. Think tank. *Encyclopedia Britannica* (13 January 2015). https://www.britannica.com/topic/think-tank (accessed 17 June 2021).

Leuz, C. 2018. Evidence-based policymaking: promise, challenges and opportunities for accounting and financial markets research. *Accounting and Business Research*, 48(5), 582–608. doi:10.1080/00014788.2018.1470151.

Levers, M-J.D. 2013. Philosophical paradigms, grounded theory, and perspectives on emergence. *SAGE Open*, 3(4), 1–6. doi:10.1177/2158244013517243.

Matsheka, T.C. 2020. Statement by the Honourable Dr. Thapelo Matsheka, Minister of Finance and Economic Development of the Republic of Botswana during the high-level political forum on sustainable development (July 2020, New York). https://sustainabledevelopment.un.org/content/documents/26833Botswana_General_Debate.pdf, (accessed 2 November 2020).

McGann, J.G. 2006. *Comparative Think Tanks, Politics and Public Policy*. Cheltenham, UK and Northampton, MA, USA: Edward Elgar Publishing.

McGann, J.G. 2015. *Think Tanks and SDGs*. Philadelphia, PA: Think Tanks and Civil Societies Program.

McGann, J.G. 2016. *The Fifth Estate: Think Tanks, Public Policy, and Governance*. Washington, DC: Brookings Institution Press.

McGann, J.G., Rafferty, J., and Viden, A. 2014. *How Think Tanks Shape Social Development Policies*. Philadelphia, PA: University of Pennsylvania Press.

McGann, J., Signé, L. and Muyangwa, M. 2017. The crisis of African think tanks: challenges and solutions. https://www.brookings.edu/blog/africa-in-focus/2017/12/13/the-crisis-of-african-think-tanks-challenges-and-solutions/ (accessed 18 August 2021).

McGann J.G., and Weaver, R.K. 2009. Think tanks and civil societies in a time of change. In J.G. McGann and R.K. Weaver (eds), *Think Tanks and Civil Societies: Catalysts for Ideas and Action* (pp. 1–36). New Brunswick, NJ: Transaction Publishers.

Mikesell, J. 2003. *Fiscal Administration* (8th edn). Belmont, CA: Thomson Learning.

Ministry of Finance and Economic Development. 2020. *2020/21–2022/2023 Economic Recovery and Transformation Plan; Sustainable and Resilient Recovery Towards High-Income Status*. Gaborone: Government Printing and Publishing.

Ministry of Finance and Economic Development (Zimbabwe). 2020. Press statement – guidelines and modalities for accessing the ZWL$18.02 billion economic recovery and stimulus package (4 June 2020). http://www.zimtreasury.gov.zw (accessed 18 August 2021).

National Academies of Sciences, Engineering, and Medicine. 2017. *Communicating Science Effectively: A Research Agenda*. Washington, DC: National Academies Press.

Parkhurst, J. 2017. *The Politics of Evidence: From Evidence-Based Policy to the Good Governance of Evidence* (1st edn). Abingdon: Routledge.

Pew Charitable Trusts. 2014. *Evidence-Based Policymaking: A Guide for Effective Government*. Washington, DC: Pew Charitable Trusts.

Pfeffer, J., and Sutton, R.I. 2006. Evidence based management. *Harvard Business Review*, 84, 62–74. https://hbr.org/2006/01/evidence-based-management.

Reid, B., and Spinks, N. 2007. *Effacing the Facts: Critical Realism and the Politics of Evidence*. Paper presented at the 3rd International Congress of Qualitative Inquiry, University of Illinois at Urbana-Champaign, 2–5 May.

Republic of South Africa. 2020. *South African Economic Reconstruction and Recovery Plan*. https://www.gov.za/sites/default/files/gcis_document/202010/south-african -economic-reconstruction-and-recovery-plan.pdf (accessed 18 August 2021).

Rousseau, D.M. 2006. Is there such thing as Evidence-Based Management? *Academy of Management Review*, 31(2), 256–269. doi:10.5465/AMR.2006.20208679.

Ruggeri, K., van der Linden, S., Wang, C., et al. 2020. Standards for evidence in policy decision-making. https://socialsciences.nature.com/posts/standards-for-evidence-in -policy-decision-making (accessed 21 June 2021).

Saltelli, A., and Giampietro, M. 2017. What is wrong with evidence based policy, and how can it be improved? *Futures*, 91, 62–71. doi.org/10.1016/j.futures.2016.11.012.

Simon, H.A. 1947. *Administrative Behavior: a Study of Decision-Making Processes in Administrative Organization* (1st edn). New York: Free Press.

Simon, H.A. 1955. A behavioral model of rational choice. *Quarterly Journal of Economics*, 69, 99–118. http://www.jstor.org/stable/1884852.

Simon, H.A. 1979. Rational decision making in business organizations. *American Economic Review*, 69(4), 493–513. https://www.jstor.org/stable/1808698.

Soll, R. 2017. *How Think Tanks Became Engines of Royal Propaganda*. https:// www.tabletmag.com/sections/history/articles/think-tanks-jacob-soll-propaganda (accessed 18 June 2021).

Stone, D. 2006. Public Policy Analysis and Think Tanks. In G.J. Fischer, F. Miller and M.S. Sidney (eds), *Handbook of Public Policy Analysis: Theory, Politics, and Methods* (pp. 149–157). Boca Raton, FL: Routledge.

Sutcliffe, S., and Court, J. 2005. *Evidence-Based Policymaking: What Is It? How Does It Work? What Relevance for Developing Countries?* https://odi.org/documents/ 1892/3683.pdf (accessed 19 August 2021).

TTCSP (Think Tanks and Civil Societies Program). 2021. Think tank of think tanks. https://www.gotothinktank.com (accessed 28 June 2021).

United Nations Namibia. 2020. *Socio-Economic Recovery Plan 2020*. https://www .na.undp.org/content/namibia/en/home/library/socio-economic-recovery-plan-2020 .html (accessed 18 August 2021).

Urban Institute. 2016. *Principles of Evidence-Based Policymaking*. Washington, DC: Urban Institute https://www.urban.org/sites/default/files/publication/99739/ principles_of_evidence-based_policymaking.pdf.

Uzonwanne, F.C. 2016. Rational model of decision making. In A. Farazmand (ed.), *Global Encyclopedia of Public Administration, Public Policy, and Governance* (pp. 78–95). Geneva: Springer. doi.org/10.1007/978–3-319–31816–5_2474–1.

Vishwanath, V.B., and Hakem Z.F. 2012. Toward a theory of evidence based decision making. *Management Decision*, 50(5), 832–867. doi .org/ 10 .1108/ 00251741211227546.

World Bank. 2020. Botswana's economic recovery efforts gets $250 million boost. https://www.worldbank.org/en/news/press-release/2021/06/11/botswana-s-economic-recovery-efforts-gets-250-million-boost (accessed 18 August 2021).

Zittoun, P. 2014. *The Political Process of Policymaking: A Pragmatic Approach.* New York: Palgrave Macmillan.

4. Think tanks in Cameroon

Jean Cedric Kouam, Francis Tazoacha and Denis A. Foretia

INTRODUCTION

Think tanks have famously played a great role in marshalling the policies of nations along the right paths through an integrated approach. In budding democracies, and emerging markets and those vulnerable to economic shocks, like that of Cameroon, think tanks can play a leading role in informing and reforming leaders. They can catalyse change by creating awareness of vital developmental issues, initiating discussions and debates, and showing policy-makers the right path to make progress in sustainable development.

Cameroon, commonly referred to as Africa in miniature, features climatological, geological, geographical, human, linguistic and cultural diversity. The country has a population of just over 25 million (World Bank, 2018), and it is the largest economy in the Central African Economic and Monetary Community (CEMAC). Cameroon is equally gifted with many natural resources (oil and gas, minerals and precious woods) and produces a range of agricultural products (coffee, cotton, cocoa, banana, rubber, maize and cassava).

Despite this economic potential, which makes it the 16th largest economy in Africa in terms of gross domestic product (GDP) and 99th out of 205 countries in the world according to a recent World Bank ranking, the country continues to face numerous governance problems which, in addition to hampering its economic development, make it increasingly vulnerable on the international scene (World Bank, 2021). In 2020, the World Bank's Doing Business ranking showed that Cameroon ranked 167th out of 190 countries in terms of ease of doing business, with a score of 46.1 and two regulatory reforms implemented. Although the government has adopted numerous strategies to promote inclusive and sustainable economic growth, achieving the goal of making Cameroon an emerging, democratic and diverse country by 2035[1] still seems distant. The country remains confronted with major challenges such as corruption, socio-political problems in the Anglophone regions of the North-West and South-West, the attacks of the Boko-Haram group in the Far North, and so on, which considerably handicap its development.

In the search for immediate sustainable solutions to the problems plaguing Cameroon today it is considered a *sine qua non* to increase the contribution of manufacturing to 25 per cent of GDP, and real GDP growth to 8 per cent (that is, 5.7 per cent per capita), as set out in the government's new National Development Strategy 2020–2030 (NDS30). This new government strategy, which operationalizes the second phase of the vision of emergence by 2035, aims to put in place favourable conditions for sustainable economic growth, and to consolidate the democratic process while respecting diversity. However, the achievement of such objectives requires the support of think tanks which are already present in the country, but which are largely ignored and/or neglected by most decision-makers. Through the policy recommendations they formulate in the various reports and studies they publish, these reservoirs of ideas and knowledge generally provide a bridge between the world of knowledge or research and that of politics or power. These non-governmental, non-profit institutions have the merit of providing clear and intuitive answers to many questions in the political, economic, technological, social, and other, domains. Unfortunately, in Cameroon, their effectiveness remains questionable and low, due to the many constraints they face.

The objective of this chapter is to highlight the role that think tanks can play in Cameroon, particularly in terms of influencing the governance processes, legislation and social protection programmes; as well as the strategies to be put in place to address the pressing issues they still face and which are hindering sustainable development in Cameroon. The chapter first presents the history of think tanks in Cameroon and their evolution over time. The next section is devoted to the categorization of think tanks according to their field of competence, affiliations, or ideological orientations. The chapter then analyses the influence of these institutions in the process of governance, legislation, social protection programmes since the creation of the first think tank in Cameroon. Finally, we identify the challenges faced by Cameroonian think tanks, and the strategies to address them.

THINK TANKS IN CAMEROON: HISTORY AND EVOLUTION

History of Think Tanks in Cameroon

It is believed that the proliferation of think tanks across the world originated with the socialist Fabian Society in the late 19th century in the United Kingdom. It sought to influence the country's public policy. Later, the meaning of 'think tank' began to change in the 1960s when they reached the United States of America (Ladi, 2015).

The origin of civil society in Cameroon can be traced back to the 1980s and 1990s, with fundamental feautures of its development including the worsening economic predicament, increasing unemployment and redundancies of civil servants with the inability of the government to create jobs or provide basic social services, more than 80 per cent devaluation of the Franc CFA, global pressure towards a more democratic and open society, and the enactment of laws of associations, cooperatives and common initiatives groups in the 1990s (Mbuagbo and Neh, 2003).

The legal instrument for operating non-governmental organizations (NGOs) in Cameroon is found in two texts: Law No. 99/014 of 22 December 1999, which explicitly governs NGOs; and Law No. 90/053 of 19 December 1990 on the freedom of association, which is a general law applicable to all forms of associations. Within the meaning of the law of 22 December 1999, a non-governmental organization is a declared association or foreign association authorized in accordance with the legislation in force and approved by the administration to participate in the execution of a mission of general interest (Nyambo, 2008). Data advanced in 2018 by the Global Go To Think Tank Index Report demonstrates that there are 28 think tanks existing in Cameroon. Out of this number, information is made available online for only 11 of them. Nine of these Think Tanks are in Yaoundé, one in Douala and one in Buea.

Even though the legal instrument for creating NGOs in Cameroon was laid down in 1990, the first think tank was present in Cameroon in 1949. This is the Research Institute for Development / l'Institut de recherche pour le développement (IRD). The fields of research at this institute include plant pathology, hydrology, pedology, botany, entomology, parasitology, field crops, animal husbandry, economics and languages. The IRD extended its work in the human sciences from the 1980s to, among other things, archaeology, sociology and demography, and studies on land, agrarian systems and education (IRD, 2023).

In 1967, the International Institute of Tropical Agriculture (IITA) was established in Cameroon. It is an award-winning, research for development (R4D) organization, providing solutions to hunger, poverty, and the degradation of natural resources in Cameroon. It works to improve livelihoods, enhance food and nutrition security, increase employment, and preserve natural resource integrity. Furthermore, in 1987, the Centre for International Forestry Research and World Agroforestry (CIFOR-ICRAF), the world's leader on harnessing the power of trees, forests and agroforestry landscapes, was established in Cameroon. It was created to address the most pressing global challenges of our time: biodiversity loss, climate change, food security, livelihoods and inequity (IITA, 2023).

Also in 1987, another think tank called the African Centre for Banana and Plantain Research (CARBAP) was established. It is based in Njombe near Douala. Its objective is to enhance the research on crops, including banana and plantains (CARBARP, 2021). Additionally, the Friedrich Ebert Foundation / Friedrich-Ebert-Stiftung (FES), a German think tank, has existed in Cameroon since 1987. This think tank, based in Yaounde, seeks to strengthen the reform-oriented societal and political forces of political parties, trade unions and civil society, and in particular to include women and young people in order to improve democratic participation in decision-making processes. One of the most prominent thank tanks in Cameroon is the African Capacity Building Foundation (ACBF), a specialized agency of the African Union. It has provided support to think tanks in Cameroon through capacity-building.

In 1994, another think tank was founded in Yaoundé, called the Center for Environment and Development / Centre pour l'environnement et Développement, Yaoundé. This organization was a response to the need for grassroots and independent voices in the policy reforms of the forest and environment sector in Cameroon and the Congo Basin. The Centre for Independent Development Research (CIDR), based in Buea, was created in 2003 with its activities focused on fostering research and outreach related to economic, business and rural development, including environmental resource management and policy guidance (CIDR, 2021). The next known think tank, founded in 2012, is the Nkafu Policy Institute, with its headquarters in Yaoundé. The mission of the Institute is to catalyse the economic transformation of Africa through an integrated approach. The main activities of the Cameroon Policy Analysis and Research Centre / Centre d'analyse et de Recherche sur les Politiques Économique et Sociales du Cameroun (CAMERCAP-PARC), based in Yaoundé, are geared towards conducting studies and applied research on topical development issues. Additionally, CAMERCAP-PARC is dedicated to fostering transparent discussions on economic and social issues and making them widely available to the public in order to improve national actors' skills through research and analysis (CAMERCAP-PARC, 2021). Finally, the African Center for International, Diplomatic, Economic and Strategic Studies (CEIDES), created in 2013 and based in Yaoundé, is a scientific association which aims to participate, in areas of very specific knowledge, to constructive reflection with a view to the rebirth of the continent (CEIDES, 2023).

Evolution of Think Tanks in Cameroon

Considering that think tanks are bodies of experts providing advice and ideas on specific political or economic problems, they are endowed with the potential to shape the world. Originally, most think tanks were created as necessary for a particular purpose, to tackle short-term necessities, and dissolved when that particular work was done. Such pioneer institutions included the Fabian Society, the Carnegie Endowment for International Peace and the Brookings Institute. These organizations had their niche in political/policy issues. Despite massive recent diversification, they project themselves as 'policy institutes'. Many now carry out research as academic institutions, while others perform advocacy; yet none of these organizations pursues knowledge for knowledge's sake.

Although the law lays down the creation of NGOs in Cameroon, including think tanks, the evolution of these entities (how they value rigorous policy research and inundate stakeholders with rapid-response policy research) remains slow, given the number that have been created and the absence of a network to harness and promote their development. Although it is reported that there are 22 think tanks in the country (see the Appendix), only a few are active in this field.

In 2007, the United States Embassy in Cameroon encouraged and established think tanks and policy planning staff as a means of addressing challenges in the Central African sub-region (Ndzesop, 2007). The rise of new think tanks in Cameroon parallels the rise of leadership in the Central African sub-region. In 2019, the Nkafu Policy Institute urged the government of Cameroon to create an enabling environment for think tanks in the country as a means to help enhance development through proper research (Nkafu Policy Institute, 2019). In December 2020, the International Center for Research and Documentation on African Traditions and Languages (CERDOTOLA) organized a symposium to create a platform for think tanks, in order to foster Cameroon's emergence by bringing together producers of ideas, to be made available to decision-makers through specialized publications.

These calls or initiatives have been vital in enhancing the growth and development of think tanks in Cameroon as a tool to shape policies and sustainable development in the country. Despite the lackadaisical approach of some of these think tanks towards promoting better policies to harness development, the government for its part is doing little or nothing to boost these institutions. There is therefore a need for the government to create an enabling environment for these institutions to play their roles as think tanks.

The development of think tanks across the world over the years is much more notable in Anglo-Saxon countries than in French-speaking countries, especially in Africa. The ranking made by the University of Pennsylvania over several years in its Global Go To Think Tank Index does not list any think tank in Cameroon (McGann, 2019). This very low showing of Cameroon's think tanks in the world inevitably reflects their limited ability to define the problems they address, as well as to formulate solid recommendations to influence the prevailing social, economic and political context. In other words, their work does not seem to have a great impact on current issues. If it is true that Cameroonian think tanks are unknown at the national and international level, it should also be recalled that they have similar characteristics to those of other countries in the world, that is, they are engaged in research activities, publication of articles, reports and policy briefs with a view to understanding the social realities of Cameroon and contributing to the reflection on major issues that hinder the collective welfare.

CATEGORIZATION OF THINK TANKS IN CAMEROON

General Information (Country, Gender of the Founder/Current Leader, Date Founded)

During a survey we conducted between 7 and 23 September 2021, 22 think tanks were identified in Cameroon. They were all created by Cameroonians, except for the Friedrich Ebert Foundation and the Institute of Research for Development (IRD) whose headquarters are in Germany and France, respectively. Of these 22 think tanks, 20 are founded by men (90 per cent), 1 by a woman (5 per cent), and 1 by a group of men and women (5 per cent); 18 per cent of these think tanks are currently led by women, compared to 82 per cent led by men (Figure 4.1). Apart from the foreign think tanks present in Cameroon, those founded by Cameroonians are mostly young, the most recent of which was created in 2019, although the oldest has existed since 1989.

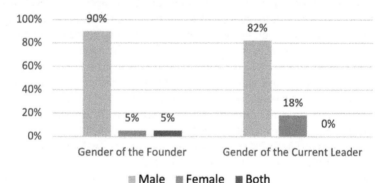

Source: Nkafu Policy Institute (2021).

Figure 4.1   *Genders of think tank founders and current leaders in Cameroon*

Categorization According to Ideological Affiliations or Orientation (Region of Location/Type of Organization/Economic Model, Staff Size)

Of the Cameroonian think tanks contacted during this survey, only 30 per cent completed the questionnaire submitted to them. Seventy-five per cent of these organizations are located in the Centre region of the country, while 25 per cent are based in the Littoral; 50 per cent of these think tanks describe themselves as a research centre/institute, 17 per cent as a civil society organization, and 33 per cent as a political think tank. The majority of these think tanks are non-profit (95 per cent), non-partisan, and are characterized by their political neutrality; while 5 per cent are profit-making. Regarding the total staff working both full- and part-time, 17 per cent reported having a staff size of between 0 and 4; 5 per cent reported that they employed between 5 and 9 people; 17 per cent reported having a staff size of between 20 and 49 people. Of these staff sizes, 50 per cent said that the percentage of women working in their organization was between 25 and 50 per cent; 50 per cent said that the percentage of women employed in their organization was less than 10 per cent of women. Figure 4.2 illustrates detailed information on think tanks in Cameroon.

The think tanks that responded to the survey questionnaires stated that influencing public policy is mainly done by engaging directly with the executive branch, notably the presidency and ministerial departments (50 per cent), as well as with the media (50 per cent). Fifty per cent of these think tanks find their engagement with policy-makers neither easy nor difficult, 33 per cent find it very difficult, while 17 per cent find it somewhat difficult. Three think tanks were revealed as the most well known among Cameroonians and having some influence on the national scene: the Center for Environment and Development (CED), the African Center for International, Diplomatic, Economic and Strategic Studies (CEIDES) and the Nkafu Policy Institute.

Categorization According to the Field and Nature of Interventions

As for the areas of intervention of think tanks in Cameroon, several specialize in specific areas and cover a specific region. They are mainly devoted to the study of public (social) policies, notably education (12.5 per cent), health (12.5 per cent), sustainable development (12.5 per cent), economic affairs (12.5 per cent), governance and democracy (25 per cent), and peace and security (37.5 per cent). The main channels of transmission of research results are radio debates (12.5 per cent); radio (12.5 per cent); public and private newspapers (12.5 per cent); social networks (12.5 per cent); and the organization's website (25 per cent). Regarding their engagement with the media (television, radio, newspapers), 33 per cent consider it neither easy nor difficult; 33 per cent find it very difficult; 34 per cent, on the other hand, answered that they find

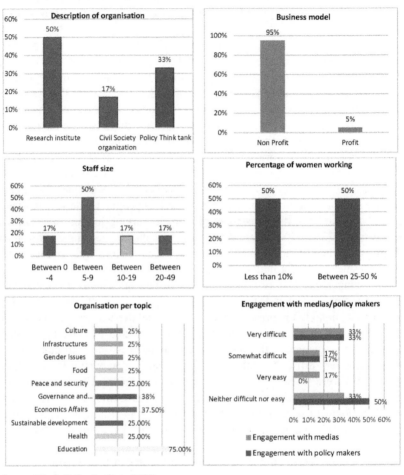

Source: Nkafu Policy Institute (2021).

Figure 4.2   Detailed information on think tanks in Cameroon

this engagement very easy (17 per cent) and somewhat easy (17 per cent). Publications include policy briefs (87.5 per cent), articles (75 per cent), opinion editorials (12.5 per cent), research reports (62.5 per cent), videos and documentaries (12.5 per cent), studies, opinion pieces and books (25 per cent).

To interact with other stakeholders, Cameroonian think tanks frequently organize public events. These events are mainly roundtables, debates, press conferences, webinars, interviews and symposia; 12.5 per cent report holding one of these events weekly, 12.5 per cent report holding them every two weeks,

12.5 per cent monthly, 25 per cent quarterly (about four times a year), and 37.5 per cent twice a year. They are 87.5 per cent autonomous and independent (that is, independent of any interest group or donor, and autonomous in their operation and funding), while 12.5 per cent claim to be funded exclusively by government grants and contracts but are not part of the official government structure.

Despite the efforts made by think tanks in Cameroon in terms of publications, public events and interventions in the media and social networks, they remain largely unknown to the general public and even to some policy-makers. However, the socio-political and security conditions that prevail in the country abound with many issues to which think tanks can contribute their work. Indeed, for think tanks to thrive in a country, the context must be sufficiently favourable, and people must agree that they are important for the formulation of policies or alternatives. In other words, they must be able to influence public life by bringing academic rigour to the study of contemporary issues. Think tanks must thus create original ideas and bring forward new options to tackle the different challenges that affect their immediate or distant environment. In the following sections, we assess the influence of think tanks in Cameroon, while highlighting the problems they still face and which hinder their growth.

INFLUENCE OF THINK TANKS IN CAMEROON

To assess the influence of think tanks in Cameroon, we interviewed a panel of 27 experts with extensive experience in the fields of research and policy. Although the sample interviewed was not very representative of Cameroonian experts in these fields, their responses nonetheless provided an indication of how Cameroonians perceive the situation of think tanks in the country. These experts were mostly young, dynamic, and working with think tanks and other research centres in Cameroon and abroad; 37.04 per cent of them said they were between 26 and 35 years old, 44.44 per cent between 36 and 45 years old, 7.47 per cent between 46 and 60 years old, and 11.11 per cent over 60 years old. They were 77.78 per cent male and 22.22 per cent female. As for the level of education of these individuals, 7.4 per cent declared having a bachelor's degree, 59.26 per cent a master's degree, and 37.04 a doctorate. They are variously employees of the public sector (15.52 per cent), the private sector (59.26 per cent), in both the public and private sectors (14.81 per cent), currently unemployed (3.7 per cent) and working as freelancers (3.7 per cent).

As for the relationship of these experts with Cameroonian think tanks, 69.23 per cent of them said that they had worked for or contributed to an activity conducted by a think tank, and the remaining 30.77 per cent said that they had never done so. The main think tanks in which these experts declared having had a relationship in the past are: CEIDES, the African Center for Research in Moral and Political Sciences, BESTRAT, Nkafu Policy Institute, Friedrich Ebert Foundation, and Cameroon Policy Analysis and Research Center (CAMERCAP-PARC). The areas of intervention of these experts interviewed included: education (40.74 per cent), health (14.81 per cent), agriculture (14.81 per cent), gender issues (33.33 per cent), sustainable development (55.56 per cent), culture (11.11 per cent), economic affairs (51.85 per cent), governance and democracy (51.85 per cent), and peace and security (29.63 per cent). Several elements were considered in the survey questionnaire to assess the impact of think tanks in Cameroon: influence in the governance process; influence in the formulation of social protection policies; and influence in legislation and regulation.

Influence of Think Tanks in the Process of Politics in Cameroon

Think tanks are considered to be non-governmental organizations that use a wide range of resources to influence the content and outcome of public policy (Abelson, 2009). Since think tanks are apolitical and independent, they should be able to influence the development of a country and ensure the collective well-being of its citizens. This is especially true of their impact on governance and policy. However, their growth remains dependent on a political system where the state does not monopolize the process of general interest, and where private organizations play an eminently important role (Michelot, 2013). In Cameroon, 34.62 per cent of the experts interviewed stated that because Cameroonian think tanks are new to the national scene, they would therefore not yet have any influence on the way policy is defined and implemented by the different parties in the country. Of the experts interviewed, 53.85 per cent believe that these think tanks have only become actors in the Cameroonian political sphere in the last 5–10 years, and 15.39 per cent of these experts believe that think tanks have been important actors in the political arena in Cameroon for more than ten years (Figure 4.3).

The influence of think tanks on policy development in Cameroon is condi-tioned by many factors. For 50 per cent of the experts interviewed, this influ-ence results in particular from the quality of the research activities carried out and published by these think tanks. In addition, 46.15 per cent believe that the performance of think tanks depends on the ability of the specialists they have at their disposal to translate complex ideas into a form that is easily understood by the general public; for 11.54 per cent, it is due to the fact that think tanks are non-partisan and independent; and for 11.54 per cent, it is due to the attention they receive from government. For these experts, this evaluation of think tanks in Cameroon depends on the quantity and quality of articles published as well as interviews in the main media (38.46 per cent), the fact that these think tanks are cited during a parliamentary session (15.38 per cent), changes observed

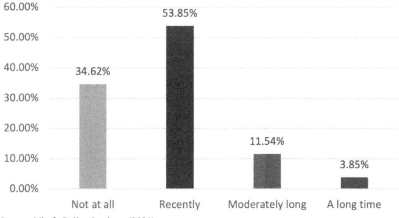

Source: Nkafu Policy Institute (2021).

Figure 4.3   *Influence of think tanks on the process of politics in Cameroon*

in public opinion (53.85 per cent), and policy reforms implemented by the government (34.62 per cent).

The participation of think tanks in political life in Cameroon remains conditioned by a number of realities. Among these realities are their ability to testify about the realities of public life before government authorities while providing policy proposals adapted to the Cameroonian context (38.46 per cent), their willingness to build strong relationships with members of the government, which is essential for lobbying activities (30.77 per cent), their ability to engage in public relations campaigns (73.08 per cent) and their ability to make sound recommendations to current problems (53.85 per cent).

Influence in the Process of Governance, Human Rights, Freedom of Expression and Economic Development

Since 2012, Cameroon has been facing numerous crises. According to experts, these crises are directly related to the governance problems affecting the country. During the survey we conducted, 69.23 per cent of experts interviewed certified that poor governance in the country is at the root of most of the crises and problems Cameroon is facing. As for the commitment of think tanks to improve governance in Cameroon, 73.08 per cent of experts supported the idea that Cameroonian think tanks are committed to this despite the fact that the results of their actions are slow to be felt. For these experts, the effects of the actions undertaken by Think Tanks to improve governance in Cameroon can only be visible if they engage directly with the executive (42.31 per cent) to present the results of their research and the means to bring about change, with parliament (34.62 per cent), with local public authorities (57.69 per cent), with the grassroots (46.15 per cent) and with the media in order to inform citizens directly (73.08 per cent). Figure 4.4 illustrates the contribution of think tanks to promote good governance, human rights/freedom of expression and economic development.

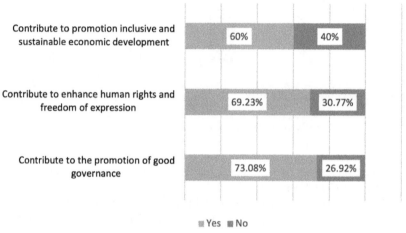

Source: Nkafu Policy Institute (2021).

Figure 4.4   *Contribution of think tanks to promote good governance, human rights/freedom of expression and economic development*

In addition, 69.23 per cent of experts interviewed said that Cameroonian think tanks play an important role in improving the situation of human rights and freedom in Cameroon, while 30.77 per cent said the opposite. The ability of these think tanks to conduct objective and free intellectual reflections on the one hand, and to produce publications on issues relating to democracy, civil liberties, elections and the conduct of economic affairs, to name but a few, could further contribute to the promotion of freedom of expression and human rights in the country. Indeed, 50 per cent of the experts interviewed felt that Cameroonian think tanks sometimes find it difficult to maintain a certain independence in research; 20.83 per cent felt that it was very difficult; 20.83 per cent felt that this independence of think tanks in research would be neither difficult nor easy; and only 8.34 per cent felt that it was easy. This difficulty of think tanks to conduct independent and free research also has many impli-cations for their performance and ability to influence the conduct of economic policy. In this sense, only 60 per cent of the experts interviewed affirmed that Cameroonian think tanks manage to contribute to promoting inclusive and sustainable economic development, while 40 per cent affirmed the opposite.

THE CHALLENGES FACED BY THINK TANKS IN CAMEROON

The weak presence of Cameroonian think tanks on the national and interna-tional scene is linked to a number of challenges that they face and that naturally have profound repercussions for their performance or their ability to influence political action. Among these challenges, the issue of funding appears to be the main obstacle: 87.5 per cent of the experts interviewed maintain that one of the major challenges facing think tanks in Cameroon is finding a funding mechanism that can enable them to function. As for the sources of funding for these think tanks, 37.5 per cent of the think tanks that responded to the survey questionnaire affirmed their dependence on foreign or state funding, although they sometimes tailor their thinking to the interests of donors. For 75 per cent of the think tanks surveyed, finding an adequate funding mechanism would allow them to operate effectively. For the remaining 25 per cent, the effectiveness of think tanks in Cameroon would rather result from the pooling of available knowledge and the networking of the various experts employed there. In addition to limited access to funding, Cameroonian think tanks face other challenges. These include difficulty in maintaining qualified or compe-tent staff, difficulty in recruiting experienced staff, and difficulty in producing quality work. Solving the problem of funding within Cameroonian think tanks would naturally help to overcome these difficulties, while equipping them with the capacity to adapt to the changing environment within which they operate (McGann, 2011). According to CODESRIA (2017), access to funding for think tanks will solve the problem of recruiting and mentoring young research-ers who are competent and committed to managing programs, formulating projects on current issues in society but which are not yet in the headlines but which, when they are, will attract the attention of decision-makers. Figure 4.5 illustrates other difficulties faced by think tanks in Cameroon.

CONCLUSION AND POLICY RECOMMENDATIONS

The role of think tanks is undisputed in the world today. These mostly apoliti-cal, independent, non-profit (that is, non-financial) think tanks are very active in defining the general interest, a role traditionally assigned to state institu-tions (Michelot, 2013). Their primary function would thus consist neither in

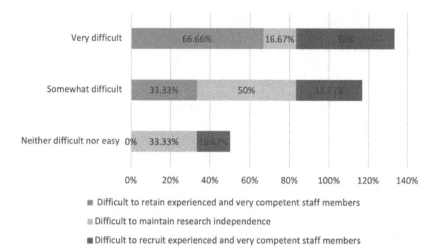

Source: Nkafu Policy Institute (2021).

Figure 4.5   Other difficulties of think tanks in Cameroon

traditional basic research nor in applied research or development, but more in acting as a bridge between knowledge and power, and between science and the legislator, in very broad fields of interest (Dickson, 1971).

This chapter aimed to take an inventory of think tanks in Cameroon in order to assess the impact of their actions in the country. After surveys of existing think tanks on the one hand, and of certain Cameroonian experts with a good knowledge of research, the political system and the way think tanks operate in Cameroon and in the world on the other, it was found that Cameroonian think tanks have very little influence on the prevailing socio-political and economic environment. This is mainly due to the economic conditions in which they were created and are evolving, but above all to the political climate, which is not conducive to their development.

Think tanks in Cameroon face several other challenges that hinder their growth, including their capacity and ability to make appropriate recommendations to decision-makers on current and obvious issues that divide the country (the socio-political crisis in the Anglophone regions of the country, insecurity in the Far North and East regions, poor governance, unemployment, public debt, and so on). These challenges include limited access to funding. Indeed, most of the funds that Cameroonian think tanks receive come from abroad.

According to many Cameroonian experts, finding a solution to the limited access to funding for Cameroonian think tanks would address other problems that Cameroonian think tanks still face. These include their ability to retain qualified or competent staff, to recruit experienced staff and therefore to produce quality work. However, the solution would not be limited to finding funding, but would also require that this funding allows them to produce ideas to legitimately influence public discourse.

NOTE

1. Cameroon has set itself the ambition of achieving emergence by 2035. This vision is broken down into three indicative phases: Phase I (2010 to 2019) has the overall objective of modernizing the economy and accelerating growth; Phase II (2020–2027) has the overall objective of achieving middle-income status; Phase III (2028–2035) has the overall objective of becoming a new industrialized and emerging country (by increasing the share of the secondary sector to over 40 per cent of GDP).

REFERENCES

Abelson, D. (2009). *Do Think Tanks Matter? Assessing the Impact of Public Policy Institutes*, 2nd edn. Montréal, McGill-Queens University Press.
CAMERCAP-PARC (2021). Centre D'analyse et de Recherche sur les Politiques Économique et Sociales du Cameroun, Yaounde, Cameroon. https://www.africaportal .org/content-partners/centre-danalyse-et-de-recherche-sur-les-politiques-economiques -et-sociales-du-cameroun-camercap-parc/.
CARBARP (2021). Food and Beverage manufacturing. http://www.carbapafrica.org.
CEIDES (2023). African Center for International, Diplomatic, Economic and Strategic Studies. https://www.ceides.org/.
CIDR (2021). Centre for Independent Development Research. Yaounde, Cameroon. http://www.cidrcam.org/about_us.
CODESRIA (2017). Comment le CODESRIA est devenu le think tank N°1 d'Afrique. https://www.scidev.net/afrique-sub-saharienne/news/codesria-premier-think-tank -afrique-subsaharienne/.
Dickson, P. (1971). *Think-Tanks*. New York: Atheneum.
IITA (2023). International Institute of Tropical Agriculture, Cameroon. iita.org.
IRD (2023). Institut de Recherche pour le Developpement (IRD). http://www.ird.fr.
Ladi, S. (2015). Think tank. *Encyclopedia Britannica*. https://www.britannica.com/ topic/think-tank.
Mbuagbo, T. and Neh, C. (2003). Civil society and democratization: the Cameroonian experience. African Journal of Social Work, 18(2): 133–148.
McGann, James G. (2011). 2011 Global Go To Think Tank Index Report. TTCSP Global Go To Think Tank Index Reports. https://www.researchgate.net/publication/ 304089437_2011_Global_Go_To_Think_Tanks_Index_Report.
McGann, James G. (2019). 2018 Global Go To Think Tank Index Report. TTCSP Global Go To Think Tank Index Reports. https://repository.upenn.edu/think_tanks/ 16.
Michelot, Martin (2013). Les modes d'influence des *think tanks* dans le jeu politique américain. *Politique Américaine*, 2(22): 97–116.
Ndzesop, I. (2007). The place of Cameroon in US policy toward Central Africa after the events of September 11, 2001. Yaounde, Cameroon: Institut des Relations Internationales du Cameroun.

Nkafu Policy Institute (2019). Why FACTS and think tanks matter. Nkafu events, January. Why FACTS and Think Tanks Matter - Nkafu Policy Institute. https://nkafu .org/m-events/why-facts-and-think-tanks-matter/.

Nkafu Policy Institute (2021). Why FACTS and think tanks matter. Yaounde, Cameroon. https:// nkafu .org/ nkafu -event/ why -facts -and -think -tanks -matter -in -cameroon/.

Nyambo, J. (2008). The legal framework of civil society and social movements. https:// codesria.org/IMG/pdf/Chapter_2.pdf.

World Bank (2018). The World Bank in Cameroon. https://www.worldbank.org/en/ country/cameroon/overview.

World Bank Group (2021), Data for better lives. World Development Report. https:// openknowledge.worldbank.org/bitstream/handle/10986/35218/9781464816000.pdf.

APPENDIX 4-A

Table 4A.1   *Think tanks in Cameroon*

Think tanks in Cameroon	Sex of founder	Gender of current leader	Areas of action	Date of creation	Institutional affiliation	Type
African Center for International, Diplomatic, Economic and Strategic Studies (CEIDES)	Male	Male	International Relations, Diplomacy, Economy and Strategy	2012	Independent	Non-Profit
Center for Analysis and Research on Economic and Social Policies of Cameroon (CAMERCAP-PARC)	Male	Male	Public policy, finance, youth employment, statistics, civil society, private sector, education, environment, natural resources, governance, social development, technology, transportation, etc.	2013	State of Cameroon	Non-profit
Friedrich Ebert Foundation (Cameroon Office)	Male	Female	Peace and security, migration and economic transformation processes	1925	Social Democratic Party of Germany (SPD)	Non-profit
Observatory of the Foreign and National Press (Open Cameroon)	Male	Male	Education/youth, communication, economic intelligence, innovation, prospection.	2005	Independent	Non-profit

Think tanks, governance, and development in Africa

Think tanks in Cameroon	Sex of founder	Gender of current leader	Areas of action	Date of creation	Institutional affiliation	Type
CAPE Cameroun	Male	Male	Economy, politics, defense/security, health, social, technology, infrastructure, and others	2019	Independent	Non-profit
African Centre for Research in Ethics and Political Science (CARES-MP)	Male	Male	Political and economic governance, society	2018	Independent	Profit
African Centre for Banana and Plantain Research (CARBA	Male	Male	Improvement of production systems, conservation and valorization of genetic resources, disease control, agriculture, processing	2001	Intergovernmental institution, Conference of Ministers of Research and Development of the countries of West and Central Africa (COMRED / COA)	Non-profit
Center for environnent and Development	Male	Male	Forest governance, mining and large infrastructure projects, land tenure and sustainable agriculture, community rights, climate change/ REDD	1994	Independent	Non-profit

Think tanks in Cameroon	Sex of founder	Gender of current leader	Areas of action	Date of creation	Institutional affiliation	Type
Centre for Independent Development Research (CIDR)	Male	Male	Its area of focus is to deliver innovative and effective research, technical assistance, and decision support services that build human and institutional capacity and promote sustainable economic and social development	2003	Independent	Non-profit
Nkafu Policy Institute	Male	Female	Economic affairs, health policy, education policy, science and technology, governance and democracy, peace and security	2012	Independent	Non-profit
Education Research Network for West and Central Africa (ERNWACA)	Female	Female	Education	1989	Intergovernmental institution	Non-Profit
Center for International Forestry Research (CIFOR)	Male	Male	Climate change; energy, gender, justice and tenure; sustainable landscapes and livelihoods; value chains, finance and investments	1993	Intergovernmental institution	Non-profit

Think tanks in Cameroon	Sex of founder	Gender of current leader	Areas of action	Date of creation	Institutional affiliation	Type
Research for Enterprise, Industries, Technology and Development (EITD Research)	Male	Male	Development and Economic Policy; Enterprise and Industry; Engineering Science and Technology; Primary HealthCare; Education; Environment and Production; and Field services and technical support	1992	-	Non-profit
Bureau of Strategic Studies (BESTRAT)	Male	Male	Strategy and security	2017	Independent	Non-profit
Institute for Governance in Central Africa (IGAC)	Male	Male	Public affairs management in African countries		Independent	Non- profit
Institute of Research for Development Cameroon (IRD)	Male	Male	Environment, human sciences, archaeology, agriculture; etc; the research themes specific to Cameroon are: health and well-being of populations, Earth system and biodiversity, social dynamics	Since 1949 in Cameroon	France	Non-profit
Central African Centre for Libertarian Thought and Action	Male	Male	Areas of research water, energy and transportation sectors	2014	Independent	Non-profit

Think tanks in Cameroon	Sex of founder	Gender of current leader	Areas of action	Date of creation	Institutional affiliation	Type
Open Cameroun	Male	Male	Intelligence and innovation	2005	Independent	Non-profit
The Okwelians	Formed by a group	Male	Governance (institutions and decentralization; public finance management; sub-regional and regional integration, foreign policy and diplomacy, power/ citizens relationship (civil society, transparency, corruption, etc); peace and security; economy (employment, innovation	2000	Independent	Non-profit
The Muntu Institute African Humanities and Social Sciences	Male	Male	industrialization, infrastructure, energy and digital); society (health, education, culture and environment)	2017	Independent	Non-profit
Cameroon Think Tank Network (CTTN)	Male	Male	Research, Social Sciences, Humanities, Conferences and Symposia	2020	Independent	Non-Profit
Paul Ango Ela Foundation for Geopolitics in Central Africa (FPAE)	Formed by a group	Female	Intelligence and innovation, think tank network of Cameroon	1999	Independent	Non-profit

5. Think tanks, governance and development: the Ghanaian perspective

Frank L.K. Ohemeng and Joseph R.A. Ayee

INTRODUCTION

The proliferation of think tanks (TTs) has become a key feature of the Ghanaian polity. Although their exact number is unknown, there is evidence of the influence of TTs in governance and development, especially since the return to constitutional governance in 1993. The policy space created by the return to constitutional rule and the global pursuit of development and democratic governance, which includes the need for effective citizen participation in policy development and implementation (Choudhary, 2022), has created the enabling environment in which TTs continue to carve a niche for themselves in governance and development. The questions the chapter intends to answer are: How have these institutions continued to influence governance and development in Ghana? What are the major challenges they face in their quest to achieve their objectives? How can these challenges be addressed?

This chapter seeks to answer these questions and to show that despite some significant challenges that these institutions continue to face, they have become major policy actors in influencing policy development and implementation. Thus, through their efforts, they have been able to highlight governance and development deficits in the country. The chapter examines four main areas in which TTs continue to contribute to governance and development: policy development in general, the fight against corruption, electoral politics, and community development. In addition, the chapter discusses some of the challenges facing these institutions and suggests ways that government can help them in governance and development.

The information used in this chapter was mostly derived from both primary and secondary sources. The primary sources focused on documentary analysis (Bowen, 2009) from government sources, newspaper reports, and annual reports and the websites of some of the TTs. Secondary sources are from published materials from some of these institutions, as well as published papers about them and their role in national development.

The chapter is organized as follows. We begin our discussion by first explaining the concepts of governance and development. This enables us to situate the Ghanaian case in the broader discussion of these ideas. Next, we examine the history and development of TTs in Ghana. This is necessary in the sense that although the idea of TTs is quite a recent phenomenon in the country (Ohemeng, 2005, 2014), a careful examination shows that such institutions existed prior to constitutional rule in 1993. We then discuss the terrain of TTs in the country, before identifying some areas in which these institutions continue to play major roles, as part of governance and development. We conclude the chapter with future suggestions on how to study these institutions, and ways in which they can continue to influence governance and development in the country.

GOVERNANCE AND DEVELOPMENT: A BRIEF DISCUSSION

Governance and development are two concepts that perhaps have been over-used, not only in the academic literature, but also in the general discourse in recent years, despite their long histories. In addition, there is a relationship between the two concepts, because conditions of poverty, economic stagnation, lack of political stability, lack of priorities and obstacles to sustainable development have been blamed on ineffective governance (Jreisat, 2011). As Werlin (2003: 329) rightly pointed out, 'Governance rather than natural resources is the primary reason for the wealth and poverty of nations'. It would therefore be naïve to have a thorough discussion about them here. Nevertheless, it is important for the concepts to be explained in the context of our discussion.

What then is governance? Scholarly agreement on the concept is rare. More so, several different adjectives, such as 'good' (Roy and Tisdell, 1998), 'good enough' (Grindle, 2007) 'value or public value' (Bryson et al., 2014), 'collaborative' (Bianchi et al., 2021; Ansell and Gash, 2008; Douglas et al., 2020), and a host of others, have been used to describe it, thereby making it difficult to pinpoint out exactly what is being discussed. At the same time, it has been found across different disciplines and used differently in these contexts, thus making the idea an ambiguous one to define. It is not surprising that Frederickson (2007) bemoaned the fact of the idea being found everywhere.

It is believed that the idea was first conceptualized by Cleveland (1972) to look at how future organizations may operate. In short, his idea was related to organizational activities. Cleveland (1972: 13) then proposed what governance is about:

> [t]he organizations that get things done will no longer be hierarchical pyramids with most of the real control at the top. They will be systems – interlaced webs of tension in which control is loose, power diffused, and centers of decision plural. Decision-making will become an increasingly intricate process of multilateral brokerage both inside and outside the organization which thinks it has the responsibility for making, or at least announcing, the decision. Because organizations will be horizontal, the way they are governed is likely to be more collegial, consensual, and consultative.

Today, this notion has moved beyond what Cleveland perceived as organizational development to examine how society governs itself, especially the broader steering of societal affairs from the well-known feudal system, characterized by 'chieftain or king towards a broader base of elected representatives, managers, bureaucrats and interest group leaders' (Michalski et al., 2001: 7).

Another perspective which has led to confusion is the notion of good governance. In the literature, good governance concerns the significant role of other sectors in the national polity to enhance effective accountability and policy-making (Grindle, 2007). It depicts the traditional 'two heads are better than one' notion, leading to what has been described as collaborative governance (Ansell and Gash, 2007; Bianchi et al., 2021). It is therefore about the diffusion of authority in the society. In this sense, it concerns the exercising of authority through political and institutional processes that are transparent and accountable, and encourage public participation in the governance process. This notion further shows the diffusion of authority to societal actors, thus moving away from the traditional idea of an elite, defined as the governance of the ruling class. Thus, the OECD (1995: 14), for instance, sees the concept as encompassing 'the role of public authorities in establishing the environment in which economic operators function and in determining the distribution of benefits, as well as the relationship between the ruler and the ruled'.

A closer look at the current literature shows that the term 'governance' can be used in a narrower sense as a synonym of 'government' (Pierre and Peters, 2000). According to Fröhlich and Knieling (2013: 13), the use of the term in this sense signifies 'softer' forms of regulation, that are not characterized by hierarchical government decisions, but through the inclusion of private stakeholders in problem resolution processes. Thus, the term denotes the blurring of boundaries between state and society. Not everyone, however, accepts this view. For instance, Bryant (2018: 1) categorically says that 'governance is not government, although government at any level can potentially become part of a governance process'.

In a broader perspective, governance is not the antonym of government, but rather something that emphasizes collaboration among interdependent or non-state actors, the growth of horizontal relationships, networking, decentralization, and indirect provision of government services through contractual relationships with private and non-profit organizations (Wachhaus, 2014: 574). In this sense, the idea connotes a generic term defining the entity of 'all co-existing forms of collective regulation of societal circumstances: from institutionalized civil society self-regulation through various forms of cooperation between public and private stakeholders to sovereign action by governmental stakeholders' (Mayntz, 2006: 15). In this broad definition, governance is seen as the coordination of social actions and not as a distinction from hierarchical regulation or control (Mayntz, 2004; Benz, 2005; Heinelt and Kübler, 2005).

In this chapter, we take the broader view of governance to indicate the collaboration of government and other entities in society including the private for-profit and not-for-profit organizations. This broader view goes beyond good governance, for example, which is more about the managing of a state's economy (World Bank, 1992). Some literature has described this broader view as 'shared or joint governance', to indicate the range and structure of policy-making between government and other players in the economy (Provan and Kenis, 2008). According to Mirvis and Googins (2013), shared governance signifies an important shift in the relationship between the public and private sectors by turning attention from government as a state function, to governance by multiple institutions, and thus from the workings of the regulatory state to a relational state. They go on to explain that shared governance involves a fuller range of actors setting 'direction for society', the exercise of authority by both state and non-state institutions, and interactions between the state and private interests beyond traditional rule-making and compliance (Mirvis and Googins, 2013: 233). The core idea of shared governance is collaborative decision-making, and that the best public goods should be provided by the government and the public together. This process involves multiple stakeholders, empowers citizens, and strengthens public trust in government. Scholars have pointed out that shared governance is citizen-centred instead of bureaucracy-centred, and the key to this is citizen participation (Nan and Yang, 2022).

From this broader perspective, other scholars have described governance and shifting relationships as network governance (Wang and Ran, 2021). Networks in this sphere are about the interdependent structures linking several organizations and other entities, without hierarchy or critical leverage (Provan and Kenis, 2008). Consequently, network governance is defined as 'entities that fuse collaborative public goods and service provision with collective policymaking' (Isett et al., 2011: i158). This policy-making process and the fusing of service provision, and thus the success of this collaborative approach, are based on the principles of trust, reciprocity, negotiation and mutual inter-dependence among actors (Provan and Kenis 2008; Liu, 2022). Wang and Ran (2021: 3) say that 'in the context of the public service delivery, network governance is usually equated as governance since governance takes place within networks of complex interactions between public and non-public actors'.

Another perspective of this broader definition is that of collaborative governance (Ansell and Gash, 2007; Bianchi et al., 2021; Huxham et al., 2000). Collaborative governance denotes the idea of an all-hands-on deck approach for the development of societies, since societies continue to face 'wicked problems' (Bianchi et al., 2021; Head, 2008; Head and Alford, 2015), which makes it difficult for one sector, especially government, to address; especially where governments have limited bureaucratic and technical capacities. Wang and Ran (2021: 3) define it 'as the collaboration of different organizations from public, private and civic sectors working together as stakeholders based on deliberative consensus and collective decision making to achieve shared goals that could not be otherwise fulfilled individually'. This broader view is necessary since government continues to recognize the different roles of different institutions in the developmental process.

It is instructive to note that a governance system consists of three elements, namely: structure (power, authority, the capacity of institutions, centralization versus decentralization, citizen representation, and so on), process (the constitution, rules and methods of policy and decision-making) and outcomes (performance in the areas of service delivery, attaining of sustainable development and improving civil society, accountability and transparency) (Jreisat, 2011).

CONCEPTUALIZING AND ANALYSING DEVELOPMENT: WHAT THE LITERATURE SAYS

One of the most difficult concepts to be defined in the literature is development. This is because the idea means different things to different people in different fields of study. For example, when an economist speaks of development, it would mean something different than it does to the political scientist. The same applies to a psychologist or sociologist or anthropologist. Thus, it is imperative to first identify the field that we intend to focus on here. When we think about development, we are talking about both economic and political developments. The economic understanding of the concept focuses on the economic wellbeing of the individual. For instance, it may look at questions such as the level of poverty, the ability to promote good health, and so on. Political development, however, looks at how citizens may have the freedom to engage in political activities, to participate in the deliberation of issues that affect their daily lives, as well as the evolution and effectiveness of state institutions. Development then generally implies 'movement or growth over time along some specified set of dimensions from one state of these dimensions to another' (Willner, 1964: 471). This continuum is about moving from an unacceptable level to a higher, more desirable state of human endeavour. It is from this perspective that modernization theorists, for example, talk about development as moving from primitive society to a modern one, where improved technology and institutions are the order of the day. Development in this trajectory is seen in economic and political terms.

Economically, defining development is still up in the air, ever present in policy circles and in academic research. It is said that part of the problem in defining economic development is that it 'is often conflated with development and growth ... in both policy and academic debates' (Feldman et al., 2016: 7). Feldman et al. (ibid.) see economic development as different from economic growth, with the former focusing on 'quality improvements, risk mitigation, innovation, and entrepreneurship that place the economy of a higher growth trajectory', while the latter is about quantitative numbers. Consequently, they define economic development as 'the development of capacities that expand economic actors' capabilities'. This definition focuses on the capabilities of individuals and society in general in generating economic growth to enhance the wellbeing of society. This is what Sen (1993, 1999, 2009) had in mind when he developed his capability theory, which focuses on individuals' ability to develop their capabilities to improve their economic growth.

We define economic development by adapting Adelman's definition. Adelman (2000) says that economic development deals with the combination of: (1) self-sustaining growth; (2) structural change in patterns of production; (3) technological upgrading; (4) social, political and institutional moderniza-tion; and (5) widespread improvement in the human condition. The definition is all-encompassing and will enable us to identify what TTs are doing to help government promote economic development, especially to improve human conditions, and address such wicked problems as poverty and climate change that are having detrimental effects in developing countries.

It has been said that development is political. This is because 'improving the quality of people's lives and their access to resources and opportunities depends on the decisions that society makes (and who makes those decisions) about the allocation and distribution of scarce resources' (Pycroft, 2006: 1). Making such meaningful decisions depends on the quality of the state in each territory. Hence, political development is seen in the light of the 'universali-zation of the nation-state system' and 'national growth' or 'nation' (Kumar, 1978). If so, then what is political development?

Political development is another confusing concept in the social sciences. It is more difficult to define than economic development. For some scholars, political development is a subfield of political science (Bates, 2015). It is this which has led to so many different definitions being propounded, with some founded simply on political ideology, such as Marxism. It would be naïve to go through these numerous perspectives of political development. Pye (1965) highlights ten such definitions. He goes on to say that political development shares three broad characteristics, which are the concern with equality, the capacity of the political system, and differentiation or specialization of governmental organizations. He further notes that these characteristics are generally related to certain issues, such as equality to the political culture, the problems of capacity to authoritative governmental structures, and the question of differentiation to non-authoritative structures.

Almond and Powell (1966: 34) define political development as 'the increased differentiation and specialization of political structures and the increased secularization of political culture'. This definition links political development as the movement to democratic rule, rather than anti-democratic governance (LaPalombara, 1963). To Almond and Powell (1966), political development is concerned with increased effectiveness and efficiency of the performance of the political system, and its capabilities to achieve what it is intended to do, which is more about the promotion of human dignity. They mention five capabilities of a political system: extractive capability, regulative capability, distributive capability, responsive capability and symbolic capability.

The link between political development and bureaucracy is also well articulated in the literature (LaPalombara, 1963). Riggs (1963) looks at how bureaucracy and bureaucratic interests affect political development; not how the declared political aims of officials impinge on politics, but how the existence and self-interest of bureaucratic institutions affect, directly or indirectly, the growth of political institutions. To scholars who accept this view, 'efficient administrative machines can be used ... to promote development' (Parsons, 1957: 179). Following this, Taylor (1972: 104) defines political development as:

> [t]he growth of an impartial civil service and differentiation in the structures of government, the maintenance of stability and the provision for orderly change in leadership, fundamental changes in the style of thought, the increase of responsiveness in the personnel and institutions of government and the development of grassroots democracy, national integration that overrides primordial conflicts and brings purposive action to the state and its people, the provision of defence – military, economic, cultural – against the outside world, or simply constitutional development, the growth of rules by which authoritative decisions can made.

From the above, we see political development as the ability of the state to make substantial decisions for the development of its citizens. Until recently, however, such decisions were seen as the preserve of state institutions, in particular the political executive and the civil service.

Unfortunately, the inability to meet the expectations and aspirations of society, especially given the numerous crises, led to the call for citizen participation, especially in developing countries, as a part of political development. In these countries, the move from authoritarian systems to democratic governance led to the opening up of both the political and policy spaces, to enable civil society to be part of their economic and political development. It is this opening which has led to the emergence and the important role of TTs in political development, which we intend to subsequently analyse.

We thus see development from political, economic, sociological and cultural perspectives. Politically, development encompasses the ability of political institutions to endanger good governance by creating an environment that brings society together. This is achieved with strong political institutions, and the objective is to be able to develop policies and programmes to address wicked societal problems. Economic development, as explained above, addresses the economic needs of the society. For example, the ability to engage in policies to reduce poverty and enhance the welfare of citizens can be placed in this area. Sociological, social development is linked to both political and economic development. Generally, it is about improving the wellbeing of every individual in society so that they can reach their full potential. Thus, from a sociological point of view, development is concerned about the process or set of processes characterized by general sustainable economic growth and sets of natural, human, technological, cultural, financial and organizational conditions (Oberle, 1972).

On the other hand, cultural development is about the identity of people and how they see themselves. Scholarly interest in culture and development indicates how they control their destinies and how things reflect their particular experiences. Consequently, it is believed that 'where people's beliefs, ideas, meanings, and feelings … are not taken into consideration and respected, then we cannot speak about human development' (Tucker, 1996: 4).

THE TERRAIN OF THINK TANKS IN GHANA: AN OVERVIEW

The definition given to TTs determines their history and development in Ghana. For example, if one defines them as universities without students (Weaver, 1989), then TTs are not necessarily new in the Ghanaian policy and political environments. On the other hand, if these organizations are defined as 'independent, non-profit, research-oriented institutes, among whose primary objectives are to examine and comment on a wide range of public policy issues' (Abelson, 1992: 851), then one can argue that they are a more recent phenomenon in Ghana (Ayee, 2000; Ohemeng, 2005). Since we are interested in the latter, this section will focus on their emergence and development, rather than on the former, which have been part of the country's main public universities.

The first independent private TT to be established in Ghana is the Institute of Economic Affairs (IEA) in 1989. At that time, Ghana was still under military authoritarian rule, and the policy space was limited despite the existence of some civil society organizations (CSOs). While the idea of citizen participation in development had been the mantra of the then ruling Provisional National Defence Council (PNDC), the idea appeared in what is now known as the district assembly concept and other grassroots citizen participation initiatives. At the national level, policy-making continued to be dominated by politicians and technocrats in the civil service, with assistance from international experts, especially from the World Bank and the International Monetary Fund (IMF), and the donor community in general. The influence of these external institutions had become significant with the adoption of the structural adjustment programme (SAP) in 1983 (Foli and Ohemeng, 2021). This, however, does not mean that these external officials or bureaucrats had not formerly been present in the policy-making process in Ghana (Foli, 2016; Libby, 1976).

The establishment of the IEA set the pace for the development of other TTs. This development, however, coincided with the return to constitutional governance in 1993. This political development opened both the political and the policy spaces for CSOs to emerge as strong policy actors, as it was realized that government could not be the sole repository of ideas for policy-making and policy implementation. Thus, 'in Ghana, democratization encouraged the emergence of critical civil society organizations (including think tanks), which helped to stabilize and enhance democratic institutions' (Datta et al., 2010: 54). Consequently, there has been a rise of firms, advocacy groups, public relations firms and non-traditional media sources that continue to produce and support the production and circulation of ideas for government and the society at large in policy-making, governance and development (Acquah, 2021).

In addition, this period marked the height of neo-liberalism, a political ideology spearheaded by the United States and the United Kingdom, which called for the 'hollowing out' of the state in order to enable both the private for-profit and non-profit sectors to play meaningful roles in governance (Milward and Provan, 2000). Another important development was the change in direction of the World Bank and the IMF in their relationship with countries in the Global South when it came to governance. These institutions, after years of supporting authoritarian regimes, changed course and called for new ways of governing, which came to be referred to as 'good governance' (Grindle, 2007; Kiely, 1998). Good governance focused on the liberalization of the political space with the introduction of liberal democracy, the upholding of human rights, and citizen participation in policy-making (Cilliers, 2021; Leftwich, 1993).

It is within this general ambiance that TTs strongly emerged and continue to rise in Ghana. Currently, it is difficult to pinpoint the exact number of these institutions in the country. Part of the problem in identifying these institutions stems from their fuzzy description and agendas vis-à-vis other CSOs (Acquah, 2021). In other words, while it is easy to identify such institutions in the developed world based on their activities (research), in Ghana and other developing countries such institutions have extended their reach to other areas of national polity, including advocacy and the provision of developmental projects to communities.

In the 2020 Global Go To Think Tank Index Report, McGann (2021) identified 44 TTs in Ghana. Unfortunately, this number does not provide a clear picture of the actual count of these institutions in the country. The number includes some institutions affiliated to the government, or simply government TTs, while some newly emerging ones were not included in the count. Another difficulty in knowing the actual number is that there is no registry with the various government agencies such as the Registrar-General's Department, the Ghana Revenue Authority, or even the Ministry of Employment and Social Welfare, redesignated as Ministry of Employment and Labour Relations, which have oversight responsibilities of these institutions. It has therefore become easy for some people to set up these institutions for reasons best known to them.

Based on the fluid demarcations amongst these institutions, Ohemeng (2015) categorized TTs in Ghana into three different classes or groups. These are: publicly funded or government-affiliated or quasi-governmental; independent local institutions; and independent private organizations with international dimensions. The latter two falls under what the literature describes as autonomous and independent/quasi-independent institutions, which is the focus of this chapter. However, it is important that we briefly discuss these for the sake of brevity.

Publicly funded or government-affiliated or quasi-governmental TTs are part of the government structure and are based in a government institution. A good example is the Ghana Urbanisation Think Tank, which is situated within the Ministry of Local Government, Decentralization and Rural Development and co-chaired by the chief director at the Ministry and a professor from the publicly funded University of Ghana. Quasi-governmental TTs are funded by government grants but are not part of the government structure. This is the case of the Institute of Statistical, Social and Economic Research, also based at the University of Ghana. There are numerous examples of these types of institutions in Ghana. These institutions, however, may have some level of autonomy, especially when it comes to generating extra funds to support their work. These institutions are mostly created by Acts of Parliament as extensions to institutions of higher learning. Considered integral to subvented organizations in the public sector, they are mostly found in the country's public universities, although some have started to spring up in the ministries and other governmental institutions. Their subvented status means that they receive state funding, including the salaries of all employees. As part of the university system, they are expected to offer courses that relate to university teaching. While such institutions can solicit external funding, whatever they receive goes directly to the main university account system. They are not in a position to use externally sourced funding, or any other funding in paying the remuneration of employees, for instance. This is because such remunerations are covered by the government.

The institutions constituting this class of TTs were first created by the then Nkrumah government immediately after the country gained independence in 1957, and have been continued by subsequent governments to the present. Apart from the Institute of Statistical, Social and Economic Research (ISSER), based at the University of Ghana, there are also the Centre for Development Studies, the Cocoa Research Institute, and the Council for Scientific and Industrial Research, among others (Mbadlanyana et al., 2011).

The second group of TTs is the independent local private ones. What differentiates these TTs from the other two groups is that their activities are completely restricted to issues in Ghana. While some have some relations with similar or sister organizations outside the country, as well as serving as satellite offices of others (Amoah, 2012), their focus is on development in Ghana. They are considered as 'public policy research and advocacy institutions set up and maintained by an individual or group of individuals without government support directly or indirectly in any shape or form' (Amoah, 2012: 6–7). In a nutshell, they transcend TTs as research institutions or reservoir of ideas, to engage in advocacy on behalf of the poor.

Despite this, some are closely connected to government, or even have disguised affiliation with some political parties based on their founders and membership. Examples of such institutes include the Danquah Institute and Institute of Fiscal Studies, whose primary efforts are for the purpose of helping the government they support to design and initiate policies for national development. For example, the Danquah Institute continues to serve as a policy research organization for the New Patriotic Party (NPP). Similarly, the Institute of Fiscal Studies helps to promote local development, but it is more pro-National Democratic Congress (NDC).[1] Their so-called 'independence', therefore, can be questioned. Thus, we see them as being different from what may be considered to be traditional non-governmental organizations that maintain close contact with their constituencies (Kamstra and Knippenberg, 2014).

On the other hand, there are others that continue to preserve this semblance of independence by not being affiliated (whether formally or informally) to any political party. As a result, their focus has always been on national development irrespective of the government in power. Such organizations include IMANI, Third World Network (TWN), Institute of Democratic Governance (IDEG), Centre for Health and Social Services (CHSS) and a host of others. Nevertheless, some of these TTSs, for example, the Centre for Democratic Development (CDD)-Ghana, and Integrated Social Development Centre (ISODEC), have established several community projects that tend to bring them closer to the grassroots. ISODEC has since the early 1990s helped to deliver rural water and sanitation services in many parts of the country.

The third category is independent private TTs with international affiliations. Bajenova (2022) has described these TTs as transnational institutions, as their activities cut across nations or beyond the confines of one state. This group can be further divided into two separate entities. The first are TTs that although established and based in Ghana, not only work across the West African subregion, but also look at issues across the continent. Good examples of such TTs are the African Centre for Economic Transformation (ACET), the Kofi Annan International Peacekeeping Training Centre, the African Barometer, the International Center for Evaluation and Development (ICED), and a host of others. The second group are organizations that may be described as surrogates for TTs based in the Western world. Their presence in Ghana is evidenced by the establishment of offices there. Examples of these institutions are Transparency International (TI), the Tax Justice Network (TJN), International Food Policy Research Institute (IFPRI), the International Growth Centre (IGC)-Ghana, and West Africa Network for Peacebuilding (WANEP). An important characteristic of these institutions is that they employ not only Ghanaians, but also people from the rest of the continent, as well as expatriates from their parent organizations. At the same time, their mother organizations can send personnel to work for a set period. Local officials can also be sent to parent organizations for training and knowledge development. Be that as it may, there is growing awareness of the proliferation of these institutions, and the recognition of them as major players in different spheres in governance and development, since the policy space was opened with the ushering in of the Fourth Republic in 1993.

GOVERNANCE AND DEVELOPMENT IN GHANA: THE ROLE OF THINK TANKS

In this section, we examine how TTs continue to promote governance and development in Ghana. Unlike traditional non-governmental organizations, whose activities can be found in almost every sphere of society, TTs are more concentrated in Accra, the capital of Ghana, with a few others found in other regional capitals. They are more concerned with political, economic and social developments as part of governance in the country. Consequently, these institutions can be categorized as being economic or political in focus although the activities they undertake in these spheres significantly overlap because of their policy focus. In this section we look at how TTs have been promoting political, economic and social development in Ghana.

Political Development and Governance

A major issue addressed by the majority of TTs in Ghana is political develop-ment and governance, as explained earlier. Indeed, the genesis of TTs focused on this aspect of development with the emergence from authoritarian regimes to democratic governance. In many cases, this movement created the space for political discussion which focused more on how to consolidate what many called the fragile democratic dispensation in the early 1990s (Botchway, 2018; Gyimah-Boadi, 2009).

The seemingly uncomfortable notion of returning to authoritarian rule based on previously failed democratic experiments since independence continued to weigh on the minds of Ghanaians after the inauguration of the Fourth Republic in 1993. It was this political jitteriness that led TTs to develop various strategies in helping to move Ghana to democratic consolidation (Abdulai and Crawford, 2010; Arthur, 2010). Some of these measures include the development of the Inter-party Advisory Committee (IPAC). The focus of the IPAC is to bring together the Electoral Commission (EC), political parties and CSOs with the view of building electoral consensus, effective election management system, and political reforms towards democratic consolidation. Over the years, and through the IPAC, various initiatives have been taken up which have helped Ghana to consolidate its democracy.

One of the major achievements of electoral reforms spearheaded by TTs is the acceptance and deployment of biometric machines to register and authenti-cate voters by election stakeholders to ensure the integrity of, as well as reduce the controversies surrounding, electoral outcomes (Ayee, 1997; Boafo-Arthur, 2008; Frempong, 2012). Indeed, a key controversy in every democracy is how votes are cast and electoral outcomes determined in a credible and transparent manner. The integrity of electoral success hinges on this, as we continue to witness in the United States and some developed democracies. This reform became necessary after the NPP and other parties rejected the outcome of the 1992 general election on the grounds of electoral and voting malpractices (Gyampo, 2017; NPP, 1993), and has helped in achieving democratic consol-idation in Ghana.

In Africa, large-scale elections are characterized by violence, intimidation and electoral disputes (Ani and Uwizeyimana, 2022; Bekoe, 2012; Bob-Milliar, 2014; Borzyskowski and Kuhn, 2020; Leonard, 2009; Kumah-Abbiw, 2017; Mueller, 2011; Oduro, 2021; Söderström, 2018). The causes of this violence, intimidation and fear are the lack of political knowledge among the electorate, and the lack of good election monitoring systems. How have TTs helped to mitigate this and ensure that voters cast their ballots without fear of violence and intimidation, and that the result of the electoral outcome is accepted by all in Ghana? Two main strategies developed by these institutions are the establishment of independent election monitoring teams known as the Coalition of Domestic Election Observers (CODEO), and improving the quality of the campaign and the credibility of the electoral process through political messaging and marketing. CODEO is an independent and non-partisan network of civil society groups, faith-based organizations and professional bodies which observe Ghanaian elections, established in 2000 under the auspices of CDD-Ghana. The network helps to mobilize citizens of Ghana to actively participate in the electoral process and to complement the efforts of the EC in ensuring transparent, free, fair and peaceful elections. The efforts by election observers have made it easier for losing candidates and parties to generally accept the outcome of the electoral process, thus enhancing democratic consolidation and peacebuilding (Oduro, 2021).

As already noted, electoral fear and violence may emerge from the lack of political knowledge about the general political management, including political campaigns, the rules governing the electoral processes, and the role of political parties, as well as the EC. To ensure that this knowledge is well disseminated, TTs continue to play various roles to improve the quality of the campaign and the credibility of the electoral process. For example, in 2012, the IEA sponsored and facilitated the signing of the Political Parties Code of Conduct for elections, which serves to guide the activities of the political parties during the campaign and to help defuse tension. With the collaboration of other TTs, presidential debates are held prior to elections, and candidates also use the platform to appeal for peace. In addition, TTs spearheaded the signing of a symbolic peace pact between the presidential candidates of the two leading parties, the NPP and NDC, to commit to use legal means in the case of electoral disputes. This led to the election petitions of both the NPP and the NDC in 2012 and 2020, respectively, in which the outcomes of the elections held in those years were challenged in the Supreme Court. TTs have thus contributed to the continuous expansion of the political space for good governance.

In all, the involvement of TTs in the promotion of political governance and development has led to the consolidation of Ghana's democracy, which has enabled it to receive accolades across the world. As a result, international institutions continue to praise Ghana and score the country very high in their rankings. For example, Freedom House scores Ghana at 80/100 on Global Freedom Scores, with 35 and 45 on political rights and civil liberties, respectively. In all, experts and members of TTs continue to be increasingly engaged by government on political developments, as well as some political parties to author various sections of their manifestos for governance.

Think Tanks and Economic Development

While the majority of TTs are engaging in political development, they are also very much interested in how Ghana is governed to achieve economic development and enhance the wellbeing of citizens. In fact, the first few major TTs in the country began as economic institutes focusing on how they could help government to develop better economic policies, to promote economic welfare including poverty reduction to tackle wicked problems (Ohemeng, 2005). Thus, in addition to some state-sponsored TTs, these private institutions have become the main producers of local, non-governmental research evidence in the economic development space. They continue to apply scientific methods to the gathering, analysis and reporting of different types of evidence on economic development using primary qualitative and quantitative data.

Consequently, over the years, TTs have helped government to develop economic policies for growth in two areas that we would like to focus on. These are industrial policy development, and the management of oil in the broader sense. Their activities have focused on the promotion of accountability and transparency as part of economic growth initiatives. For example, the IEA has hosted a series of events on gains made in promoting transparency and accountability, factors affecting economic growth, and the public's perception of socio-economic and governance conditions in Ghana. In addition, ISSER through its annual flagship publication, *The State of the Ghana Economy*, discusses developments in various sectors of the Ghanaian economy including fiscal development, financial and monetary sector, international trade and payments, agricultural, industrial and services sectors. Similarly, the IFS in its policy briefs and roundtables has examined government's fiscal and monetary policies as well as the extractive sector, and their implications for socio-economic development.

Another key area of TTs in economic development is the designing of and advising on public policies aimed at promoting industrialization and supporting private sector-driven industrial development and sustained economic growth, and the management of natural resources for development. TTs have therefore become important contributors to the content of policy, key in ensuring quality standards and effective performance in policy and programme implementation (Ohemeng and Ayee, 2016; Owoo and Page, 2017).

A major important area of interest is the crafting of policies to manage Ghana's oil as a way of reshaping the government's approach to industrial development. Under the new Industrial Development Strategy, industry is projected to grow at an average annual rate of 20.3 per cent, propelled by growth in the construction sector, infrastructure development in the oil sector, and production of gas to power thermal generation. Yet, many felt that this growth would not be achieved without a good management framework. Owoo and Page (2017) are of the view that with the discovery of oil in commercial quantities, and demands from the business community, there has been intense pressure on the government to maximize participation by domestic firms in the resource development and management. The government responded to this pressure by setting the objectives of achieving a minimum level of local equity participation of 5 per cent in all petroleum investments, and 90 per cent local content in the supply of inputs to the petroleum sector, by 2020. Consequently, a Local Content Bill was introduced in Parliament in 2007, but its passage was delayed until 2013. Nevertheless, TTs and other CSOs continue to point out the lack of transparency between the oil industry and the government during the time the legislation was in Parliament. Their inputs have therefore led to the effective development of local content policies in the industry, which seems to have enabled Ghana to 'get it right' in the fight against the resource curse that continues to hinder economic growth on the continent (Amoako-Tuffour et al., 2015).

THINK TANKS, CORRUPTION AND DEVELOPMENT IN GHANA

One of the obstacles to development in developing countries is corruption. It is defined as:

> the abuse of public office for private gain, including bribery, nepotism and misap-
> propriation; extra-legal efforts by individuals or groups to gain influence over the
> actions of the bureaucracy; the collusion between parties in the public and private
> sectors for the benefit of the latter; and more generally influencing the shaping of
> policies and institutions in ways that benefit the contributing private parties at the
> expense of the broader public welfare (López-Claros, 2015: 35)

Indeed, many have described corruption as a social cancer (Beniwal, 2012; Feil, 2021; Olken and Pande, 2012), as it kills development and destroys prosperity (López-Claros et al., 2020). Consequently, the need to fight corruption has been of paramount importance to almost everyone.

In Ghana, it has been noted that the country loses millions of dollars every year through corruption, an amount that could enhance the country's development. In 2016, the Heritage Foundation (2016), a United States-based TT, noted that Ghana is losing the battle against corruption. The government's inability to decisively commit to tackling persistent political corruption suggests that funds earmarked for social intervention programmes to help alleviate the hardships of the poor are unlikely to reach the target beneficiaries (Asomah,

2018). In 2022, Ghana was ranked 72nd on the Transparency International (TI) Corruption Perceptions Index, with a score of 43 points out of 100 unchanged since 2020.

As a result, various TTs have aimed at fighting this social cancer. For example, a newly formed TT, the Solidaire Ghana (SG), has the sole aim of fighting corruption and abuse of rights of the citizenry, and is interested in helping to shape policy formulation and advocate good governance.

How are TTs fighting corruption in Ghana? TTs have joined forces with other CSOs such as the Ghana Integrity Initiative (GII) (the local chapter of TI) and Ghana Anti-Corruption Coalition (GACC), and developed the anti-corruption group to draw the attention of the government, Ghanaians and development partners to the state of affairs of the country. Through the efforts of these TTs, various institutional frameworks have been developed in fighting the disease. A good example is the passage of the Right to Information Act in 2018. The RTI Act is seen as a major tool in the fight against corruption, as it is believed that the ability of citizens to freely obtain public information from public organizations can lead to the exposure of corrupt officials (Adu, 2018). Furthermore, TTs such as CDD-Ghana, IDEG and Imani-Ghana joined forces with the GII and GACC to push Parliament to approve in 2014 the National Anti-Corruption Action Plan (NACAP), which has become the blueprint to combat corruption.

In Ghana, article 21(1) (f) of the 1992 Constitution specifically guarantees the right to information, subject to certain qualifications and the necessary laws in the country. Unfortunately, government since 1993 has used many tactics to avoid the passage of an RTI law. For instance, the first RTI draft bill was prepared in 1996, but never got passed. It then underwent various reviews in the 2000s, but never got tabled in Parliament. In 2010, a bill was tabled in Parliament but was not passed. After a series of back-and-forth over the years, the bill was finally passed and assented in 2019, nearly 20 years after it began its journey (Ohemeng, 2023).

The initiation and the pressure to pass the bill was the effort of CSOs spearheaded by the IEA, which drafted the initial bill and was later joined by the CDD-Ghana. Seeing that their initial efforts were not yielding the needed results, these two organizations formed a coalition with other TTs such as the Commonwealth Human Rights Initiative (CHRI) that became known as the RTI Coalition. With their collective efforts, they managed to put substantive pressure on government, assisting in drafting and reviewing the bill, engaging with individual parliamentarians over the years until the bill was finally passed. Thus, the effort of this coalition made it possible for the RTI, an instrument considered vital for the consolidation of democracy and reducing corruption, to be passed into law in Ghana, thus helping to overcome government inertia on an important issue.

THINK TANKS AND DEVELOPMENT ADVOCACY

Almost all TTs in Ghana perceive themselves as policy advocacy institutions. Policy advocacy means developing and pushing government to adopt policies, including pro-poor policies for development. Policy advocacy is defined variously as comprising 'purposive efforts to change specific existing or proposed policies or practices on behalf of or with a specific client or group of clients' (Ezell, 2001: 23), or 'any attempt to influence the decisions of any institutional elite on behalf of a collective interest' (Jenkins, 1987: 297), or simply as 'intentional activities initiated by the public to affect the policy making process' (Gen and Wright, 2013). While TTs engage in policy advocacy, they also undertake what may be described as advocacy for development.

Advocacy for development concerns a wide range of activities conducted to influence decision-makers at different levels, with the overall aim of combating the structural causes of poverty and injustice. The idea thus goes beyond influencing policy, and aims for sustainable changes in public and political contexts. This work includes awareness-raising, legal actions and public education, as well as building networks, relationships and capacity (Barrett et al., 2016; Morariu and Brennan, 2009). TTs such as the CDD and ISODEC continue to enhance developmental awareness affecting societies. For instance, ISODEC has been at the forefront of girl-child education at the local level, helping communities to understand the need to educate girls rather than giving them in marriage at a young and tender age. Similarly, the CDD in Northern Ghana is ensuring the development of sustainable agricultural and other practices in addressing poverty reduction. Some of these TTs have also teamed up with traditional chiefs to address local cultures that continue to impede development, especially those affecting girls (Afrifa and Ohemeng, 2021).

SOME CHALLENGES OF THINK TANKS

Notwithstanding the contributions of TTs to governance and development in Ghana through policy entrepreneurship and thought leadership, they face two major challenges. First is the perception that they are not neutral, but rather partisan, leading to some of their findings and recommendations being dismissed, especially by a political party that regards these as not favourable to its cause or interests. This has led to the questioning of the methodology used to arrive at those findings and recommendations. This criticism appears frivolous. Indeed, a few TTs such as the Danquah Institute and Institute for Fiscal Studies (IFS) were founded by some members and sympathisers of the NPP and NDC, respectively. However, the majority of them, such as the IEA, CDD-Ghana, IDEG and Imani-Ghana, cannot be said to be partisan because they have employed some leading figures of the two major parties (the NPP and NDC) as either research fellows or board members. The IEA, for instance, used to have the late Justice D.F. Annan (first Speaker of the Parliament of the Fourth Republic) as the chair of its board of directors; while Professor Kwamena Ahwoi (a former minister in the NDC government) was a research fellow at the time the NDC was not in power. So too were Professor Daniel Adzei-Bekoe (former chairman of the Council of State) and B.J. da Rocha (founding member and first national chairman of the New Patriotic Party), who served on the IEA board of directors and as a senior fellow, respectively. The partisan tag against TTs in Ghana is symptomatic of the growing politicization and polarization of national issues in the country since the Fourth Republic, and the lack of a culture of debate and dissent.

The second major challenge is the inadequate funds at the disposal of TTs, and their lack of sustainability to undertake their activities. All the TTs are funded by foundations, development partners and, in some cases, local corporate bodies. Funding from these sources is cyclical and depends on the current interests of the benefactors, which therefore makes funding unsustainable and unreliable. In addition, where funding was available, it was tied to conditions that some of the TTs have complained of as not flexible enough to enable them to undertake equally important activities. The inadequate funding has led most TTs to scale down their activities, thereby reducing their vibrancy.

How can these two challenges be addressed? In the case of the partisanship tag against the TTs, there is the need to deepen a culture of debate and dissent in the country, while the political parties must endeavour to depoliticize issues and look at national issues from a non-partisan lens. This in itself entails the forging of a shared national vision, which has been missing since the advent of the Fourth Republic, leading to policy discontinuity despite a constitutional stipulation that 'as far as practicable, a government shall continue and execute projects and programs commenced by the previous Governments' (Republic of Ghana, 1992: Article 35(7)). Furthermore, the TTs themselves should undertake self-introspection to determine how to address the negative perception. In terms of inadequate and unreliable funding, the TTs themselves will need to diversify their current funding sources through a proper diagnosis, to become more ingenious and innovative in revenue mobilization through other local and international sources.

CONCLUSION

This chapter has shown that governance and development overlap, and both cut across economic and political developments. As a result, the chapter has examined areas of governance that are depicted by both economic and political developments in which TTs have played and continue to play a meaningful role in Ghana.

This chapter has outlined the role of TTs in governance and development. In so doing, it has examined areas related to good governance and economic development, as well as issues related to righting corruption and development advocacy. In the area of corruption, the role of TTs as watchdog has enabled them to continuously expose abuses and infractions in the country and bring them to public attention. Development-wise, they have assisted communities, especially in ventures to enhance poverty reduction, as well to address cultural practices which are detrimental to the society.

As already discussed, TTs began to flourish in Ghana with the movement from an authoritarian regime to a democratic one in 1993. Significantly, the initial focus of these earlier established institutions was on political development, with the hope of helping Ghana to move from electoral to consolidated democracy. These TTs believed that without political stability, as well as strong institutions, achieving economic development may be a mirage. Their approach therefore epitomized that of the World Bank and the IMF, which after years of promoting economic development at the expense of political development belatedly realized the importance of the state, without which economic development could not be achieved. Thus, to the World Bank and IMF, to promote and protect the market or neo-liberalism, a strong political development is required in the form of a capable state that could protect property rights and ensure accountability in governance.

TTs in Ghana are interested in both political and economic development. Consequently, they do not restrict their activities to one sphere of influence. For example, the IEA may be seen as largely focusing on economic issues, even though it undertakes more activities in political development in Ghana. Similarly, the CDD may be seen as a pro-political development organization, but that is not the case. Thus, focusing on the names of these institutions and what they do can be deceptive.

The chapter also identified two key challenges facing the TTs, namely their partisan tag, and inadequate and unsustainable sources of funding. These can be addressed through the repositioning of the TTs themselves, and a change largely on the part of the political parties in the way politics should be conducted.

NOTE

1.   The NPP and NDC are the two dominant political parties in Ghana.

REFERENCES

Abdulai, A.-G., and G. Crawford (2010) 'Consolidating democracy in Ghana: progress and prospects?', *Democratization*, 17(1), 26–67.

Abelson, D.E. (1992) 'A new channel of influence: American think tanks and the news media', *Queens Quarterly*, 94(4), 849–72.

Acquah, E. (2021) 'The future of African think tanks', in J. McGann (ed.), *The Future of Think Tanks and Policy Advice Around the World* (27–31). Cham: Palgrave Macmillan.

Adelman, I. (2000) 'Fifty years of economic development: what have we learned?', Paper presented at the Annual Development Conference, Washington, DC: World Bank.

Adu, K.K. (2018) 'The paradox of the right to information law in Africa', *Government Information Quarterly*, 35(4), 669–674.

Afrifa, S., and F.L.K. Ohemeng (2021) 'Traditional chiefs as institutional entrepreneurs in policy making and implementation in Africa', in G. Onyango (ed.), *Handbook of Public Policy in Africa* (128–138). New York: Routledge.

Almond, G.A., and G.B. Powell (1966) *Comparative Politics: A Development Approach*. Boston, MA: Little, Brown & Company.

Amoah, L.A.G. (2012) 'Private think tanks, international networks and public policy formation in a democratizing Ghana (1980–2010): an exploratory interrogation', a research report for Civil Society Research Facility Ghana, Institute of Statistical, Social, and Economic Research (University of Ghana), and Centre for International Development Issues Nijmegen (Radboud University Nijmegen).

Amoako-Tuffour, J., T. Aubynn and A. Atta-Quayson (2015) 'Local content and value addition in ghana's mineral, oil, and gas: is Ghana getting it right? Accra: Ghana: African Center for Economic Transformation.

Ani, K.J. and D.E. Uwizeyimana (2022) 'Introducing elections and electoral violence in Africa', K.J. Ani and V. Ojakorotu (eds), *Elections and Electoral Violence in Nigeria* (1–10). Singapore: Springer Nature.

Ansell, C., and A. Gash (2008) 'Collaborative governance in theory and practice', *Journal of Public Administration Research and Theory*, 18(4), 543–571. https://doi.org/10.1093/jopart/mum03.

Arthur, P. (2010) 'Democratic consolidation in Ghana: the role and contribution of the media, civil society, and state institutions', *Commonwealth and Comparative Politics*, 48(2), 203–226.

Asomah, J.Y. (2018) 'Ghana in search of government accountability in controlling political corruption: are the private mass media part of the solution or the problem?' Unpublished Doctoral Dissertation, Department of Sociology, University of Saskatchewan Saskatoon, Canada.

Ayee, J.R.A. (1997) 'The December 1996 general elections in Ghana', *Electoral Studies*, 16(3), 416–427.

Ayee, J.R.A. (2000) *Saints, Wizards, Demons, and Systems: Explaining the Success and Failure of Public Policies and Programmes*. Accra: Ghana Universities Press.

Bajenova, T. (2022) 'Transnational think tank networks: multipliers of political power or a new form of expertise monopolies at the European level', *Administrative Theory and Praxis*. Online First: DOI:10.1080/10842806.2022.214746.

Barrett, J.B., M. van Wessel and D. Hilhorst (2016) *Advocacy for Development: Effectiveness, Monitoring and Evaluation*. Wageningen: Wageningen University.

Bates, R. (2015) *When Things Fell Apart: State Failure in Late-Century Africa.* Cambridge: Cambridge University Press.

Bekoe, D.A. (ed.) (2012) *Voting in Fear: Electoral Violence in Sub-Saharan Africa.* Washington, DC: United States Institute of Peace Press.

Beniwal, A. (2012) 'Corruption: a social disease', Indian Journal of Political Science, 73(1), 85–96.

Benz, A. (2005) 'Public administrative science in Germany: problems and prospects of a composite discipline', *Public Administration*, 83(3), 659–668.

Bianchi, C., G. Nasi and W.C. Rivenbark (2021) 'Implementing collaborative governance: models, experiences, and challenges', *Public Management Review*, 23(11), 1581–1589.

Boafo-Arthur, K. (2008) *Democracy and Stability in West Africa: The Ghanaian Experience.* Uppsala: Department of Peace and Conflict Research, Uppsala University.

Bob-Milliar, G.M. (2014) 'Party youth activists and low-intensity electoral violence in Ghana: a qualitative study of party foot soldiers' activism', *African Studies Quarterly*, 15(1), 125–152.

Borzyskowski, I. von, and P.M. Kuhn (2020) 'Dangerously informed: voter information and pre-electoral violence in Africa', *Journal of Peace Research*, 57(1), 15–29.

Botchway, T.P. (2018) 'Civil society and the consolidation of democracy in Ghana's fourth republic', *Cogent Social Sciences*, 4(1), 1452840.

Bowen, G.A. (2009) 'Document analysis as a qualitative research method', *Qualitative Research Journal*, 9(2), 27–40.

Bryant, C. (2018) 'Government versus governance: structure versus process', *EchoGéo*, 43, http://journals.openedition.org/echogeo/15288.

Bryson, J.M., B.C. Crosby and L. Bloomberg (2014) 'Public value governance: moving beyond traditional public administration and the new public management', *Public Administration Review*, 74(4), 445–456.

Choudhary, N. (2022) 'Development governance', in A. Farazmand (ed.), *Global Encyclopaedia of Public Administration, Public Policy, and Governance* (3179–3193). Cham: Springer Nature.

Cilliers, J. (2021) *The Future of Africa: Challenges and Opportunities.* Cham: Springer Nature.

Cleveland, H. (1972) *The Future Executive: A Guide for Tomorrow's Managers.* New York: Harper & Row.

Datta, A., N. Jones and E. Mendizabal (2010) 'Think tanks and the rise of the knowledge economy their linkages with national politics and external donors', in A. Garcé and G. Uña (eds), *Think Tanks and Public Policies in Latin America* (46–72). Buenos Aires: Fundación Siena and CIPPEC.

Douglas, S., C. Ansell, C.F. Parker, E. Sørensen, P. 't Hart and J. Torfing (2020) 'Understanding collaboration: introducing the collaborative governance case databank', *Policy and Society*, 39(4), 495–509.

Ezell, M. (2001) *Advocacy in the Human Services.* Belmont, CA: Brooks/Cole.

Feil, H. (2021) The cancer of corruption and World Bank project performance: is there a connection? *Development Policy Review*, 39(3), 381–397.

Feldman, M., T. Hadjimichael, L. Lanahan and T. Kemeny (2016) 'The logic of economic development: a definition and model for investment', *Environment and Planning C: Politics and Space*, 34(1), 5–21. https://doi.org/10.1177/0263774X15614653.

Foli, R. (2016) 'Transnational actors and policy making in Ghana: the case of the Livelihood Empowerment Against Poverty', *Global Social Policy*, 16(3), 268–286.

Foli, R. and F.L.K. Ohemeng (2021) 'The role and impact of international bureaucrats in policy making in Africa', in G. Onyango (ed.), *Handbook of Public Policy in Africa* (117–127). New York: Routledge.

Frederickson, H.G. (2007) 'Whatever happened to public administration? Governance, governance everywhere', in E. Ferlie, L.E. Lynn Jr and C. Pollitt (eds), *The Oxford Handbook of Public Management* (282–304), Oxford: Oxford University Press.

Frempong, A.K D. (2012) *Electoral Politics in Ghana's Fourth Republic: In the Context of Post-cold War Africa*. Accra: Freedom Publication.

Fröhlich, J. and J. Knieling (2013) Conceptualising climate change governance. In J. Fröhlich and J. Knieling (eds), *Climate Change Governance* (9–26). Heidelberg: Springer Berlin,

Gen, S. and Wright, A.C. (2013) Policy advocacy organizations: a framework linking theory and practice. *Journal of Policy Practice*, 12(3), 163–193.

Grindle, M.S. (2007) 'Good enough governance revisited', *Development Policy Review*, 25(5), 533–574.

Gyampo, R.E.V. (2017) 'The state of electoral reforms in Ghana', *Africa Spectrum*, 52(3), 95–109.

Gyimah-Boadi, E. (2009) 'Another step forward for Ghana', *Journal of Democracy*, 20(2), 138–152.

Head, B.W. (2008) 'Wicked problems in public policy', *Public Policy*, 3(2), 101–118.

Head, B.W. and J. Alford (2015) 'Wicked problems: implications for public policy and management', *Administration and Society*, 47(6), 711–739.

Heinelt, H. and D. Kübler (2005) *Metropolitan Governance in the 21st Century: Capacity, Democracy and the Dynamics of Place*. London: Routledge.

Heritage Foundation (2016) *2016 Index of Economic Freedom: Promoting Economic Opportunity and Prosperity*. https://www.heritage.org/index/pdf/2016/book/index_2016.pdf.

Huxham C., S. Vangen, C. Huxham and C. Eden (2000) 'The challenge of collaborative governance', Public Management: An International Journal of Research and Theory, 2(3), 337–358. https://doi.org/10.1080/14719030000000021.

Isett, K.R., I.A. Mergel, K. LeRoux, P.A. Mischen and R.K. Rethemeyer (2011) 'Networks in public administration scholarship: understanding where we are and where we need to go', *Journal of Public Administration Research and Theory*, 21(suppl_1), i157–i173. https://doi.org/10.1093/jopart/muq061.

Jenkins J.C. (1987) 'Nonprofit organizations and policy advocacy', in W.W. Powell (ed.), The Nonprofit Sector (296–318). New Haven, CT: Yale University Press.

Jreisat, J. (2011) 'Governance: issues in concept and practice', in D.C. Menzel and H.L. White (eds), *The State of Public Administration: Issues, Challenges and Opportunities* (424–438). New York and London: M.E. Sharpe.

Kamstra, J. and L. Knippenberg (2014) 'Promoting democracy in Ghana: exploring the democratic roles of donor-sponsored non-governmental organizations', *Democratization,* 21(4), 583–609. DOI:10.1080/13510347.2012.751975.

Kiely, R. (1998) 'Neoliberalism revised? A critical account of World Bank conceptions of good governance and market friendly intervention', *International Journal of Health Service*, 28(4), 683–702.

Kumah-Abiwu, F. (2017) 'Issue framing and electoral violence in Ghana: a conceptual analysis', *Commonwealth and Comparative Politics*, 55(2), 165–186.

Kumar, S. (1978) 'The concept of political development', *Political Studies*, 26(4), 423–438.

LaPalombara, J. (ed.) *Bureaucracy and Political Development* (SPD-2), Vol. 2. Princeton, NJ: Princeton University Press.

Leftwich, A. (1993) 'Governance, democracy and development in the Third World', *Third World Quarterly*, 14(3), 605–624.

Leonard, D.K. (2009) 'Elections and conflict in Africa: an introduction', *Journal of African Elections*, 8(1), 1–12.

Libby, R.T. (1976) 'External co-optation of a less developed country's policy making: the case of Ghana, 1969–1972', *World Politics*, 29(1), 67–89.

Liu, Y. (2022) 'Public trust and collaborative governance: an instrumental variable approach', *Public Management Review*. DOI: 10.1080/14719037.2022.2095003.

López-Claros, A. (2015) 'Removing impediments to sustainable economic development: the case of corruption', *Journal of International Commerce, Economics and Policy*, 6(1), 1550002.

Lopez-Claros, A., A.L. Dahl and M. Groff (2020) *Global Governance and the Emergence of Global Institutions for the 21st Century*. Cambridge: Cambridge University Press.

Mayntz, R. (2004) 'Mechanisms in the analysis of social macro-phenomena', *Philosophy of the Social Sciences*, 34(2), 237–259.

Mayntz, R. (2006) 'From government to governance: political steering in modern societies', in D. Scheer and F. Rubik (eds), *Governance of Integrated Product Policy: In Search of Sustainable Production and Consumption* (1–8). London: Routledge.

Mbadlanyana, T., N. Sibalukhulu and J. Cilliers (2011) 'Shaping African futures: think tanks and the need for endogenous knowledge production in Sub-Saharan Africa', *Foresight*, 13(3), 64–84.

McGann, J.G. (2021) '2020 Global Go To Think Tank Index Report', TTCSP Global Go To Think Tank Index Reports, 18. https://repository.upenn.edu/think_tanks/18.

Michalski, W., R. Miller and B. Stevens (2001) 'Governance in the 21st century: power in the global knowledge economy and society', in OECD (ed.), *Governance in the 21st Century* (7–26). Paris: OECD.

Milward, H.B. and K.G. Provan (2000) 'Governing the hollow state', *Journal of Public Administration Research and Theory*, 10(2), 359–379.

Mirvis, P.H. and B. Googins (2013) 'Toward shared governance for sustainability: U.S. public and private sector roles', *Building Networks and Partnerships*, Organizing for Sustainable Effectiveness, Vol. 3, (227–260). Bingley: Emerald Publishing.

Morariu, J. and K. Brennan (2009) 'Effective advocacy evaluation: the role of funders', *The Foundation Review*, 1(3). https://doi.org/10.4087/FOUNDATIONREVIEW-D-09–00031.1.

Mueller, S. (2011) 'Dying to win: elections, political violence, and institutional decay in Kenya', *Journal of Contemporary African Studies*, 29(1), 99–117.

Nan, R. and Y. Yang (2022) 'Who is willing to participate in local governance? Modernization of shared governance in China', *Sustainability*, 14, 14899. https://doi.org/10.3390/su142214899.

New Patriotic Party (NPP) (1993) *The Stolen Verdict: Ghana, November 1992 Presidential Election: Report of the New Patriotic Party*, Accra, Ghana: The Party.

Oberle, W.H. (1972) 'A sociological view of "development"', paper presented at the 3rd World Congress of Rural Sociology, Baton Rouge, Louisiana, August, 2–27.

Oduro, F. (2021) 'The changing nature of elections in Africa: impact on peacebuilding', in T. McNamee and M. Muyangwa (eds), *The State of Peacebuilding in Africa: Lessons Learned for Policymakers and Practitioners* (163–180). Cham: Palgrave.

OECD (1995) *Participatory Development and Good Governance*. Paris: OECD.

Ohemeng, F.L.K. (2005) 'Getting the state right: think tanks and the dissemination of new public management ideas', *Journal of Modern African Studies*, 43(3), 443–465.

Ohemeng, F.L.K. (2015) 'Civil society and policy making in developing countries: assessing the impact of think tanks on policy outcomes in Ghana', *Journal of Asian and African Studies*, 50(6), 667–682.

Ohemeng, F.L.K. (2023) 'Think tanks as collective policy entrepreneurs and the art of policy making in Ghana', in M. Kpessa-Whyte and J. Dzisah (eds), *Public Policy Making in Ghana: Conceptual and Practical Insights* (161–180). Cham: Springer.

Ohemeng, F.L.K. and J.R.A. Ayee (2016) 'The "new approach" to public sector reforms in Ghana: a case of politics as usual or a genuine attempt at reforms?', *Development Policy Review*, 34(2), 277–300.

Olken, B.A. and R. Pande (2012) 'Corruption in developing countries', *Annual Review of Economics*, 4, 479–509.

Owoo, N.S. and J. Page (2017) 'Industrial policy in Ghana: from a dominant state to resource abundance', in E. Aryeetey and R. Kanbur (eds), *The Economy of Ghana Sixty Years after Independence* (176–191). Oxford: Oxford University Press.

Parsons, M.B. (1957) 'Performance budgeting in the Philippines', *Public Administration Review*, 17(3), 173–179.

Pierre, Jon and B. Guy Peters (2000) *Governance, Politics and the State*. Basingstoke: Palgrave.

Provan, K.G. and P. Kenis (2008) 'Modes of network governance: structure, management, and effectiveness', *Journal of Public Administration Research and Theory*, 18(2), 229–252.

Pycroft, C. (2006) 'Addressing the political dimensions of development', *The Governance Brief*, Issue 14. https:// www .adb .org/ sites/ default/ files/ publication/ 28635/governancebrief14.pdf.

Pye, L.W. (1965) 'The concept of political development', *Annals of the American Academy of Political and Social Science*, 358, 1–13.

Republic of Ghana (1992) *Constitution of the Republic of Ghana, 1992*. Accra: Ghana Publishing Company.

Riggs, F.W. (1963) 'Bureaucrats and political development: a paradoxical view', in J. Palombara (ed.), *Bureaucracy and Political Development* (SPD-2), Vol. 2 (120–167). Princeton, NJ: Princeton University Press.

Roy, K.C. and C.A. Tisdell (1998) 'Good governance in sustainable development: the impact of institutions', *International Journal of Social Economics*, 25(6/7/8), 1310–1325.

Sen, A. (1993) 'Capability and well-being', in M. Nussbaum and A. Sen (eds), *The Quality of Life* (30–53). Oxford: Oxford University Press.

Sen, A. (1999) *Development as Freedom*. Oxford: Oxford University Press.

Sen, A. (2009) 'The economics of happiness and capability', in L. Bruni, F. Comim and M. Pugno (eds), *Capabilities and Happiness* (16–27). Oxford: Oxford University Press.

Söderström, J. (2018) 'Fear of electoral violence and its impact on political knowledge in Sub-Saharan Africa', *Political Studies*, 66(4), 869–886.

Taylor, C.L. (1972) 'Indicators of political development', *Journal of Development Studies*, 8(3), 103–109.

Tucker, V. (1996) 'Introduction: a cultural perspective on development', *European Journal of Development Research*, 8(2), 1–21.

Wachhaus, A. (2014) 'Governance beyond government', *Administration and Society*, 46(5), 573–593.

Wang, H. and B. Ran (2021) 'Network governance and collaborative governance: a thematic analysis on their similarities, differences, and entanglements', *Public Management Review*. DOI: 10.1080/14719037.2021.2011389.

Weaver, K.R. (1989) 'The changing world of think tanks', *Political Science and Politics*, 22(3), 563–578.

Werlin, H.H. (2003) 'Poor nations, rich nations: a theory of governance', *Public Administration Review*, 63(3), 329–342.

Willner, A.R. (1964) 'The underdeveloped study of political development', *World Politics*, 16(3), 468–482.

World Bank (1992) *Governance and Development*. Washington, DC: World Bank.

6. Think tanks and policy visibility during the COVID-19 responses in Kenya

Japheth O. Ondiek and Gedion Onyango

INTRODUCTION: AN INSTITUTIONAL THEORY IN PERSPECTIVE

In her book *How Institutions Think*, Mary Douglas argues that human thinking is anchored within an institution. Different institutions influence individuals to think differently while responding to different emotions or issues (Douglas 1986). In this way, institutions do not think independently, set goals and build themselves (ibid.). Instead, contends Mary Douglas, as they are being constructed, individual ideas are fashioned into a common shape to prove their legitimacy by sheer numbers. Thus, institutions can create linkages, think and forget just like humans inhabiting them. *How Institutions Think*, provides a true sense of viewing institutions such as think tanks and how they work, or their capability to influence policy agendas. Harcourt et al. (2005) define institutions as consisting of standardized and conventional patterns of behaviour across and within organizations. They notably provide meaning to social order and exchange. These entail some behavioural patterns that comprise industry and organizational standards, norms and routines. Institutions play critical roles in understanding the state–society relationship. They are the epitome of modern human civilization's highest form of organizing society and its conflicting interests (March and Olsen 1989; North 1990). In Max Weber's view, institutions as bureaucracies are an 'iron cage' due to the end effects of increased bureaucratization and rationality of institutions in ordering modern society (Barker 1993; DiMaggio and Powell 1983; Douglas 1983).

In public policy, institutions are the venues for government action (Baumgartner and Jones 1991; Stone and Ladi 2017). They assign identities and order interests; hence, they are the primary link between the government, citizens and different citizen groups (North 1990). Institutional stability determines the effectiveness of public service delivery and the government's quality (Rothstein and Teorell 2012). It is mainly through ordered collective interests and actions, guided by a set of values and rules (or institutions), that groups within the state can effectively engage in public affairs or influence government action (Liang et al. 2007; Meyer and Rowan 1977).

Most notably in public policy, the growth of formal institutions in influencing public affairs shows how different groups organize themselves within the state to influence government action. In this age, this demonstrates modernity in society's development and the state's maturity. Therefore, in the developing political contexts of Africa, the proliferation of institutions such as think tanks shows that political systems are becoming relatively more open, hence creating democratic policymaking processes (Ohemeng 2005). Moreover, even though most African states still wrestle with evidence-based and expert-led policymaking, the surge in think tanks since the 1980s shows an increased interest in scientific approaches to policymaking (Mitullah 2021; Shrum 2001).

The need for evidence-informed government action has seen the numbers of think tanks grow in response to most societies' growing complexities and problems today. It is assumed that to govern societies and address emerging wicked problems, more comprehensive data and reliable research is needed to make informed decisions ('tHart and Vromen 2008). Africa is no exception to this global trend. According to the 2020 Global Go To Think Tank Index Report, there are approximately 679 think tanks in sub-Saharan Africa, with South Africa and Kenya hosting most of these (McGann 2021).

Put differently, the proliferation of non-state institutions or think tanks in Kenya, as elsewhere, shows the modern African state's growing rationalistic pluralist nature (Ohemeng 2005). Thus, despite challenges related to the resilience of autocratic governance norms in Africa, different social groups are developing the capability to organize themselves within the state along with varying policy and political interests. This has also been complemented by the African state's growing capacity to transform society into its own image in the last 20 years (Hyden and Onyango 2021; Onyango 2022).

At the same time, we cannot confidently overstate the role of think tanks in shaping public policy processes in Africa, given the loose and sometimes hostile relationships between the government and civil society groups, including think tanks (Kimenyi and Datta 2011). Because of this, think tanks have learnt to tread carefully in their engagements so as not to provoke the government. This means that think tanks can easily choose silence over voice on policy issues if the political environment does not favour them. Besides, an evidence-based policy process that think tanks seek to promote is not something most African governments are keen on, hence the prevailing gap between the producers and consumers or the demand side of knowledge (Onyango and Hyden 2021; AfDB 2011).

Furthermore, most influential non-governmental think tanks are not home-grown, or are not being funded locally. Instead, they tend to have stronger links with outside development actors, or they seem to primarily promote donor interests over those of the public (Harcourt et al. 2005; Kelstrup 2016). As such, these think tanks advocate for out-of-context policy models and paradigms in African contexts that sometimes bring them into collision with the government. Notably, the proliferation of think tanks in Africa, mainly in Kenya, came with a surge in donor funding and foreign investments, especially after the 1990s following the return of multiparty politics. This implies that the analysis of think tanks in African contexts, as elsewhere, should place them within the broader political contexts: governance environments (Kimenyi and Datta 2011).

It is essential, however, to emphasize that whether formed by the government or individual actors, think tanks across Africa are central actors in public policy processes (Ohemeng 2015). This is the main logic undergirding institutional theory: individual choices are structured primarily by rules, norms and schemes for particular purposes (North 1990; March and Olsen 1989; Douglas 1986). The institutional theory considers individuals' and organizations' attitudes, beliefs and behaviours to be strongly influenced by various interactions and networks (Scott 2001). These can be found in the workings of think tanks in Africa and Kenya.[1]

In this way, institutional theory particularly informs an understanding of the role of think tanks in influencing public policy, mainly policy visibility. In this chapter, we delve into the dimensions of policy visibility and the role of think tanks during the COVID-19 responses by the Ministry of Health in Kenya, using an institutionalist perspective. In doing so we investigate different activities, strategies and processes that think tanks devised or engaged in to increase public awareness of Kenya's COVID-19 policy guidelines and contents. Even though it is not easy to measure the influence of think tanks (Weidenbaum 2010), we generally explore their specific roles during COVID-19 responses to know their position in public policy processes and governance in Kenya. Typically, institutional analysis is essential to this end, considering that globally, the COVID-19 pandemic has tested the role of institutions, including think tanks (McGann 2021; Morales 2021; Garsten 2013).

Following this introduction, this chapter is organized as follows. First, we introduce our working definition of think tanks and how this ties together with the policy visibility approach to policy implementation. Next, we provide a brief background of think tanks in Kenya, then tender a discussion of different case studies. We draw a two-part conclusion: addressing challenges confronted by think tanks during the COVID-19 pandemic, and making recommendations for addressing these challenges. Based on our belief that think tanks are here to stay, African governments should devise effective strategies for their engagement, and a place for think tanks in public policy processes at all levels.

We have selected four outstanding think tanks in Kenya to explore their roles during the COVID-19 pandemic. These are the Kenya Medical Research Institute (KEMRI) and Kenya Institute of Public Policy Research and Analysis (KIPPRA), which are government think tanks; Amref Health Africa; and the Africa Population and Health Research Center (APHRC). Amref and APHRC are non-governmental humanitarian and research organizations, respectively. Our empirical analysis draws on documentary analysis of these think tanks' publications and media outlets, including Twitter and other social media engagements by the selected think tanks.

UNDERSTANDING THINK TANKS AND POLICY VISIBILITY ASPECTS

During the pandemic, think tanks and experts worldwide were instrumental in advising and in generating data. This was also the case in Kenya (see Babu 2020; Mitullah 2021). Specifically, think tanks played essential roles in dealing with:

> 1) the public health crisis; 2) preparing national and international strategies for economic recovery and revitalization; 3) identifying innovative and inclusive public and private intervention strategies to help vulnerable groups; 4) fostering international cooperation by creating rapid, responsive and resilient systems to respond to future crises; and 5) new operating models for think tanks – research, communications and funding (Babu 2020, p. 19)

Nevertheless, the pandemic also exacerbated the 'survival game' arising from underfunding and other challenges (Babu 2020).

These challenges notwithstanding, think tanks promoted policy visibility of government initiatives meant to counter the COVID-19 pandemic. These policy visibility aspects include knowledge sharing/exchange (research, reports, and so on), policy advising, policy communication (dissemination of reports, debates, breaking down technical information, and so on) and partnerships (training, learning and translation) to inform COVID-19 policy responses effectively in Kenya. In this way, think tanks' role is the explanatory variable, and policy visibility is dependent. We assume that think tanks frame actors' imaging of policy problems, knowledge, choices, approaches, interests, and capabilities to engage with other stakeholders or citizens. For example, a think tank's policy domain or objective may inherently limit its scope of operations, and its norms, values, and audiences to prioritize and stakeholders to reach out for. Also important to this aspect is the broader organizational context where think tanks operate and how they influence or become influenced by their environment.

Conceptually, think tanks appear heterogeneous and are used to characterize various group organizations, including those aligned with political profiles and unambiguous advocacy ideologies ('tHart and Vromen 2008; Stone and Ladi 2017; Ohemeng 2005; Weidenbaum 2010). Consequently, there has been a proliferation of self-declared think tanks and independent policy institutes with specific economic, health and environmental care agendas. This chapter's institutional theorizing of think tanks allows us to consider three ways of viewing them, regarding policy visibility components. First, think tanks are historically, normatively, legally and socio-politically positioned institutions that promote particular policy agendas touching their sectors, interests and purposes. Second, we consider think tanks as collectivities of individual interests and values with specific expertise organized to assert influence over the government, politicians, other groups and general society's conduct. Third, they also include constituent policies. Thus, the government creates a policy advisory body to enhance an expert and evidence-driven public policy process in public institutions through a constitutional Act. In this manner, think tanks range from research organizations and non-governmental organizations, especially donor-affiliated, to quasi-autonomous units and semi-governmental agencies within the government (Stone 2007). In addition, there are think tanks affiliated with political parties, universities and for-profit corporate entities (McGann 2019).

Therefore, think tanks are associations of professionals, either in government or outside it, that conduct research and activism in various fields (Sartor 2019). Social and economic policy, politics and government, the environment, health, agriculture, science and technology, are typical examples. 'Policy visibility' is an umbrella term describing 'activities, strategies, and processes that enhance the exposure or prominence of public policy design and contents to the general populace and concerned parties' (Onyango 2019, p. 1). It underscores knowledge exchange processes between actors and target groups, sound policy communication and ownership by institutions concerned, and policy legitimation strategies. In addition, 'policy-visibility prescribes strategies that integrate behavioural, environmental, and structural organisational and political dimensions of policy. This may, in turn, influence policy contents' communication and transfer and translation processes' (Onyango 2019, p. 3).

From a policy visibility standpoint, institutions are central and think tanks should establish synergies to enhance coordination between and among different actors regarding policy content such as COVID-19 guidelines and behaviours. Policy communication is a critical component of policy visibility. It includes dissemination and interpretations of less technical policy guidelines, identification of deficiencies, dynamics and pitfalls in policy transfer (institutionalization, coordination, and so on), and translation (internalization and learning) by policymakers (Onyango 2019, p. 2). Institutions such as think tanks must partner and network to enhance policy visibility with the government's policy-hosting institution and other stakeholders. Improving policy visibility involves 'breaking institutional *silos* that characterize most policy errors, accidents, and anomalies, which could also specifically emanate from uninformed cognitive responses due to the lack of adequate exposures or promotion of policy contents and objectives' (ibid., p. 3).

In light of policy visibility, the role of institutions such as think tanks in shaping social actors' behaviours concerning COVID-19 are broadly looked into. This provides a perspective that can be instrumental in assessing and shaping policymakers and citizens' attitudes and positions regarding a particular policy problem. Within a broader interorganizational context, institutional theory explains the reasons and processes for organizational behaviour and the effect that organizational behaviour produces. For think tanks, the institutionalist argument means that they compete for 'social and economic fitness' because their success and survival depend not only on technical efficiency, but also on their ideas, perceived social appropriateness, practices, services and service practices. This way, legitimacy becomes a critical resource that think tanks must extract from their institutional environment (Powell and DiMaggio 1991).

In improving policy visibility, it is ideal for think tanks to engage with the 'emerging public': young professional students who may soon use policy implementation structures. In reality, think tanks should explore avenues to engage specialized groups such as events, conferences and interactive workshops to engage with the emerging public. This engagement with the public can benefit think tanks in informing the public, keeping policy discussions rolling, ensuring accountability even when governments change, and wisely contributing to a culture of research-based evidence in policymaking. For example, in Kenya, KIPPRA and KEMRI are primarily involved in engaging young academia, professionals and students in a series of policy discussions.

Also, policymakers, including think tanks, should ensure that essential policy contents are well abstracted for stakeholders and the public. Think tanks may use media framing as a policy visibility strategy to tackle issues linked with complex policy structures. For example, they should aspire to enhance the visibility of technical components of COVID-19 policies to stakeholders and targeted groups. This can be done by using simple yet effective strategies that comprise radio talks, TV series, posters and debates, instead of delving into bureaucratic processes such as executive seminars and conferences, executive training and resource mobilizations (Onyango 2019). Similarly, evidence-based policy training must be adequate to deter uncertainties, conspiracies and deficits in understanding COVID-19 policies, occasioned by a lack of communication.

Think tanks can improve the capacity of public administrators to complement their roles in disseminating policy and research outcomes on COVID-19, including using social media platforms to enhance policy visibility. Even though think tanks may formulate structural policy programmes, policy visibility may encounter setbacks, especially when proper identification and trade-offs between government stakeholders, political leaders, media and the targeted audience need to be properly informed. Therefore, think tanks should be instrumental in complementing traditional processes such as civic education, seminars in influencing public decisions, and adopting citizen-oriented and bottom-up policy advocacy campaigns.

To influence policy visibility, frame-building activities and frame settings are approaches that think tanks need to explore with media organizations to improve public understanding of complex policy settings. In addition, think tanks' promotional and advocacy streams should span digital advertisements, and contemporary communication channels such as Twitter and Facebook series, films and documentaries, and forming channels of e-mail communications to communities of practice.

THINK TANKS IN KENYA: A BACKGROUND

The phenomenon of think tanks is common in Kenya. It goes back to the colonial state and became more prominent during decolonization. In that era, various groups and experts advised and mobilized professional groups to influence government action (Leys 1975). However, like most African backgrounds, Kenya is still dealing with colonial legacies, problems of development, and democratization challenges. Thus, it is marked by a combination of nascent democracies and authoritarian remnants, and think tanks remain a largely undefined political object associated with actors in development cooperation. Also, the diversity of think tanks operations in Kenya varies according to the environment in which they operate and the issues they promote.

While some emerged from non-governmental actors, others operate in traditional environments of civil participation; some have evolved from university research centres such as the Institute of Development Studies at the University of Nairobi, and others have grown out of social movements. Also, while some, such as KIPPRA, have ties with the government, others, such as the Center for Multi-Party Democracy (CMD-Kenya), are aligned with political parties. Some fit the quasi-independent or autonomous units category within governments or business corporations. Table 6.1 summarizes think tank affiliations in Kenya grouped according to the Global Go To Think Tank Index Report's categorization (McGann 2019).

Table 6.1   Typology of think tanks affiliation in Kenya

Category	Definition	Examples
Quasi-independent think tanks	Controlled by an interest group, donors and contracting agencies who say how the institutions are run. They are completely autonomous from the government.	Institute of Economic Affairs (IEA)
Autonomous and independent think tanks	Mainly independent of one interest group, including donors. They are entirely autonomous in terms of operations and funding from the government.	African Institute for Development Policy (AFIDEP), Africa Policy Institute (API), Institute of Policy Analysis and Research (IPAR), Africa Economic Research Consortium, Partnership for African Social and Governance Research (PASGR)
University-affiliated	Policy research-oriented institutions controlled at the university level. Clearly attached as a functionary wing or department in the university.	Institute of Development Studies (IDS), University of Nairobi
Quasi-governmental think tanks	Semi-autonomous institutions. Government grants and contracts exhaustively fund them. However, they do not form a formal structure within the government.	Kenya Institute for Public Policy Research and Analysis (KIPPRA) Kenya Medical Research Institute (KEMRI)
Political party-affiliated	Wings affiliated with political parties.	Institute of Economic Affairs – Kenya Centre for Multiparty Democracy
Corporate (for-profit) think tanks.	Business organizations oriented for profit in public policy research consulting.	The Inter Region Economic Network (IREN).

Think tanks' formation and divergence in the legal constitution place their role in Kenya in a cross-sectional matrix of politics, academia and public policy influence. Similarly, think tanks' roles also extend to providing ancillary services that help them to propel their policy work into decision-making through research, funding, and training members of political parties. Therefore, as often noted in the nature of think tanks, there is critical confusion generated by the diverse activities and functions of these institutions in Kenya, presenting a dilemma in defining their specific roles. Over the past two decades, this has compounded their hybridity forms and dramatic proliferation (Stone and Ladi 2017).

Kenya has witnessed a remarkable growth of think tanks since the 1990s following the democratization wave. They currently stand at over 53 think tanks of various categories (see Table 6.1). The history of think tanks in Kenya goes back to the colonial period, especially in agriculture, health and livestock, demonstrating development patterns over the years (Leys 1975; Kimenyi and Datta 2011). We argue that Kenya's settler economy, and later sticking with capitalism over socialism immediately after independence, could also have created an environment that naturally enhanced the emergence of think tanks. To borrow Kimenyi and Datta's (2011, p. 7) description of the same situation across African countries, in 'the early years of independence, former colonial research institutions [in Kenya] were reconfigured to promote growth and development at "home". [The Kenyatta government] invested considerable sums of money in expanding state infrastructure, including research and development'.

These institutions included the Nairobi Chamber of Commerce (Kenya National Chamber of Commerce and Industry since 1965), the Agricultural Finance Corporation (AFC), the Agricultural Development Corporation (ADC), the Kenya Association of Manufacturers, the Institute for Development Studies (IDS), the University of Nairobi, and religious missions, among others. These institutions acted as think tanks on particular policy areas during the colonial state period and the early years of independence. For example, Colin Leys noted, concerning the transfer of land to large-scale African farmers in the 1960s, that the 'government's policy had been formulated by a special working party of officials and outside experts which seems to have foreseen the likelihood of a clash with the farmers, without appreciating its seriousness' (Leys 1975, p. 109).

Following the reintroduction of multiparty politics in the 1990s, and the fall of the Kenya African National Union (KANU) government in 2002, there has been a proliferation of think tanks in Kenya. These have come in different typologies covering governmental think tanks such as KIPPRA, formed in the mid-1990s, and university-affiliated, professional associations-affiliated, political party-affiliated, and non-governmental institutions. In Kenya, the essential functions of these think tanks have been around public policy issues and political reforms exploring the broad spectrum of ideas, concepts and theories that underpin democratic governance.

Considering this, both external and homegrown think tanks have increased in Kenya. Some think tanks in the former category extend donor governments' engagements with local actors. These donor government affiliated think tanks in Kenya include Germany's Konrad Adenauer Stiftung (KAS) and the United States Ford Foundation. Here, we also find think tanks that function as country/ regional branches of independent international think tanks and political parties such as the Population Council and Institute of Economic Affairs. Under the category of homegrown think tanks are those created by individual experts and professional groups, political parties and those created by the government and local universities. Given the financial strain that public universities in Kenya have undergone, especially since the 2000s, university-affiliated think tanks have been generally for profit generation (Muchunguh 3 May 2021).[2] Those created by political parties, mainly the Centre for Multiparty Democracy (CMD-Kenya), aim to build the capacities of political parties in Kenya.

In contrast, government think tanks such as KEMRI and KIPPRA are primarily involved in generating scientific information and data-driven public policy. Those created by individual experts or groups and universities focus on policy advice, advocacy, research and training, such as the African Population and Health Research Centre (APHRC) and African Institute for Development Policy (AFIDEP). Some are mainly created by professional groups, such as the Kenya National Chamber of Commerce and Industry; these offer consultancy and advocate for members' interests in government policy.

Therefore, the proliferation of think tanks demonstrates Kenya's development and governance processes. However, there is a deep imprint of donor dependence in the most prominent policy-focused think tanks. Indeed, besides being funded by the government, government-affiliated or university-affiliated think tanks are heavily dependent on donor funding. The same can be said for the individually created think tanks, and those operating as branches of international think tanks. Consequently, their policy agenda must align with donors' policy priorities. This has partly led to a hostile relationship between some think tanks and the government, especially if the government's agenda does not align with donor priorities, leading to stringent regulations on think tanks regarding their funding sources.

In general, despite the well-researched developments in examining think tanks' role in developed countries, there has been little attention to the role of think tanks and public policy in Kenya. In a critical review of think tanks in Kenya, it is not new to conclude that they have shaped policy space, political discourse, economic policy direction, policy communication and visibility. However, the leeway remains to effectively influence policy direction on the political system's political interests and structures. However, the state and the government in Kenya are rapidly transforming, especially following the implementation of the 2010 Constitution (Onyango and Hyden 2021). The 2010 Constitution introduced devolved government structures, further expanding governance spaces and the demand for expert-oriented and data-driven public policy processes by the government (Mitullah 2021). Therefore, the role of think tanks is increasingly crucial in enhancing policy visibility under these changing environments in Kenya. Unfortunately, workers, representatives and these modern organizations are not yet equipped to handle their responsibilities.

SALIENT CHALLENGES CONFRONTED BY THINK TANKS IN KENYA

Critical challenges remain. Civil society components, for example, have reportedly been withdrawn from a couple of devolution-strengthening programmes in Kenya, at the government's request. However, think tanks must contend with political realities in their respective regions. They need the internal capacity to traverse dynamic terrain and generate information. This situation may encourage more internationally connected think tanks with access to resources and power to bargain with the government and influence public policy, compared to local think tanks in Kenya. Also, the core funding is being phased out, especially following the advent of the COVID-19 pandemic. Indeed, generally, foreign funders have been under pressure to reduce their funding for civil society; this is particularly true for those attempting to influence policy (McGann and Weaver 2017), and think tanks in Kenya are no exception. Just a few funders can provide core support, which think tanks can use for long-term programmatic and strategic goals, and even fewer are willing to fund projects with overheads built in.

In addition, the national government loosely collaborates with independent organizations and think tanks; and it underutilizes think tanks' strategic resources. This is primarily a factor of a need for more understanding of the essence of think tanks, and the deep-seated history of distrust by the government (Kimenyi and Datta 2011). Even though their expertise is widely regarded, political and security institutions in many countries often view think tanks as agents of unknown forces. Behind this mistrust there are intertwined concerns about independence and support. As mentioned in regard to elsewhere in Africa, donor pressure to show effect has made it challenging for think tanks working in a hazy policy space in recent years (Mbadlanyana et al. 2011).

Various players, including private sector risk advisory companies, consulting firms and one-person think tanks, have increased the competition. Thus, most Kenyan think tanks have a long way to go in terms of shaping decision-making. Others, especially politicians, have further challenged non-partisan think tanks' independence, particularly regarding their funding sources. It is a common misconception that a donor's support determines the think tank's agenda. Although this may be true for some single-donor organizations, well-established think tanks with a diverse donor base are less susceptible: they have succeeded in collaborating with government institutions to shape their policies, mainly by providing technical advice and funding.

No matter what their nature, think tanks have a lot to offer governments, private and non-profit industries, and international partners working in Africa, thanks to their ability to conduct independent studies, form strong peer networks, and recruit highly trained and skilled people from diverse professional backgrounds (Mbadlanyana et al. 2011). Most of their research is open to the public, but most of their work is private. Though secrecy is a sign of a long-term trusting relationship with a client, independent think tanks should still prioritize the public good over the interests of a select few.

This overview has shown that think tanks work in diverse settings in Kenya and the rest of the developing world. Some work in communities where political engagement is a tradition; in others, non-governmental actors have minimal influence; in yet other contexts, they advise and promote government policies. Against this backdrop, this chapter examines the role that selected think tanks in Kenya have played in enhancing components of policy visibility in the context of COVID-19 responses, by discussing how they enhanced the policy visibility of COVID-19 guidelines. This case analysis can present insights for understanding think tanks' general contributions to Kenya's policy governance.

DISCUSSION

This discussion is based on the following questions:

1. How have Kenyan think tanks enhanced policy communications regarding COVID-19 guidelines?
2. How have think tanks shared knowledge, and how has this impacted upon enforcement and behaviour regarding COVID-19 regulatory policies?
3. How do think tanks in Kenya engage in partnerships, and how has this impacted upon the effectiveness of regulatory policies targeting the COVID-19 pandemic?

Case 1: Kenya Institute of Public Policy Research and Analysis (KIPPRA)

According to the Global Go To Think Tank Index Report 2020, the Kenya Institute for Public Policy Research and Analysis (KIPPRA) is the second-best think tank in sub-Saharan Africa. KIPPRA is involved in capacity development, retooling skills for technocrats and integrating young professional programmes (YPP) in the policy process, government operations, mentoring, research methodology, and macro-economic modelling. In addition, the KIPPRA Act 2016 anchors its role in the space of public policy research to 'develop capacities in public policy research and analysis and assist the government in the process of policy formulation and implementation'. KIPPRA has created a public policy knowledge management repository portal where all policy briefs, publications, abstracts, chapters, articles, county economic reports and journals are shared.

This platform has made KIPPRA feature prominently as the second-best public policy think tank for quality policy research and analysis in Africa. Its documents are more visible online than others, and reach a wider readership via free online access. To enhance dissemination and communication of COVID-19 policy, KIPPRA has been instrumental in supporting research, policy briefs, economic modelling and capacity building, and strengthening counties on mitigating the economic effects of COVID-19. The government and county governments have depended on KIPPRA policy products for economic recovery modelling for the counties. KIPPRA has consistently produced policy monitors to ensure continuous knowledge sharing, from March 2020 to June 2021. Additionally, KIPPRA is actively hosting webinars related to COVID-19, and has participated in and organized six virtual webinars to discuss COVID-19 economic policy towards recovery. In knowledge sharing, KIPPRA hosted a webinar symposium for think tanks to discuss their role in COVID-19 and how they could continue to be instrumental in formulating policies supporting recovery from COVID-19.

The think tank recognizes its mandate in developing wider capacities for policy implementation, evaluation, timely policy research and analysis, policy engagement and communication on public policy, and developing and maintaining a reservoir of knowledge on public policy, in contributing to national development goals. KIPPRA had shown consistency in policy communication even before the pandemic started, and outlined a clear category of knowledge products for public consumption, some of which do not directly reflect COVID-19. Even though it has not been at the forefront of dealing with COVID-19 policy communications, it has been instrumental in producing and sharing knowledge products.

For instance, KIPPRA has produced 250 discussion papers, 12 article journals, 12 Kenya economic reports, 21 policy monitors and newsletters, and 151 policy briefs in its public policy repository.[3] KIPPRA has also consistently produced quarterly policy monitor editions focusing on implications of socio-economic and measures taken to deal with the COVID-19 pandemic in Kenya. The secondary review shows that KIPPRA remains one of Kenya's most robust think tanks in terms of policy dissemination and communication. In the social media space, specific policy communication and advocacy of COVID-19 were limited. For example, on Twitter and Facebook, KIPPRA has 6811 and 574 followers, respectively, and had only made 46 Twitter communications on COVID-19 guidelines between March 2020 and June 2021. The think tank's influence in social media is limited when compared to Amref Health Africa, KEMRI and APHRC on issues regarding COVID-19 guidelines.

KIPPRA has partnered with fellow think tanks to enhance the capacity of policy production, knowledge management, and adaptive policy research and capacity development in COVID-19. For example, it partnered with the HORN Institute, KATIBA Institute, KEMRI and APHRC to organize webinars on economic recovery. KIPPRA has also partnered with county governments to enhance their recovery efforts towards the effects of the pandemic by conducting workshops, dissemination of county budget briefs, and training on the COVID-19 Economic Re-Engineering and Recovery Strategy. Similarly, it has partnered with the United Nations Development Programme (UNDP), UN Women-Kenya, World Bank Kenya, and the German development agency Deutsche Gesellschaft für Internationale Zusammenarbeit GmbH (GIZ) to create a socio-economic recovery strategy. The analysis shows that KIPPRA's partnership choice was based on enhancing policy visibility, capacity building, and strengthening COVID-19 research and funding towards developing socio-economic recovery models for counties and the national government.

Case 2: The African Population and Health Research Center (APHRC)

APHRC is a think tank and research institution mandated to generate policy-driven evidence specifically to improve the well-being and health of the African population. It has created a legacy impact in research capacity strengthening, policy communication and engagements. This has been evident through its scientific analysis, data-driven health analytics and socio-economic evidence during COVID-19.

APHRC has strategically increased linkages and partnerships with universities, the private sector and research institutions to build upcoming research think tanks, training and fellowships, and increase capacity to mitigate the effects of COVID-19 within communities. For example, in 2020, 22 partner institutions were enrolled to work with APHRC in different categories. For instance, APHRC joined partnerships with Amref, the African Institute for Development Policy (AFIDEP), the African Women's Development and Communications Network (FEMNET) and the Hewlett Foundation to discuss mitigation measures for COVID-19. APHRC also engages with civil society, technical partners, the Ministry of Health (MoH), policy actors and communities to reach people across the continent with COVID-19, including disseminating innovative communication products on COVID-19.

Specifically, APHRC and the University of Witwatersrand in South Africa have collaborated with the Consortium for Advanced Research Training in Africa (CARTA) to nurture research and policy leaders, scholars and world-class researchers in undertaking doctoral training. As such, APHRC has sustained and grown its think tank portfolio by churning policy-oriented and research personnel actively involved in evidence-based research and policy implementation during COVID-19. With partnerships, think tanks have also experienced increased grants and funding success rates from external partners, largely in syncronization with increased COVID-19 activities. In the Annual Performance Review Report of the 2017–2021 APHRC strategic plan, it was acknowledged that grants and funding were at the peak during COVID-19. The 2021 report revealed that financial mobilization increased by 55 per cent compared to the previous three years covered in the strategic planning (APHRC 2021).

With COVID-19-related institutional pressures, APHRC was forced to adopt alternative means of conducting business. Traditional and physical presence conferences were abandoned. Virtual programs such as Zoom, Blue Jeans and Google Meet were used to disseminate research and policy outcomes, data collection and virtual mentorship programmes. COVID-19 also unsettled the way think tanks operate. For instance, APHRC adopted check-in centres where human resources organized monthly wellness programs, mental wellness, physical, emotional and counselling sessions for staff working remotely. Despite COVID-19 disruption, APHRC has intensified its presence in social media and online spaces, especially on Facebook and social media, to communicate policy and reach a wider audience. For example, APHRC has 10 700 Twitter and 16 881 Facebook media followers, with consistent messaging, including COVID-19-related policy outputs, webinars, conferences and article posts. Since March 2020, when COVID-19 was first reported in Kenya, APHRC has consistently appeared on Twitter, with 55 communicated policy briefs, webinar series, messaging on vaccine programming and trials, and COVID-19 data reaching a wider audience.

APHRC is a think tank specializing in health policy outcomes and has been instrumental in enhancing policy communication and programmes informed by evidence since the pronouncement of COVID-19. APHRC developed guidelines on training and disseminating COVID-19-related information across knowledge management centres, research and data collection, and policy engagement strategies with the public to strengthen policy visibility. Its knowledge management portfolio has included continuous learning and sharing best practice lessons to achieve impact, and systematic tracking and analysis of knowledge management products produced during COVID-19 were conducted.

Through joint advance seminars (JAS), capacity building in research, conferences, publications and webinar series, APHRC has been instrumental in disseminating and producing evidence-based COVID-19 mitigation measures and policy briefs. This has largely contributed to the behaviour change. Through CARTA programmes and fellowships, 172 fellows were enrolled on the PhD and post-doctoral programmes in 2020 to continue conducting quality research and policy dissemination. For instance, APHRC led the development

Table 6.2   General research outputs in 2020 by units in APHRC

	HSH	MCW	PDRH	UWB	DME	WARO	EYE	AAD	RCS	PEC	TOTAL
Published papers	32	28	24	15	8	3	1	1	4	2	118
Policy briefs	0	1	0	3	?	3	3	1	0	0	13
Technical reports	0	2	0	0	0	2	1	0	0	0	5
Book chapters	1	1	0	3	0	0	0	0	0	0	5
Fact Sheet	0	2	1	0	0	0	0	0	0	0	3
Supplements	2	0	0	0	1	0	0	0	0	0	3
Books	0	0	0	1	0	0	0	0	0	0	1
Total	35	34	25	22	11	8	5	2	4	2	148

Source: APHRC Annual Report (2020).

and knowledge synthesis instrumental to the national steering committee on COVID-19 to prepare protocols for school reopening. To enhance policy visibility, CARTA fellows have published 193 papers, ten blogs and two policy briefs to improve portfolio mitigation measures against COVID-19.

In streamlining knowledge exchange and mentorship programmes, APHRC engaged in virtual internship programmes to support COVID-19 policy communication and engagement. There was a sharp increase in research reports in 2020, with 148 scientific reports, compared to 122 in 2019 and 89 in 2018. The year 2020 saw an upsurge of projects running and new projects totalling 123, up from 88 in the previous years. Recent research projects also increased from 31 in 2019 to 57 in 2020. Table 6.2 shows increased outputs of factsheets, publications, articles, technical reports, book chapters and policy briefs during COVID-19.

Case 3: Amref Health Africa

Amref Health Africa created one of the most robust policy communication and visibility strategies towards disseminating COVID-19 information through its COVID19Africa Information Centre, created to inform the public about the prevention of COVID-19 consistently and strengthen the capacity of frontline line health workers. Amref Health Africa integrated an approach whereby all COVID-19-related information and communication, including videos, policy briefs, COVID-19 statistics, Facebook, Twitter and webinars, were accessed to enhance policy communication. To reach a wider audience with COVID-19 guidelines, Amref Health Africa developed information-friendly communication packages comprising simplified animated infographics for health workers and the public, to improve uptake. The developed briefs and infographic packages addressed the information on symptoms of COVID-19, simple ways to reduce the spread, and how COVID-19 spreads. Amref Health Africa also initiated video messaging demonstrating how to prevent and respond to COVID-19 emergencies, shocks, mitigation and overall prevention.

To target the youthful population in COVID-19 policy messaging, Amref Health Africa partnered with Youth in Action (Y-ACT) and Kenya Young Parliamentarians Association (KYPA) to launch innovative online live platforms. These included '2bonge live', to enable young people to interact and engage in real-time issues affecting them during COVID-19. Think tanks must therefore be innovative and tactful to engage different populations and create impact meaningfully. Through creative and innovative policy visibility and communication strategies, Amref Health Africa has reached 10 million young people with its communication on COVID-19 guidelines, including dominating social media on the COVID-19 challenge, mainly exhibiting 'new norm' photos on preventing COVID-19.[4] In addition, 19 videos were documented to demonstrate COVID-19 guidelines for a different audience. COVID-19 presents a new impetus for think tanks to deliberate on how best to create policy communication for different audiences, including thinking around reach, simplicity and impact.

Amref Health Africa created a unique blend of knowledge sharing and exchange platforms where basic information on COVID-19 could be accessed. One of the vibrant knowledge management and sharing platforms was https:// amref .org/ coronavirus/ social -media -toolkit/ . This portal was specifically created to enhance tacit and explicit knowledge regarding the COVID-19 guidelines. It also provides links to other important platforms, including social media, videos and factsheets containing COVID-19 statistics and packages. Virtual conferences and webinars have also become lucrative knowledge exchange platforms during the pandemic, and it organized 23 Zoom and webinar conferences on COVID-19, including four blogs.

This platform has been used to discuss emerging trends, policy outcomes and findings on the pandemic. Amref Health Africa created different channels through which COVID-19 guidelines and behaviour change could be channelled and discussed in social media streams. For example, a Twitter chat series discussion was created with partners to inform girls on how to curb early pregnancies during the pandemic, and channels #FactsnotFear, #AskDaktari and #AmrefCOVID19Response were designed to enable citizens to engage with experts on issues to do with COVID-19.

This was widely instrumental in managing misinformation on COVID-19, mythical views and truths on vaccine hesitancy, and general information on COVID-19. Amref Health Africa is widely followed on Twitter and Facebook.

It has managed to pass on and stream information concerning policy directions, newly published blogs, articles and news. Amref Health Africa has 86 365 Facebook followers from social media analytics, which translates into its wide reach on policy communication, knowledge sharing and exchange. On Twitter, 29 000 followers have also enhanced Amref Health Africa's capacity to disseminate information regarding COVID-19. The think tank dominates social media with constant messaging and communication on COVID-19 issues, and provides international statistics on COVID-19 trends.

Amref Health Africa considered local, regional and international partnerships based on enhancing capacity building and training of health workers, knowledge sharing, information and exchange, access to communities and chances of access to funds for creating better interventions for curbing the spread of COVID-19 among communities. Gitahi and Bailey (2021), in a Amref Health Africa news release published on 15 June 2021, noted that:

> By combining resources and strengths to support vulnerable communities, think tanks can work together to address challenges and aid timely access to essential health services. That partnerships are fundamental to creating a lasting health response in Africa and as such, partnerships with academic institutions, think tanks and community-based organisations can provide the evidence to inform policy, services and programmes to strengthen and better respond to reality needs of the most vulnerable during pandemic.

On several COVID-19-related strategies, Amref Health International considered cross-border and cross-sectoral collaborations with organizations such as the European Union, Global Fund Aid, Coca-Cola Beverages (CCBA), and the United Nations Children's Fund (UNICEF) to raise funds and capital support interventions for COVID-19, social protection and sexual and gender-based violence. Partnerships with the Ministry of Health, Kenya, county governments, and the National Council of Persons with Disability, have strategically supported capacity building among health workers in counties, including capacity strengthening of people with disabilities.

During the COVID-19 pandemic, think tanks have formulated strategic partnership criteria to solve specific issues, especially in technology, to enhance their capacity to strengthen communication functions. Specifically, Amref Health Africa formed linkages with innovative technology health companies to improve service delivery in the COVID-19 response, to increase the capacity of frontline health workers. For example, Leap platforms, M-Jali and Jibu Learning are COVID-19 learning and messaging platforms provided by partners, and over 8 000 health workers have enrolled on a mobile application for COVID-19 training (Bailey and Gitahi 2015).

Case 4: Kenya Medical Research Institute (KEMRI)

Kenya Medical Research Institute (KEMRI) is a state corporation think tank that has existed since 1979 to carry out health-related research, to improve human health and provide quality health research, service delivery and capacity building. The think tank has sustained a critical mass of technical personnel and scientists to mount a competitive health research infrastructure. Scimago and Elsevier recognized KEMRI as the top research institution in Africa regarding research output by world-ranking companies.[5] The think tank is also mandated to translate and disseminate research findings for evidence-based policy formulation and implementation.

Like other think tanks operating in COVID-19, the institutions have adjusted their operations to conform to the new challenges and disruptions brought about by the pandemic. KEMRI researchers have been heavily involved in COVID-19 testing, advisory and communication roles, and statistical analysis, since the coronavirus's first detection in Kenya. KEMRI was instrumental in conducting the nationwide test and analysing data to inform the announcement of daily briefings by the Ministry of Health. Similarly, it conducted rapid research on COVID-19 vaccine development in partnership with the University of Oxford, United Kingdom (UK). As the government's strategic think tank wing, KEMRI's top researchers and virologists participated in a daily media briefing on COVID-19 statistics, protocols, and understanding of different vaccines. KEMRI resorted to other communication channels to complement policy communication, including radio talk shows, television series, live debates, conferences, press releases and social media engagement. A COVID-19 policy communication regarding the discovery of genome sequencing was released through a press release dated 3 June 2020: 'PRESS RELEASE: Kenya Scientists Release Genome Sequencing for the COVID-19 Cases in Kenya Scientists in Kenya have successfully sequenced genomes of SARS-CoV-2, the virus responsible for the global COVID-19 pandemic, obtaining important information about the genetic composition of viral strains in 122 of the confirmed cases in Kenya.'

Even though KEMRI was not visible in communicating COVID-19 protocols, projections, statistics and policy recommendations on Twitter and Facebook, think tanks resorted to mainstream media (Radio and TV) due to the immediate attention this gave to their information. For example, KEMRI appeared on the news 4570 times, compared to 389 hits for APHRC, 382 for KIPPRA, and 4060 for Amref Health Africa. The use of mainstream media and live debates by KEMRI was immediately felt as the country was kept informed on COVID-19-related protocols, vaccine development and COVID-19 statistics. Even though KEMRI enjoys a considerable number of followers on Facebook at 19 783, and 32 000 followers on Twitter, only 49 specific COVID-19 policy guideline messages can be traced from the platform between March 2020 and June 2021.

KEMRI has set up a repository portal of resources, publications, journals and articles to enhance knowledge management and sharing. However, no specific update on COVID-19-related material was extracted, mainly because it has not been updated. KEMRI continuously conducts sensitization and training for the county government's staff and laboratory technicians to strengthen their capacities and preparedness. Additionally, KEMRI uses knowledge management symposiums, conferences, webinars and Zoom to discuss emerging trends on COVID-19 and vaccine trials. KEMRI organized and participated in six webinar conferences on COVID-19 between March 2020 and June 2021. On capacity-building partnerships, KEMRI and Jomo Kenyatta University of Agriculture and Technology (JKUAT) are collaborating on continuous capacity-building exchange programmes to transfer knowledge to students on different domains, including vaccine development.

KEMRI's consideration of partnership trends indicates the desire to partner with like-minded research institutions, especially in vaccine research and development. On COVID-19, KEMRI has partnered with the Japan International Development Agency (JICA), the German Development Bank (KFW), Agha Khan Hospital, and the Ministry of Health Kenya. Additionally, KEMRI has a strategic partnership with UK-based institutions such as the Wellcome Trust and Oxford University in the development of a vaccine. Apart from research and policy dissemination, KEMRI is actively involved in producing COVID-19 products, virus transport, whole genome sequencing, drug development, rapid test kits and alcohol-based hand sanitizers.

Comparison of Think Tanks

Think tanks are actively engaged in policy visibility programmes in Kenya and have increased their socio-media communication presence to drive policy visibility on COVID-19 guidelines. Our analysis reveals that Amref Health Africa has a strong presence among Facebook and Twitter users, with 86 365 and 29 000, respectively, compared to the rest of the think tanks (see Table 6.3 and Figure 6.1). For the analysis period, Amref Health Africa has shown strong visibility and has communicated 11 000 tweets, and 225 targeted COVID-19 policy guidelines. On the other hand, KEMRI, which has the greatest link to the public, with 32 000 and 19 783 followers on Twitter and Facebook, respectively, has communicated 49 COVID-19 guidelines. APHRC has also shown considerable strength on Facebook with 16 881 followers and Twitter with 10 700. It has made 11 200 Twitter communications and communicated 55 specific COVID-19 policy guidelines. Desk review and analysis show that

Table 6.3   *Comparison of data on policy visibility and communication from think tanks from March 2020 to June 2021*

Think tank visibility, knowledge management, communication and partnership	APHRC	KEMRI	KIPPRA	Amref
Twitter followers	10 700	32 000	6810	29 000
Twitter following	1109	673	398	4825
Twitter COVID-19 guidelines – visibility	83 tweets	37 tweets	51 tweets	387 tweets
Overall tweets made	11 200 tweets	2919 tweets	2714 tweets	11 000 tweets
Facebook followers	16 881	19 783	574	86 365
Facebook likes	16 576 likes	18 618 likes	537 likes	82 296 likes
Facebook COVID-19 guidelines – visibility	55 posts	49 posts	46 posts	225 posts
COVID-19 news appearance	389	4570	382	4060
Video results on COVID-19	581 videos	10 300 videos	9480 videos	10 800 videos
Policy events/ seminars, conferences, webinars	14	7	6	24
COVID-19 policy briefs/monitors	-	7	9	-
COVID-19 publications and articles	10 publications	(Not updated)	8 publications	8 publications
COVID-19 capacity building	Yes	Yes	Yes	Yes
Blogs on COVID-19	16 blogs	-	2	4
Newsletters	2	1	-	-
COVID-19 partners	13	17	8	18

Amref Health Africa dominates with 10 800 COVID-19-related news videos, followed by KEMRI with 10 300, KIPPRA with 9480, and APHRC with 389.

Think tank knowledge management strategies (Figure 6.2) have significantly impacted upon the behaviour of communities and individuals regarding COVID-19. During the pandemic, think tanks have heightened their capacity building and strength, training, conferences, webinar/zoom series, blogs, publications and policy briefs for COVID-19. From desk review analysis, webinars and Zoom dominate COVID-19 knowledge sharing at Amref Health Africa, holding 24 webinars; followed by APHRC with 14 webinars. KEMRI and

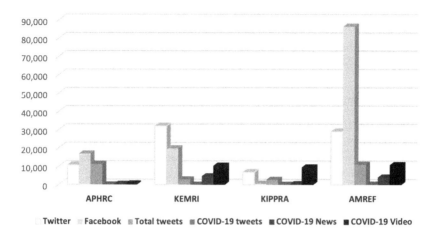

Figure 6.1   Socio-media communication and visibility of COVID-19 guidelines

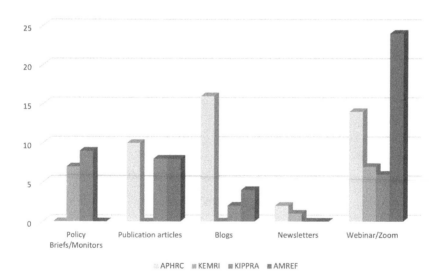

Figure 6.2   Knowledge management and sharing of COVID-19 guidelines

KIPPRA conducted seven and six webinars, respectively. At the same time, KIPPRA and Amref Health Africa have organized COVID-19 knowledge management information and platforms for policy sharing and dissemination. From the analysis, KEMRI produced 7 policy briefs while KIPPRA managed to produce 9 COVID-19 related policy briefs. During the period, there were no available data for APHRC and Amref respectively.

Regarding COVID-19 publications and articles, APHRC has produced ten, while KIPPRA and Amref Health Africa has produced eight. Blogging on COVID-19 regulations has featured 16 blogs from APHRC, four from Amref, and two from KIPPRA. COVID-19-related newsletters received little attention, with two newsletters being produced and disseminated by APHRC, while KEMRI has one.

CONCLUSION: NOTABLE CHALLENGES FACING THINK TANKS IN KENYA

Sustainability and financing are two of Kenyan think tanks' most pressing issues. Unfortunately, funding is often unequally allocated in the think tank sphere, inadequate, intermittent and unpredictable, compounded by the reality that African think tanks rely excessively on foreign support (Mbadlanyana et al. 2011). In addition, the struggle amongst nations, think tanks and government officials for foreign financial capital, and the private sector's minimal participation, contribute to the scarcity.

African think tanks are confronted with several obstacles to their autonomy. The prospect of political opposition or cooperation by government entities is the first threat to think tank independence. This danger is especially extreme in non-competitive systems and emerging democracies. Public authorities or the opposition often give think tank leaders positions or contracts if they were not previously active associates or executives of political parties. Additionally, some members of the public believe that think tanks operate for the government or the opposition, and distrust them. When think tanks lack consistent independence and enforcement strategy, they risk being agents to advance the special interests of specific donors seeking to promote their policy agenda.

The efficiency of some African think tanks' outputs falls short of internationally accepted expectations, jeopardizing their long-term viability. Some think tanks need to produce work that meets international quality requirements (Mbadlanyana et al. 2011). This is usually due to a scarcity of well-trained academics, communication and growth experts, and think tank administrators and leaders, in terms of quantity and consistency. After training, staff members often quit after some years to take better-paying jobs in the private sector, foundations and foreign organizations. African think tanks face a challenge in ensuring meaningful effects through strong policymakers and public participation (McGann et al. 2014; McGann 2016). Restricted media visibility, low engagement with and connections to politicians, limited capacity to communicate misaligned interests, lack of confidence, and limited responsiveness to immediate demands, are all barriers to be addressed.

RECOMMENDATIONS

Even though think tanks face multifaceted challenges in their progression, policy communication and visibility remain key in policymaking and implementation processes to improve citizen participation, governance, and think tanks' vibrancy. With the enhanced role of digital communication and social media, think tanks have opportunistic space to roll out their evidence-based findings, including publishing policy and research findings in a digital-friendly manner for a wider audience. It can also be noted that think tanks need to explore innovative dissemination strategies and combine efforts for significant global funding. This calls for think tanks to collaborate to create a sustainable future and build a common voice, even for funding. To guarantee the greatest influence and contribution to Africa's success, they should accelerate the transfer of best practices among peers, particularly concerning the next generation of skilled leaders, strategic planning, and interaction with the public and policymakers.

On the other hand, the future of African think tanks is also uncertain. Many reputable think tanks have vanished, and the future of the existing ones is in jeopardy. According to reports, 30 per cent of Africa's think tanks may cease to exist by 2030. Think tanks must consider venturing into entrepreneurship to sustain their policy-driven and research work. Furthermore, based on data collected on African think tanks, the civil society and think tanks programme reports that 60 per cent of African think tanks are highly susceptible and at risk of disappearing due to brain drain, staff turnover and unstable funding. Donors need to reduce the micro-level effect on think tanks by dealing with institutions rather than individual consultants, to ensure structural arrangements for institutional continuity. It is further recommended that multilateral institutions, donors and independent financial institutions consider collaborating with think tanks rather than competing in research and policy-driven processes. The essence and scale of the think tank crisis pose a significant threat to long-term African transformation. Indeed, the change in perception over the last two decades, from an Africa in perpetual crisis to an Africa on the rise, can be attributed partly to the work of African think tanks, which have created a more robust and more complex perception of policy options for strengthening policy and governance.

NOTES

1.   See http://www.fahamu.org/ep_articles/3-more-lessons-from-working-with-african-think-tanks/ (retrieved on 15 June 2021).
2.   'Think tank formed to rescue public universities from financial woes', retrieved on 16 June 2021 from https://nation.africa/kenya/news/education/think-tank-formed-to-rescue-public-universities-from-financial-woes-3385262?view=htmlamp.
3.   http://repository.kippra.or.ke/handle/123456789/9. KIPPRA has developed a Public Policy Repository (PPR) that will provide its stakeholders with a one-stop shop for national and county government policy documents.
4.   https://amref.org/coronavirus/social-media-toolkit/. Information extracted from the AMREF COVID-19 Response Information Centre on 19 June 2021.
5.   https://www.kemri.org/wp-content/uploads/2019/11/Kenya-Scientists-Release-Genome-Sequencing-for-the-Covid-19-Cases-in-Kenya.pdf.

REFERENCES

African Development Bank Report (2011). Private Sector Development as an Engine. https://www.afdb.org/sites/default/files/documents/publications/african_development_report_2011.pdf

APHRC (2020). Annual Report: Navigating the New Normal. https://aphrc.org/wp-content/uploads/2021/07/APHRC-Annual-Report-2020.pdf.

APHRC (2021). Annual Performance Review Report. https://aphrc.org/wp-content/uploads/2022/06/Annual-Performance-Review-Report-2021_20.06.2022-_F.pdf.

Babu, S. C. (2020). Revitalizing Policy Think Tanks in Developing Countries: COVID-19 Challenges and Opportunities. Agrilinks. 21 May. https://www.agrilinks.org/post/revitalizing-policy-think-tanks-developing-countries-covid-19-challenges-and-opportunities.

Bailey, A. and Gitahi, G. (2015). Covid-19 Fuelling Partnerships to Boost Health Systems. https://newsroom.amref.org/news/2021/06/covid-19-fuelling-partnerships-to-boost-health-systems/.

Barker, J.R. (1993). Tightening the Iron Cage: Concertive Control in Self-Managing Teams. *Administrative Science Quarterly*, 38, 408–437. http://dx.doi.org/10.2307/2393374.

Baumgartner, F.R., and Jones, B.D. (1991). Agenda Dynamics and Policy Subsystems. *Journal of Politics*, 53(4), 1044–1074.

Burkhardt, M.E. (1994). Social Interaction Effects Following a Technological Change: A Longitudinal Investigation. *Academy of Management Journal*, 37(4), 868–896.

DiMaggio, P.J., and Powell, W.W. (1983). The Iron Cage Revisited: Institutional Isomorphism in Organisational Fields. *American Sociological Review*, 48, 147–160.

Douglas, M. (1986). *How Institutions Think*. Sycracuse, NY: Sycracuse University Press. Routledge.

Garsten, C. (2013). All about Ties: Think Tanks and the Economy of Connections. In Garsten, C., and Nyqvist, A. (eds), *Organisational Anthropology: Doing Ethnography in and among Complex Organisations*. London: Pluto Press, 139–154.

Harcourt, M., Lam, H., and Harcourt, S. (2005). Discriminatory Practices in Hiring: Institutional and Rational Economic Perspectives. *International Journal of Human Resource Management*, 16(11), 2113–2132.

Hyden, G., and Onyango, G. (2021). Kenya: A Comparative East African Perspective. In Onyango, G., and Hyden, G. (eds), *Governing Kenya: Public Policy in Theory and Practice*. London: Palgrave Macmillan, 257–277.

Kelstrup, J.D. (2016). *The Politics of Think Tanks in Europe*. London: Routledge. https://www. coleurope.eu/politics-think-tanks-europe.

Kimenyi, M.S., and Datta, A.K. (2011). Think Tanks in Sub-Saharan Africa How the Political Landscape has Influenced Their Origins. London: Overseas Development Institute.

Leys, C. (1975). *Underdevelopment in Kenya: The Political Economy of Neo-Colonialism*. London: Heinemann Publishers.

Liang, H., Saraf, N., Hu, Q., and Xue, Y. (2007). Assimilation of Enterprise Systems: The Effect of Institutional Pressures and the Mediating Role of Top Management. *MIS Quarterly,* 31(1), 59– 87.

March, J.G. and J.P. Olsen (1989). *Rediscovering Institutions*. New York: Free Press.

Mbadlanyana, T., Sibalukhulu, N., and Cilliers, J. (2011). Shaping African Futures: Think Tanks and the Need for Endogenous Knowledge Production in Sub-Saharan Africa. *Foresight*, 13(3), 64–84. doi: 10.1108/14636681111138776.

McGann, J. (2016). *Think Tanks*. Washington, DC: Brookings Institution Press.

McGann, J. (2019). *Think Tanks, Foreign Policy and the Emerging Powers*. Cham: Springer International Publishing. http://dx.doi.org/10.1007/978-3-319-60312-4.

McGann, J. (2021). *The Future of Think Tanks and Policy Advice around the World*. Palgrave Macmillan. https://doi.org/10.1007/978-3-030-60379-3.

McGann, J., Viden, A., and Rafferty, J. (2014). *How Think Tanks Shape Social Development Policies*. Philadelphia, PA: University of Pennsylvania Press.

McGann, J., and Weaver, R. (2017). *Think Tanks and Civil Societies* (1st edn). New York: Routledge and CRC Press.

Meyer, J.W., and Rowan, B. (1977). Institutionalised Organisations: Formal Structure as Myth and Ceremony. *American Journal of Sociology*, 83, 340–363.

Mitullah, W.V. (2021). The Powers of Agenda-Setting: The Role of Politicians and Experts. In Onyango, G., and Hyden, G. (eds), *Governing Kenya*. Cham: Palgrave Macmillan. https://doi.org/10.1007/978-3-030-61784-4_4.

Morales, J. (2021). Global Think Tanks. Policy Networks and Governance. *Estudios Públicos*, 1–8. doi: 10.38178/07183089/0854201102.

North, D.C. (1990). *Institutions, Institutional Change and Economic Performance*. Cambridge: Cambridge University Press.

Ohemeng, F. L. K. (2005). Getting the State Right: Think Tanks and the Dissemination of New Public Management Ideas in Ghana. *Journal of Modern African Studies*, 43(3), 443–465. http://www.jstor.org/stable/3876063.

Ohemeng, F. L. K. (2015). Civil Society and Policy Making in Developing Countries: Assessing the Impact of Think Tanks on Policy Outcomes in Ghana. *Journal of Asian and African Studies*, 50(6), 667–682. https://doi.org/10.1177/0021909614535917.

Onyango, G. (2019). Policy-Visibility and Implementation in Public Administration. In Farazmand, A. (ed.), *Global Encyclopedia of Public Administration, Public Policy, and Governance*. https://doi.org/10.1007/978–3-319–31816–5_3867–1.

Onyango, G. (2022). *Routledge Handbook of Public Policy in Africa*. London: Routledge.

Onyango, G., and Hyden, G. (eds) (2021). *Governing Kenya: Public Policy in Theory and Practice*. London: Palgrave Macmillan.

Powell, W.W., and DiMaggio, P. (eds) (1991). *The New Institutionalism in Organizational Analysis*. Chicago, IL: University of Chicago Press. http://catdir.loc .gov/catdir/toc/uchi051/91009999.html.

Rothstein, Bo, and Teorell, Jan (2012). Defining and Measuring Quality of Government. In Holmberg, Sören and Rothstein, Bo (eds), *Good Government: The Relevance of Political Science*. Cheltenham, UK and Northampton, MA, USA: Edward Elgar Publishing, 13–39.

Sartor, J. (2019). Corporate Think Tanks. *Controlling*, 31(1), 77–78. doi: 10.15358/0935–0381–2019-1-77.

Scott, W.R. (2001). *Institutions and Organisations* (2nd edn). Thousand Oaks, CA: SAGE.

Shrum, L. J. (2001). Processing Strategy Moderates the Cultivation Effect. *Human Communication Research*, 27(1), 94–120. https://doi.org/10.1111/j.1468-2958.2001 .tb00777.x.

Stone, Diane (2007). Recycling Bins, Garbage Cans or Think Tanks? Three Myths Regarding Policy Analysis Institutes. *Public Administration*, 85(2), 259–278. https:// doi.org/10.1111/j.1467-9299.2007.00649.x.

Stone, Diane, and Ladi, Stella (2017). Policy Analysis and Think Tanks in Comparative Perspective. In Brans, Marleen, Geva-May, Iris, and Howlett, Michael (eds), *Handbook on Comparative Policy Analysis*. Routledge. https:// doi .org/ 10 .4324/ 9781315660561.

'tHart, Paul, and Vromen, Ariadne (2008). A New Era for Think Tanks in Public Policy? International Trends, Australian Realities. *Australian Journal of Public Administration*, 67(2), 135–148. https://doi.org/10.1111/j.1467-8500.2008.00577.x.

Weidenbaum, M. (2010). Measuring the Influence of Think Tanks. *Soc*, 47, 134–137.

7. Think tanks, governance and development in Nigeria

Dhikru Adewale Yagboyaju and Omosefe Oyekanmi

INTRODUCTION

Governance and development are interwoven and interconnected, both in theory and in practice. Development, especially in terms of the well-being of citizens of a particular country and their livelihoods, can be described as an end, while governance through effective policies is the means through which development aspirations and goals are actualized. Knowledge-based and knowledge-driven economies and sustainable development, in which the roles of intellectuals and, in particular, think tanks have been variously identified, have become the focus in today's world. In Nigeria, policy-makers have since the country's independence in 1960 seen research as essential input for socio-economic and political transformation. They have therefore aided the establishment of more than 69 research institutions (public and private)[1] with diverse research functions and objectives, in addition to the various departments of planning, research and statistics (PRS) existing in ministries and parastatals at different governmental levels. Many of these research institutes exist in the form of think tanks or development-centred organizations to policy authorities.

Given this, research has been conducted with outputs from these institutions impacting differently on socio-economic and political development policies as well as other strategies in Nigeria. In the public category, there are the Nigerian Institute of Social and Economic Research (NISER), Nigerian Institute of International Affairs (NIIA) and National Institute for Policy and Strategic Studies (NIPSS), among others; while the Nigerian Economic Summit Group (NESG), Centre for Democracy and Development (CDD) and Ibadan School of Government and Public Policy (ISGPP), among others, represent the private category of research institutes and think tanks in Nigeria. Research issues that have been discussed by these institutions and outfits relate, among others, to: health care delivery, especially in primary and secondary sectors; internal and external security; physical infrastructure; population and demographic problems; rural and urban development, incorporating housing and waste disposal; national educational policies; macro-economic and fiscal policies; trade and currency exchange rate determination; industrial development; governance reforms, including the issue of the nature and character of corruption in the country; political parties and the party system.[2]

Despite these, Nigeria has in the recent past decades not only been ranked poorly in international human development and prosperity indexes such as United Nations (UN) Human Development Index (HDI), the Legatum Institute's Annual Prosperity Index (API) and the Mo Ibrahim Index of African Governance (IIAG), but also classified at different times as a failed state.[3] This is a serious matter, demanding more scholarly attention. However, this is not to say that think tanks have not been criticized in other societies. For example, according to Rich (2004: i), while the number of think tanks active in American politics has 'more than quadrupled since the 1970s', their influence has 'not expanded proportionally'. Instead, the known ideological proclivities of many, 'especially newer think tanks', and their aggressive efforts to obtain high profiles, have come to 'undermine the credibility with which experts and expertise are generally viewed by public officials'. In many cases, think tanks have become 'more marketing than research organisations', with 'styles of behaviour that mimic interest groups more than universities'. This, in part, pointed to concerns connected to think tanks in the United States, at a point, becoming organizations that turn experts into advocates and policy information into ammunition. For Rich (2004: i), the once-real boundaries between experts and advocates in American policy-making had become 'blurred'.

This chapter, therefore, sets out to address two basic objectives: the first is to establish the nexus between think tanks, governance and development; the second is to analyse the effectiveness of selected think tanks (public and private) in actualizing the aspirations of governance and development goals in Nigeria. Using qualitative methods of data gathering and analysis, data was generated and analysed from primary and secondary sources. Primary data was collected through key informant interviews (KIIs) from three think tanks within the private and public spaces in Nigeria, while the secondary sources of data were journals, books, published and unpublished materials and online sources.

Following from this introductory section, the rest of the chapter is structured as follows. The next section covers definitional/conceptual issues and a review of the literature. This is followed by a section on the effectiveness of think tanks in actualizing governance and development in Nigeria. The chapter closes with a conclusion and recommendations.

DEFINITIONAL/CONCEPTUAL ISSUES AND REVIEW OF LITERATURE

The concept of governance is one with broad interpretations. It can be viewed from the simple perspective of efficiency and rationality in allocating and deploying resources within any organization or social system, to the more complex definition as the process of steering a country or the global society toward the realization of collective and often contradictory goals (Yagboyaju and Okoosi-Simbine, 2020: 160).

In defining the concept of governance, the Legatum Institute (2021), the IIAG (2016), the UNDP (2007) and the World Bank (2007) share certain positions. In this respect, the World Bank provides a framework that enunciates six dimensions of governance. These are:

- Voice and accountability (VA): measuring perceptions of the extent to which citizens of a country are able to participate in selecting their government, as well as freedom of expression, freedom of association, and a free media.
- Political stability and absence of violence (PV): measuring perceptions of the likelihood that the government will be destabilized or overthrown by unconstitutional or violent means, including politically motivated violence and terrorism.
- Government effectiveness (GE): measuring perceptions of the quality of the public services, the quality of the civil service and the degree of its independence from political pressure, the quality of policy formulation and implementation, and the credibility of the government's commitment to such policies.
- Regulatory quality (RQ): measuring perceptions of the ability of the government to formulate and implement sound policies and regulations that permit and promote private sector development.
- Rule of law (RL): measuring perceptions of the extent to which agents have confidence in, and abide by, the rules of society, and in particular the quality of contract enforcement, property rights, the police and the courts, as well as the likelihood of crime and violence.
- Control of corruption (CC): measuring perceptions of the extent to which public power is exercised for private gain, including both petty and grand forms of corruption, as well as capture[4] of the state by the elite and private interests.

These dimensions concentrate on political or public governance. However, governance as a concept cannot be reduced to government, as there exist other levels of governance outside of the core government. These can be categorized as economic and social governance. Scholars (Yagboyaju and Okoosi-Simbine, 2020; Oyeshile and Offor, 2016; Yagboyaju, 2016; Simbine and Oladeji 2010; Hyden and Bratton, 1992; Chazan, 1992) are in agreement on the relevance of the categorization of these aspects of governance. Economic governance involves the private sector and its relationships to the policies, processes and organizational mechanisms that are necessary to produce and distribute goods and services. Social governance, whose authority is the civil society, includes families, citizens, non-profit organizations and non-governmental organizations. It relates to a system of values and beliefs that are necessary for social behaviours to happen and for public decisions to be taken. Important to note in all of this is the essence of social order that is implied.

In this light, it is appropriate to note that governance can be effective, ineffective or poor, and there are causal relationships between the character of governance and development outcomes. According to Kaufmann et al. (1999: 4), it has been observed that better development outcomes such as 'higher per capital incomes, lower infant mortality and higher literacy' are the products of better governance. Conversely, poor or ineffective governance leads, according to Rogers and Hall (2003: 2), to 'increased political and social risks, institutional failure and rigidity and a deterioration in the capacity to cope with shared problems'. The issue of ineffective governance can hardly be separated from the problem of poor leadership. From Achebe (1983) and Shahadah (2012), to Yagboyaju (2015), the argument about the relationship between poor leadership and underdevelopment in Nigeria and around Africa has been consistent. This problem of poor leadership in Africa has been closely linked to corruption, greed, nepotism, indiscipline, economic regression, poverty and outright theft, that have left the region 'more or less stagnant after decades of self-rule' (Simbine and Oladeji, 2010: 807). It is implied that there is a higher likelihood that underdevelopment will produce weak political leadership through electoral democracy, leading to a vicious cycle.[5]

Development, in view of the multifarious contextual usage of the concept, is a term which does not lend itself to a universal or ultimate definition. It can be described simply as an improvement or advancement. It involves being more mature, more complete, more organized or more transformed. Todaro (cited in Yagboyaju, 2022: 47) has described development as a 'multidimensional process involving the reorganization and reorientation of the entire economic and social system'. This, in addition, involves improvement in income and output, as well as 'radical changes in institutional, social and administrative structures, and popular attitudes, customs and beliefs'. While economic growth, which emphasizes numerical strength in terms of finances, physical infrastructure and other material resources, is embedded, it must be noted that development focuses more on the living conditions and well-being of people.

It is in this light that the idea has been espoused of a set of linked freedoms[6] as building blocks for development.

Other similar opinions about the concept of development include that of the UN, expressed in particular in the Millennium Development Goals (MDGs) and the Sustainable Development Goals (SDGs).[7] In both programmes, the focus of what constitutes development is on the eradication of extreme poverty and hunger; reduction of diseases that lead to economic hardship; addressing infant and maternal mortality; addressing issues relating to malaria, HIV/AIDS and tuberculosis, among others; combating gender-related issues of violence; and advancement of democratic governance (UN, 2000; Anger, 2010; Elliot, 2013).

Nigeria, despite the country's endowment in terms of human resources and natural resources in crude oil, in particular, has not had a significant presence in actualizing development aspirations and goals. On a comparative note, Norden and Scandinavian countries such as Norway, Sweden, Denmark, Finland and Ireland, as well as several others in continental Europe with less endowments than Nigeria, have performed much better in development indexes.[8] In supporting this, Kastelli et al. (2023) claims that because of their improved ability to conduct extensive industrial research that can affect national policy change, these think tanks have the potential to support sustainable industrial development. In other words, without focusing on the unique peculiarities of these European states and Nigeria, a critical factor to development and governance is the ability of a country's think tank to carry out far-reaching research that determines governmental policies. What this implies, in line with the earlier assertion on the relationship between leadership, governance and development, is that these countries, like others around the world with better development rankings, are more effectively governed than Nigeria, based mainly on the engagement of think tanks.

Looking at the Asian experience, Nachiappan et al. (2010) states that think tanks in Asia were mostly a result of the regional dynamics that formed between them, and the state of development in the country. McGann (2007), however, differentiates between academic-oriented think tanks and policy-oriented think tanks. According to him, the former focus on long-term issues and are usually scholarly and have objective research standards; while the policy-oriented think tanks such as NISER are predominantly to service policy-makers and address contemporary policy issues. Ladi (2011), however, believes that not much is done by these policy-oriented think tanks in terms of legitimizing the aims of decision-makers and governance structure, by making available actual data and arguments.

Actualizing and sustaining development goals requires planning, objective analysis and evaluation. This is an aspect of critical thinking, the forte of intellectuals who dominate think tanks. In the opinion of Rich (2004: i), think tanks are organizations committed to 'objective analysis of policy problems', with a view to charting appropriate directions. Much has been written about the functions of intellectuals, especially in their categorizations by Antonio Gramsci,[9] as both traditional and organic intellectuals. What can be teased out from the views of Olaopa (2022), Adamolekun (2016, 2005) and Jinadu (2002) about intellectuals is that they have a special responsibility, saddling them with the role of 'developing higher level manpower, among other important roles in national development' (Jinadu, 2002: 178). In another vein, while Nachiappan (2013) contends that think tanks are significantly influenced by their institutional context, Merke and Pauselli (2015) emphasize that think tanks are not isolated from politics but are part of the very fabric of society in which they exist and function. Stone (2017), further states that national political cultures and institutional arrangements strongly determine the type of think tanks that take root, and the character of their policy involvement, contending that no contextual factors are more significant in influencing the development of think tank systems. In effect, the environmental settings of think tanks, be they policy-oriented or academic-oriented, are not significant in determining the outcome of think tanks in influencing governance and development. This is largely informed by the beliefs of government officials that think tanks should serve policy objectives (Bardauskaitė, 2022). Nonetheless, as Wang and Li (2018) avers, with the rise of contemporary think tanks, made up of specialists from several fields, think tanks with less influence from government will perform better. This somewhat justifies the effectiveness of think tanks in developed and first world countries where the influence of government and government officials is minimal compared to third world countries such as Nigeria. Hence, the promotion of development and good governance is a function of the independence of think tanks.

As such, in dealing with national or international challenges with comparatively better outcomes, non-support from the government or commercial sectors to think tanks has greater potential to impact upon development and good governance. In general, think tanks are essential in determining the development priorities of countries. They offer evidence-based perceptions and suggestions that can help to guide policy choices, develop capability, and advance policy reforms that can hasten economic growth, lessen poverty, enhance governance and promote development in the long term.

While there is a substantial amount of literature on think tanks and their role in governance and development, much of this is focused on developed countries. As it stands, there are inadequate studies on the role of think tanks in the Global South, such as Nigeria, where development challenges are more acute. Similarly, there is limited consideration of the institutional, political and environmental context of think tanks. Thus, the institutional, political and environmental settings of public and private think tanks in Nigeria, and how these affect their ability to influence governance and development, is the gap that this chapter intends to fill.

EFFECTIVENESS OF THINK TANKS IN ACTUALIZING GOVERNANCE AND DEVELOPMENT IN NIGERIA

Since Nigeria's independence in 1960, think tanks have existed, with many research institutes formed by the government to offer technical guidance on various policy matters. Chief among these organizations include the Centre for Management Development (CMD), the National Institute for Policy and Strategic Studies (NIPSS), and the Nigerian Institute of Social and Economic Research (NISER).

With the advent of globalization, more think tanks started to emerge in the 1980s, showing the growing significance of a knowledge-based economy to good governance and development. These think tanks, which concentrated on themes such as economic development, governance and security, were founded with the assistance of international organizations and foreign governments. Over the years, the importance of think tanks in Nigeria has increased, given the nation's numerous problems such as economic instability, corruption and security threats. Though think tanks have been crucial in addressing these concerns, their effectiveness in advancing the nation's growth by offering evidence-based analyses and recommendations, centred on topics such as security, governance and economic development, remains debatable. Hence, the establishment of think tanks in Nigeria and their role in actualizing their mandate is crucial. For instance, the functions of think tanks in Nigeria can be inferred from the mission statement of NISER, which states: 'NISER's responsibilities include coordinating social and economic research in federal universities. The institute also carries out independent research on social and economic issues. It provides consultancy services to the government based on research findings' (https://niser.gov.ng).

The functions of public think tanks in Nigeria are not fundamentally different from those of their counterparts in the private and non-governmental realm. An expert from a renowned think tank on democracy and governance within the private realm asserts that their organization has consistently conducted research that supports knowledge generation with the intention to influence public policy debates.[10] However, motives may differ in terms of whether they are profit-driven or not. In other words, most of the government think tanks are not driven by profits or rewards, since they are basically funded by the government. Nonetheless, this does not suggest that public think tanks do not conduct research for donor agencies and international organizations. For instance, a respondent from a government think tank in Ibadan avers:[11]

> The Institute is also allowed to support other developmental agencies or institutions, such as the UN agencies such as UNDP [United Nations Development Programme], UNICEF [United Nations Children's Fund], FAO [Food and Agriculture Organization] and particularly in areas that require research support or areas for a need assessment, in areas of end of product evaluation to determine the extent to which a political intervention should have met the stated objectives. Based on this mandate, we also do trainings, specialised trainings for agencies particularly government agencies, private agencies in the area of conducting research entirely, data analysis, methodology training and all that and even how to analyse those data that they have generated, to write the report. And so, we have done that for several MDAs (Ministries, Departments and Agencies).

Before closing this section of the chapter, a brief discussion of the analytic frame is necessary. With its focus on think tanks as institutions, the choice of institutionalism as a theoretical framework is appropriate. The framework anchors its analyses on the role of institutions and organisations. In the public sphere, these include the legislature, the executive and the judiciary, as well as the civil service, ministries, departments and agencies (MDAs), political parties, and the party system, interspersing. Such institutions are studied to unveil persistent patterns of activities, constitutional and legal arrangements, especially as they relate to functions and powers of the institutions (Onah, 2010; Leeds, 1981). The commonality of the purpose of government[12] compels inter-agency relationship and cooperation between these institutions.

The institutional approach has been criticized for being too formalistic and for neglecting the informal aspects of organizations, which are also important in political analyses. The institutional approach was relegated temporarily, especially with the emergence of the behavioural movement and the behavioural approach. However, there has been a resurgence of the institutional approach,[13] Historical institutionalism has also emerged. This is a relatively new approach that uses institutions to find sequences of social, political and economic behaviour and change across time. It is a comparative approach to the study of organizations, and does this by relying on case studies (Sanders, 2008; Steinmo, 2008).

Governance effectiveness in developed societies, some of which have been mentioned in the development indexes cited earlier in this section, is an indication of something fundamental about the relationship between the environment and the political systems housing these governance structures. This also applies to countries in which the state is described as captured, as well as others that are classified as fragile or failed. The environment, consisting of historical, geographical, technological and socio-cultural factors, has been emphasized in the ecological approach[14] to analyses in political science, public administration and administrative sciences. This implies that think tanks in Nigeria can only perform their roles to the extent permitted by the environment, or ecology, within which they operate. In establishing the linkages between the research setting and the government setting as it relates to governance, a respondent from the public realm succinctly states:[15]

> The objective is to support government in decision making using evidence from our studies and we have done that for a couple of years, you know since the establishment of the institute, but based on the mandate or the act establishing the institute, the institute is only tasked with the responsibility to provide policy advice through the development of the policy brief which is shared with the government and so that is where the responsibility of the institute to the government stops and so it is the responsibility of the government to take it up from there, to use the brief in order to design activities of policies and also implement it.

From the foregoing, the intervention of public research institutes in governance or government policies cannot go beyond the production of policy briefs. For private research institutes, their institutional setting permits them to push for advocacy, which may not be within the mandate of public-owned research institutes. This is reiterated by a respondent from a private think tank:[16]

> Through research, partnerships, and capacity building, advocacy is a critical component of all our strategies. To do this, we have built alliances, coalitions, and networks to influence policy outcomes and reaffirm commitments to a reform agenda. We have also consistently conducted researches that support knowledge generation, and which have influenced public policy debates. These take the form of reports, policy briefs and commentary pieces. Partnerships with organisations working on issues related to our core mandate help amplify a collective voice, ensure the effective use of mobilised resources and bypass obstacles that emerge.

Still on the differences between the institutional settings of private and public research institutes, another stakeholder from the public space states:

> And so that is where we are, aiming at ... like last year we submitted over 50 policy briefs and it is hard to see which one government has really taken upon to implement and so currently there is effort to, how do I put it now, effort to revise our Act where the mandate of the institute is stated to include activities related to advocacy and lobbying and so to some level of implementation. Because what I told them (members of management staff) the last time is to adopt advocacy ... because that is the difference between the non-governmental organizations and a government agency. They can engage a consultant to do small piece of research and based on the findings they pick that up and begin to advocate for it and be moving from one office to another and with that they can implement some policy change but our mandate doesn't work like that, so what I was suggesting to them is to have some kind of

MOU [Memorandum of Understanding] with some NGOs [non-governmental organizations].

The many factors in the environment in which think tanks operate in Nigeria that are discussed include: the colonial beginning of the state and, by extension, its institutions; lack of political will; 'hit and run' policy processes, constituting confusion and uncertainties; indiscipline and corruption; low level of education, enlightenment and exposure to technology; inadequate funding. This is complemented by the responses from the KIIs.

The effects of colonial rule and the colonial beginnings of Nigeria on the performance of the modern state and its institutions have been well documented.[17] The main point to draw out of this perspective is the prevalence of an amoral value system which gives rise to corruption, abuse and exploitation of public office to serve private ends, ethnicity and 'reliance on patron–client networks for legitimacy' (Osaghae, 2002: 18). A research professor from a notable public research institute highlighted some of the corrupt actions that play out in the award of research projects to their institute, stating that:[18]

> So, the point is that the political will is not there, and self-interest is another issue. Most of these things you are saying ... at the point where projects should be given to people that can actually make change, people that can actually contribute based on their knowledge and experience, you say 'No', this person is not my person, if I bring in my person whatever he will be doing I will get it and he will have something for himself. So, there are lots of study for instance that the institute can do for government and ordinarily, government would want us to do the work and send it back to them, but NO, the person in charge will look for smaller consultancy firms with 3 or 5 persons that will give them something in return and they will do it and whatever comes in, they said they have done it.

Such offices, including public and private think tanks, are often personalized, making the actualization of their objectives difficult or unattainable. This implies that focus is more on 'research' which favours or enhances the interests of those in charge. Deploying a buzzword, it lacks the political will to address issues of the public good or interest. Respondents from public and private institutions are of the opinion that apart from the unwillingness of some policy-makers to give credit to research organizations, and the inability of policy-makers to translate research outcomes to clear government policies, the politicization of research outputs further widens the research–policy nexus. Stressing the unethical role of government in research output, a respondent from a government research institute puts it this way:[19] 'the research uptake is very poor from government. That is to say, adopting the research findings, adopting some policy briefs in designing some interventions or even some policies is still very low and there is also very low appreciation of importance of research in decision making.'

Yagboyaju (2019: 5) notes the complication of the confusion and uncertainties that often typify policy conception in Nigeria, by the 'hit and run' research outputs, especially from the personal interests of researchers. When research outcomes are predetermined, such exercises lack strong evidence of rigour. However, there is also the problem of relevance of research outputs to public policy, which has confronted social scientists in particular.[20] Many researchers in this category focus more on a basic understanding of issues; while for some others, research has become 'an industry in itself' (Nzuki et al., 2013: 2). On the significance of issue-based research, especially as it relates to the value of the research focus or the title to governance and policy, a researcher suggests that modifications to the title may be tenable in the event where government suggests non-researchable topics. According to them:[21]

> sometimes we come up with some research titles based on the emerging issues but some other times the government could also come up with research titles based on their own development within the period and so once they bring their own for instance, we look at it, we see how researchable it is and if it is not researchable we look for a way out or rework it based on exactly what they have in mind and based on that we can now rework those titles in order to be able to bring out something reasonable from that kind of research and so once we have the titles we will share with them particularly at the point we have to develop the budget and so we have all the titles.

This problem of relevance of research is connected to the issue of lack of recognition for local content in addressing local problems. It implies the introduction of policy solutions from elsewhere.[22] Ake (1981: 32–33) traces the origin of this problem, in post-colonial societies, to the problem of 'economic dependence on former colonial masters, the fact of political independence notwithstanding'.

The role of education, enlightenment, exposure and technology in the relationship between think tanks and those at the core of public policy processes cannot be underestimated. At the time of writing in 2022, 23 years after the 1999 commencement of Nigeria's Fourth Republic, it is hardly conceivable to separate the country's encounter with a development conundrum, and the general attitude to education and technological breakthroughs. There is evidence[23] in support of the thesis that formal education or skill is not prioritized in electing representatives to policy-formulating offices in Nigeria. The result is that while a large percentage of the electorate consider factors other than education in electing their representatives, the latter can only give what they have, part of which is disdain for an emphasis on knowledge-driven political governance. This is not to say that contempt for research-based public policies and, in particular, research outcomes from think tanks, is restricted to only civilian dispensations in Nigeria. For example, the Ibrahim Babangida and Sani Abacha military regimes of 1985–1993 and 1993–1998, respectively, showed preference for policy inputs from the research units of government MDAs. Being conventional civil servants, officials in these units of the MDAs have mostly been careful not to be seen as offensive towards or too critical of government.[24] This aside, research by MDAs often suffers from a lack of technical skills, because it has largely been conducted by generalist administrators. Corroborating this, a respondent recounts their experience at a recent key performance indicator (KPI) meeting for public research institutes in Abuja, stating:

> there is also very low appreciation of the importance of research in decision making particularly in the level, you see most of their decisions or most of their activities, I was in Abuja last week, there is this presidential deliverables task team and so there, government has nine priority areas of focus starting from 2015 till date, some of these nine priorities some of the key informant status you know, and so the question I asked is that how did government arrive at these priorities, you know, it shouldn't be a rule of … thumb. To what level, to what extent, where these research institutions carried along. You don't just say okay because there is unemployment problem then it becomes a priority, these priorities should be empirically investigated in other to arrive at them … you don't just say, because if you should say 'Okay it is an employment problem let's begin to …' it is either you are addressing the manifestation but the problem … you are not addressing the problem.

Funding has been another critical issue, in both military and civilian dispensations. The consequences of inadequate funding, particularly in national planning and education, under which Nigerian classifies its think tanks, have been analysed by Yagboyaju (2016: 99–132). Unequivocally, funding remains a critical part of the research–policy nexus; this was stated categorically by respondents from both public and private research institutes. They claimed that limited research funding has hampered the successful process of translating research outputs into influencing government policies. For example, the whole of the country's education sector has never in the 23 years of democratization in the Fourth Republic, coinciding with the first 22 years of the 21st century, attracted beyond 10 per cent annual budgeting allocation. The effects of this can be viewed not only from the perspective of this allocation being a far cry from the 26 per cent benchmark recommended by the United Nations Educational, Scientific and Cultural Organization (UNESCO), but also in light of the fact that tertiary education, which includes think tanks in Nigeria, attracts only a fraction of the country's annual education budgetary allocation. This is at variance with the prevailing conditions in the world's emerging centres of industrial and economic prominence, such as Malaysia, Singapore and South Korea, and even in African countries such as Kenya,

South Africa and Rwanda, many of which have allocated as much as a quarter of their annual budgets to education consistently since 2010 (Yagboyaju, 2016: 127–128). Demotivation for and demoralization of research in Nigeria can, in part, be traced to this challenge of inadequate funding.

The mitigation brought about by alternative funding, especially from non-governmental organizations, has its own peculiarities. The first of these, especially for external funding from agencies such as the Ford Foundation, British Council, United States Information Services (USIS), Mac Arthur Foundation, and Swedish NGO Foundation, among others, is the challenge of incommensurability with the amount of research Nigeria requires. Secondly, coming from the common pool of support, including the United States Agency for International Development (USAID), UN and UNDP, among others, such funding could cause a kind of unhealthy rivalry rather than promoting competition among the major actors as they seek access to the funds.

The analyses above, part of which benefited from the responses in a compendium of interviews, and others,[25] discuss the responses of the KIIs on issues specifically addressed in this chapter. Issues raised by these KIIs on governance and the roles of think tanks in Nigeria include: the core objectives; actualization of these objectives; the modalities for research in the institutes; dissemination of research outcomes, enhancement of governance performance by research outputs; insulation from government interference; challenges in terms of funding; and other forms of challenges. Those whose responses are analysed are Professor Antonia T. Simbine, Professor Tunji Olaopa and Ms. Idayat Hassan of NISER, ISGPP and CDD, respectively.

CONCLUSION AND RECOMMENDATIONS

The interrelatedness between governance, development and think tanks is established in this chapter. For development to thrive, effective policies must be formulated, which can only be possible through the production of knowledge and research-induced economies. Hence, the role of think tanks is very instructive in the actualization of effective polices that can drive development. An examination of the level of development in Norden and Scandinavian countries, when compared to Nigeria which ranks poorly in several development indicators, shows that these countries have performed a lot better in development indexes based on effective governance produced through policies informed by knowledge. Thus, the role of think tanks in the research–policy nexus is responsible for the poor governance structure and, by extension, Nigeria's level of development. This assertion is premised on the fact that think tanks, whether public or private, are expected to support the government's policy design that can drive development.

However, certain factors, including the role of institutions and organizations, the environmental settings and the political systems housing these governance structures, determine the extent to which think tanks in Nigeria can perform their roles. As such, the delivery and impact of think tanks in shaping policy designs are bound by political, institutional and environmental settings of the private or public organizations. In addition, this chapter submits that the dominance of unprincipled values, inadequate funding, the absence of political will, corruption for personal gain and the patronage system, have pervaded the research–policy framework. The outcome of such deviation has produced government policies that are not guided by issue-based research, which have inadvertently shaped ineffective governance and underdevelopment in Nigeria.

It is recommended, therefore, that politicians with the political will to deliver on effective governance should be identified and supported into government. As it stands, the lack of political will remains pertinent to driving all other factors that can strengthen the research–policy nexus. To achieve this, the production of politicians with political will should be enhanced by prioritizing formal education and specialized skills as criteria for electing representatives to policy formulation offices in Nigeria.

Also, government must ensure that issues of research and development are depoliticized. Considering that socio-economic issues affect the well-being of citizens, facts and data must guide policies. To achieve this, adequate funding should be budgeted for research, as it is ideally the forbearer of development.

From the purview of the think tanks, research outcomes must emanate from fieldwork that is holistic and evidence-based, satisfying the basic criteria of rigour and science. Though the institutional and environmental settings of both public and private think tanks are distinct, performance of research institutes and organizations must be based on global best practices so as to drive development. Furthermore, beyond policy advice to the government, public think tanks should take on advocacy, which will strengthen collaborations with civil society groups in pushing for policies through informal channels.

NOTES

1. Apart from NISER, Nigeria's premier Think Tank, which was established in 1960, there have been dozens of public and private research institutes in the country. See, https://exced.ucoz.com/index/research_institutes_in_nigeria/0-69. Full list of Research Institutes in Nigeria and location (30 November 2020; accessed on 12 December 2022).
2. For example, NISER organizes monthly seminar series. In 2022 alone, it organized in collaboration with the MacArthur Foundation, 'Lived Experiences of Corrupt Behaviour in Nigeria', and a roundtable on the '2023 General Elections in Nigeria', on 24 November and 8 December 2022, respectively. This is apart from other research summits, with the 28th edition held on 14–15 December

2022. CDD is a frontrunner in activities concerning democratic advancement in the country, including operating election analysis centres (EACs) in the 2015 and 2019 Nigerian general elections.

3. According to the United States of America Fund for Peace Think Tank, countries categorized as fragile or failed lack capacity for policy formulation and implementation for sustainable development goals, including security of life and property, human rights and freedom

4. The World Bank has deployed the concept of state capture in describing the abuse of public policy processes by corrupt public officials and their collaborators, highlighting the manipulation of state institutions for personal gain, erosion of public trust, and the subversion of governance mechanisms.

5. For example, elections in Nigeria have, prior to the introduction of high technology in 2015, been characterized by malpractices such as ballot box stuffing and snatching. There have been incidences of vote buying since 2015. See Yagboyaju and Simbine (2020).

6. These, according to Amartya Sen, the 1988 Nobel Prize winner in Economics, philosopher and human development expert, include political freedoms and transparency in relations between people, freedom of opportunity, including freedom to access credit. For him, human development is about the 'expansion of citizens' capabilities to lead a reasonable life; one in which extreme poverty is banished. See Sen (1999: 1).

7. The UN launched the MDGs and SDGs in 2000 and 2015, respectively.

8. For example, rankings in the UN's HDI, and Legatuum Institute's API, among others, confirm.

9. Antonio Gramsci (1891–1937), Italian Marxist philosopher, popularized the concept of traditional and organic intellectualism. See Gramsci, Selections from the Prison Notebooks, 1971 (https://www.routledge.com).

10. KII conducted with an expert on research management on 22 December 2022 at CDD.

11. KII conducted with the a research professor on 23 January 2023 at Bodija, Ibadan.

12. The main purpose of government can be summarised to be the public good, whereby laws are made and implemented so as to aid citizens in actualizing their legitimate dreams and aspirations. See, https://www.zambianguardian.com - What is the purpose of government? (22 July 2021, Accessed on 18 December 2022).

13. Evidence is available in recent works. See Acemoglu and Robinson (2012). This work emphasises the role of institutions in determining power, prosperity and poverty levels in societies. Also, see Suberu (2018).

14. The central thesis of the ecological approach is that a public institution does not operate in vacuum and that it has a dynamic relationship with its environment, which is mutually reinforcing. John M. Gaus (1894–1969), Ferrel Heady (1916–2006) and Fred W. Riggs (1917–2008) were leading proponents of this approach. See Riggs (1961).

15. KII with a professor of knowledge management department in a public research institute on 16 December 2023.

16. KII with a senior official of a renowned private research institute in Nigeria on 23 December 2022.

17.   Among these, state–society perspectives stand out for the emphasis on connections to clientelistic/patronage and prebendal politics. See Ekeh (1975) and Joseph (1987).
18.   KII conducted with a research professor on 16 January 2023 at NISER.
19.   Ibid.
20.   The problem of relevance of social science research to public policy has been well documented in the literature. See Akinwowo (1971), Ake (1979), Ajakaiye and Roberts (1997), Ajakaiye and Falokun (2010).
21.   KII conducted with a senior researcher at NISER on 16 January 2023.
22.   Such issues have reverberated in discourses in respect of borrowed economic ideas in Africa. See Ellerman (2004).
23.   Five out of ten or 50 per cent respondents in a 2021 survey have been approached to sell their votes during recent elections in Nigeria. See Yagboyaju (2016).
24.   These military regimes have been cited, in particular, in view of the roles of the MDAs in the adoption of the structural adjustment programme (SAP) under Babangida and the Vision 2010 of the Abacha regime. There were also several feasibility studies in the downstream oil and gas industry, refineries, cement, fertilisers, iron, steel and paper production, all of which recorded insignificant success. See, Usman (2010).
25.   A Compendium of interviews granted, in 2010, by Professor S.O. Akande, then Director General (DG) of NISER, and past DGs in commemoration of the Institute's 60th anniversary celebrations (see NISEREEL, 2010), provides some tips on issues often raised in connection to policy attrition and failure in Nigeria. Past DGs interviewed are Profs. H.M.A. Onitiri (Pioneer DG), V.P. Diejomah, A.O. Phillips and D.O. Ajakaiye. The lead author in this chapter had also interacted with Antonia T. Simbine, Research Professor at NISER, then on national service at the Independent National Electoral Commission (INEC), on 5 January 2018.

REFERENCES

Acemoglu, D. and Robinson, J.A. 2012. *Why Nations Fail*. New York: Crown Publishing Group.
Achebe, C. 1983. *The Trouble with Nigeria*. Enugu: Fourth Dimension Publishers.
Adamolekun, L. 2005. Re-orienting Public Management in Africa: Selected Issues and Some Country Experiences. Economic Research Working Paper No 81. African Development Bank (www.afdb.org).
Adamolekun, L. 2016. The Idea of Nigeria – Two Challenges – Unity in Diversity and Prosperity. Convocation Lecture. Lead City University, Nigeria. 9 November.
Ajakaiye, D.O. and Falokun, G.O. 2010. Policy Research Nexus: Its Impact on Socio-Economic Development. In: S.O. Akande and A.J. Kumuyi (eds), *Nigeria at 50: Accomplishments, Challenges and Prospects*. Ibadan: NISER, pp. 871–894.
Ajakaiye, D.O. and Roberts, F.O.N. 1997. Social Research in Nigeria: The Problem of Policy Relevance. *Journal of Humanities and Social Science*. Vol. 8, No. 2: 249–268.
Ake, C. 1979. Social Science, Dependence and Underdevelopment. Presented at the National Workshop on the Impact of the Social Sciences on Policy in Nigeria, NISER, Ibadan, 4 June.
Ake, C. 1981. *A Political Economy of Africa*. London and Lagos: Longman.

Akinwowo, A.A. 1971. Linkages between Social Science Research and Decision Makers in Nigeria. *Quarterly Journal of Administration*. Vol. 2: 217–227.

Anger, B. 2010. Poverty Eradication, Millennium Development Goals and Sustainable Development in Nigeria. *Journal of Sustainable Development*. Vol. 3, No. 4: 138–144.

Anomaly, J. 2015. Public goods and government action. *Politics, Philosophy & Economics*, 14(2), 109–128.

Bardauskaitė, D. 2022. The Nexus Between the Baltic Governments and Think Tanks as Instruments of Foreign and Security Policy. *Politics*, 02633957221098019.

Chazan, N. 1992. Liberalisation, Governance and Political Space in Ghana. In: G. Hyden and M. Bratton (eds), *Governance and Politics in Africa*. Boulder, CO, USA and London, UK: Lynne Rienner, pp. 121–142.

Ekeh, P. 1975. Colonialism and the Two Publics in Africa: A Theoretical Statement. *Comparative Studies in Society and History*. Vol. 17, No. 1: 91–122.

Ellerman, D. 2004. Revisiting Hirschman on Development Assistance and Unbalanced Growth. *Eastern Economic Journal*. Vol. 30, No. 2: 311–331.

Elliot, J. 2013. *An Introduction to Sustainable Development*. New York: Routledge.

Gramsci, A. 2020. Selections from the prison notebooks. In: T. Prentki and N. Abraham (eds), *The Applied Theatre Reader* (2nd edn). United Kingdom: Routledge, pp. 141–142.

Hyden, G. and Bratton, M. (eds). 1992.*Governance and Politics in Africa*. Boulder, CO, USA and London, UK: Lynne Rienner.

IIAG. 2016. Defining Governance. *mo.ibrahim.foundation* (Posted on 17 August 2016. Accessed on 14 December 2022).

Jinadu, A. 2002. Intellectuals and Transition Politics in Nigeria. In: Browne Onuoha and M.M. Fadakinte (eds), *Transition Politics in Nigeria, 1970–1999*. Lagos: Malthouse Press, pp. 177–197.

Joseph, R.A. 1987. *Democracy and Prebendal Politics in Nigeria: The Rise and Fall of the Second Republic*. Cambridge: Cambridge University Press.

Kaufmann, D., Kraay, A. and Zoido-Lobaton, P. 1999. Governance Matters. *Policy Papers*. No. 2196. World Bank Institute.

Kastelli, I., Mamica, L., and Lee, K. 2023. New perspectives and issues in industrial policy for sustainable development: from developmental and entrepreneurial to environmental state. *Review of Evolutionary Political Economy*, 4(1), 1–25.

Ladi, S. 2011. Think-Tanks, Discursive Institutionalism, and Policy Change. In: G. Papanagnou (Ed.), *Social Science and Policy Challenges: Democracy, Values and Capacities*. UNESCO, pp. 205–220.

Leeds, C. 1981. *Political Studies*. Estover, Plymouth: Macdonald & Evans.

Legatum Institute. 2021. Prosperity Index 2021. https://www.prosperity.com (accessed 14 December 2022).

McGann, J.G. 2007. *Think Tanks and Policy Advice in the US Academics, Advisors and Advocates*. Hoboken, NJ: Taylor & Francis.

Merke, F., and Pauselli, G. 2015. In the Shadow of the State: Think Tanks and Foreign Policy in Latin America. *International Journal*. Vol. 70, No. 4: 613–628.

Nachiappan, K. 2013. Think Tanks and the Knowledge–Policy Nexus in China. *Policy and Society*. Vol. 32, No. 3: 255–265.

Nachiappan, K., Mendizabal, E. and Datta, A. 2010. Think Tanks in East and Southeast Asia. http:// www .odi .org .uk/ resources/ details .asp ?id = 5202 & title = think-tanks-east-southeast-asia.

Nzuki, M., Hassan, A. and Mbilinyi, A. 2013. Bridging the Research Policy Gap: The Impact of Research on Policy Process and Practice. *Tanzania Knowledge Network (TAKNET) Policy Brief Series*. No. 019: 1–4.

Olaopa, T. 2022. Professionals in Government: Issues in Navigating Policy Space in Nigeria. *The Guardian* (Lagos, Nigeria). 7 June. https:// guardian/ ng/ opinion/ professionals-in-government-issues-in-nigeria/.

Onah, I. 2010. *Contemporary Political Analysis*. Lagos: Concept Publications.

Osaghae, E.E. 2002. *Nigeria since Independence: Crippled Giant*. Ibadan: John Archers.

Oyeshile, O.A. and Offor, F. (eds). 2016. *Ethics, Governance and Social Order in Africa*. Ibadan: Zenith Book House.

Rich, A. 2004. *Think Tanks, Public Policy and the Politics of Expertise*. Cambridge: Cambridge University Press.

Riggs, F.W. (1961). *The Ecology of Public Administration*. CA: Asia Publishing House

Rogers, P. and Hall, A. 2003. Effective Water Governance, Global Water Partnership. *TECBackground Papers*, No. 7, p.2.

Sanders, E. 2008. Historical Institutionalism. In: S.A. Binder, R.A.W. Rhodes and B.A. Rockman (eds), *The Oxford Handbook of Political Institutions*. Oxford University Press.

Sen, A. 1999. *Development as Freedom*. New York: Alfred Knopf.

Shahadah, A. 2012. African Leadership: The Roots of Failure. https://www .africanholocaust.net/news_ah/African/leadership/html (posted on 28 April 2014; accessed on 15 December 2022).

Simbine, A.T and Oladeji, A.O. 2010. Overview, Challenges and Prospects of Governance and Political Development. In: S.O. Akande and A.J. Kumuyi (eds), *Nigeria at 50: Accomplishments, Challenges and Prospects*. Ibadan: NISER, pp. 807–884.

Steinmo, S. 2008. Historical Institutionalism. In: D.D. Porta and M. Keating (eds), *Approaches and Methodologies in the Social Sciences: A Pluralist Perspective*. Cambridge: Cambridge University Press, pp. 19–39.

Stone, D. 2017. Dynamics of Think Tank Development in Southeast Asia, Australia, New Zealand, and Papua New Guinea. In: R. Weaver (Ed.), *Think Tanks and Civil Societies*. United Kingdom: Routledge, pp. 383–410.

Suberu, R. T. 2018. Strategies for Advancing Anticorruption Reform in Nigeria. *Journal of the American Academy of Arts and Sciences*. Vol. 147, No. 3: 1–18.

United Nations (UN). 2000. *Millennium Development Goals*. New York: UN.

United Nations Development Programme (UNDP). 2007. *Human Development Report, 2007/2008, Fighting Climate Change: Human Solidarity in a Divided World*. New York: UNDP.

Usman, S. 2010. Planning and National Development. In: S.O. Akande and A.J. Kumuyi (eds), *Nigeria at 50: Accomplishments, Challenges and Prospects*. Ibadan: NISER. pp. 843–870.

Wang, H. and Li, S. 2018. The Development of Think Tanks. In: *Introduction to Social Systems Engineering*. Singapore: Springer. https://doi.org/10.1007/ 978–981–10–7040–2_10.

World Bank. 2007. *World Development Report 2007: The State in a Changing World*. Washington, DC: World Bank.

Yagboyaju, D.A. 2015. Leadership Theory. *Ibadan Journal of Peace and Development*. 5/6: 8–21.

Yagboyaju, D.A. (ed.). 2016. *Reflections on Politics, Governance and Economy in Contemporary Nigeria*. Ibadan: Ibadan University Press.

Yagboyaju, D.A. 2019. Deploying Evidence-Based Research for Socio-Economic Development Policies in Nigeria. *Africa's Public Service Delivery and Performance Review*. Vol. 7, No. 1: 1–9.

Yagboyaju, D.A. 2016. Issues in Elections and Electoral Administration in Nigeria. In: Rasheed Olaniyi and Idayat Hassan (eds), *Democracy in Two Decades, 1999–2019; Reflections on Nation Building and Development in Nigeria*. Ibadan: Swift Publications, pp. 47–69.

Yagboyaju, D.A. 2022. Nigeria: The Imperatives of Internal Security and Development Problems and Prospects. *Conflict Studies Quarterly*. 40: 43–58.

Yagboyaju, D.A. and Okoosi-Simbine, A.T. 2020. Governance and Human Security: How can Nigeria go beyond the rhetoric? *Sociology and Anthropology*. Vol. 8, No. 5: 159–169.

Yagboyaju, D.A. and Simbine, A.T. 2020. Political Finance and the 2019 General Elections in Nigeria. *Journal of African Elections*. Vol. 19, No. 1: 66–91.

8. Think tanks, governance, and development in Africa: the case of Rwanda

Eugenia Kayitesi

INTRODUCTION

Think tanks have been described as groups of experts who engage in research and advocacy in a wide range of areas including social economic policy, politics and governance, the environment, health, agriculture, science and technology (New African Magazine, 2019). The definition of a think tank has often gone beyond non-governmental organization (NGO) think tanks to include government-affiliated research institutes, university research centers, consultancies, informal groups of academics, and individuals who advise governments. Brown et al. (2014) state that think tanks fall mainly into two categories: affiliated or independent think tanks. The affiliated think tanks need a formal affiliation, usually to government or political parties, while independent organizations are autonomous. Both types of think tanks, however, exist to produce rigorous, reliable, and scientific useful research recommendations that will be disseminated to their respective audiences to inform and improve policy development and implementation for the wellbeing of citizens.

Think tanks have been credited for improving policy making and strengthening democratic institutions at local, regional, and international levels. Kimenyi and Datta (2011) argue that while providing policy advice is perhaps their underlying purpose, think tanks can have other purposes too: for instance, legitimizing government or party policies, or existing as a space for debate. Think tanks improve policy making and strengthen democratic institutions around the world through ensuring that research results inform and influence national and regional policy debate. This calls for relevant research agendas to inform decision making through research, policy analysis, and advocacy.

Today, African think tanks are playing a big role in informing global and the continental development programs of the Sustainable Development Goals (SDGs) 2030, the African Agenda 2063, and individual national development programs. Relevant data and policy analysis are empirically key for contributing to effective design and implementation of a country's development program that will harness the country's potential and resources available for sustained socio-economic development.

THE PROLIFERATION OF THINK TANKS IN SUB-SAHARAN AFRICA IN THE 1990s

Governance systems in Sub-Saharan Africa have evolved from colonial systems, where former colonial masters established research centers to enhance the development of primary commodities such as coffee, cotton and tea, which were needed to feed their home industries (Kimenyi and Datta, 2011). A working paper by the Partnership for Social and Governance Research, PASGR (2016) argued that the emergence and development of think tanks in Africa was shaped by the politics of power and external influence. The same paper posits that think tanks in Africa were first invented in the 18th century as brain trusts to solve problems and were mostly set up by the colonial masters to solve the needs of their home populations. Kimenyi and Datta (2011) argue that during the early years of independence, former colonial research institutions were reconfigured to promote growth and development at home, while new governments invested considerable sums of money in expanding state infrastructure including research and development.

After achieving independence, the colonial masters of most Sub-Saharan African countries needed to continue exerting influence over natural resources in their former colonies through neo-colonialism. Therefore, soft power in terms of governance requirements that have accompanied post-independence development aid has often required research and engagement efforts that have made think tanks relevant players in pushing this agenda, knowingly or unknowingly. From the 1980s and 1990s, African countries started undertaking structural changes in different development areas. These changes were hastened by the need for socio-economic growth, and the need for transformation in areas such as agriculture, technology and governance.

The need to put in place appropriate policies and structure favorable for the continent's social economic transformation led to a mushrooming of African think tanks in the period. McGann (2015) contends that, since the 1990s, the continent of Africa has experienced rapid economic growth at an average of 5 percent per annum, making it one of the fastest-growing regions in the world. In this period, most African countries worked hard to create an enabling environment that would reduce prevailing wars and conflicts, and improve their social and economic growth.

There was an emergence of good governance and the opening of public policy in many sub-Saharan African countries, accompanied by an information and technological revolution, the end of autocratic governments in most African states, and the increased complexity and technical nature of policy problems. The need for appropriate policies to manage and implement the new development programs in the African context, with a view to providing well-researched and proven home-grown solutions, hence became paramount, and set to play an important role on the continent. According to McGann (2015), Africa's sustained economic growth, the rise of its middle class, and a growing conviction that the continent has turned a corner, has created demand for high-quality think tanks grounded in African reality, but with access to the global body of knowledge. This was to be achieved through the provision of evidence and knowledge to facilitate and drive the continent's transformation.

Henry Rotich, Kenya's Cabinet Secretary of the National Treasury and planning, in his opening remarks at the African Think Tank Summit in Nairobi (ACBF, 2019), notes that the mushrooming of think tanks in Africa is a recent phenomenon precipitated by the presence of dynamic, political and social reforms and the need for structural adjustment. He further argues that the significant pressure to improve the African governmental policy process and governance in the recent structural adjustment era by most African countries, resulted in the creation of think tanks with the aim of strengthening research and policy linkage critical for Africa's development.

As most of these development state-minded leaders took up the mantle of leadership from post-colonial African leaders that were still largely controlled by former colonisers, the new breed of pan-African leaders in countries such as Rwanda and Ethiopia have demanded a greater say in the course of both their development and governance outcomes. These governments have implemented homegrown solutions, leading to the proliferation of government-aided but independent think tanks that are rooted in analyzing and informing policies through research. The increasing size of governments, the challenge of government-elected officials taking over the mantle of leadership from post-colonial African leaders who were still largely controlled by former colonies and demanded a greater say in national development, globalization, and the growth of state and non-state actors, led to a need for the right data and concise information that would assist the decision makers.

The proliferation of think tanks in Sub-Saharan Africa has been a result of several driving forces, namely: (1) the need for governments and development partners to have research evidence to guide public policy making; (2) efforts from private individuals who saw opportunities to benefit from the proliferation of a number of development projects being implemented by non-governmental organizations, development partners and national governments that needed to support their programs with impact evidence; (3) availability of funding from the Think Tank Initiative, which was to drive both local and development partners, causes in the civil society space that needed research evidence; and (4) communication through the mass media and the internet, increased education levels and increased civil engagement of citizens, which have raised levels of awareness among both rural and urban populations in Sub-Saharan Africa, necessitating the proliferation of think tanks which act as vehicles during engagement between citizens and policy makers.

Despite the continent's potential to spur socio-economic development in the period, the legacy of conflicts, wars, diseases, cultural practices and widely diverse development priorities and economic interests within the African countries still affect the continent's socio-economic growth. This is coupled with rapid population growth, lack of good infrastructure, limited industrialization, pandemic outbreaks such as COVID-19 and other incurable diseases (malaria, HIV, Ebola, and many others), which all still present some of the policy challenges, and call for effective leadership and governance among the African countries. Governance of a complex African continent with complex societies and an unfavorable environment still presents a big challenge to African governments and regional organizations. This therefore calls for informed decision making, and a reduction in the perceptions and fear that lead to challenges of slow policy implementation.

The need to continually implement appropriate policies and structures that are favorable for the continent's social economic transformation, led to the founding of most African think tanks in the period. The African continent needs its own narrative by use of think tanks to create solutions for African problems for its economic growth, grounded in the continent's reality for its transformation. Think tanks therefore are to play an important role of providing knowledge and innovation generation to facilitate the changes taking place in the African development, by providing evidence for policy making and strengthening policy engagement and debate on the continent.

The need for reliable data to inform policy makers on how to address these development challenges became paramount and think tanks were created to provide relevant data to policy makers and to connect them with citizens, experts, students and officials in public, private and civil society, with the aim of providing independent, informed, homegrown solutions. The African think tank agenda should assist Africa's individual states through long-term thinking and reflection, and often bold ideas, based on evidence and research that would change negative impressions about the continent and proffer solutions to persistent issues of wars and conflicts, poverty, unemployment and underemployment, diseases and pandemic outbreaks, that are badly hindering its socio-economic development. African think tanks need to ensure that voices on the continent are raised and heard in the policy making pipeline, hence harnessing issues of inclusivity and partnership nationally, regionally and internationally, and becoming an important platform in sharing knowledge and good practices that support the continent's socio-economic transformation (2018 African Think Tank Summit).

In his keynote address at the opening of the 5th African Think Tank Summit (ACBF, 2018) in Accra, Ken Ofori-Atta, Ghana's Finance Minister argued that, "given the important contributions African thinktanks play on the continent's socio-economic transformation, they need to be trusted, utilized and supported and African governments should mainstream the use of local thinktanks to deliver on their various agendas." He contends that African think tanks make significant contributions in the design, implementation, monitoring, and evaluation of innovative economic and socio-economic policies.

THE PROLIFERATION OF THINK TANKS IN RWANDA

Rwanda is a landlocked country located in the Great Lakes Region of Central Africa, with a dense population of 13.2 million people (in 2022). In the period between 1990 and 1994, the country of Rwanda experienced a devastating war and conflict that culminated in the genocide against its one of the ethnic tribes, the Tutsi in 1994. This genocide against Tutsi claimed close to 1 million people in 100 days, and more than 2 million others fled the country.

The Rwandan conflict had its roots in ethnic tensions arising from colonial tendencies as early as before 1959, where mainly one group of Rwanda's citizens, the Tutsi, were forced outside their country and fled to the neighboring countries of Congo, Uganda, Burundi, Tanzania, and many other African countries, and even beyond. For more than 30 years, this group lived as refugees in the countries of asylum. War and conflict arose when they tried to come back to Rwanda, since the then despotic Rwandan leadership did not allow them to return peacefully. The four years of war and conflict culminated in the 1994 genocide against the Rwandans of the Tutsi origin who were living in the country at the time. This left the country's civil service infrastructure and social structure devastated.

The post-conflict government led by the Rwandan Patriotic Front (RPF) took up the reconstruction and rebuilding of the society's fabric, and uniting and reconciling the Rwandan citizens affected by the deep ethnic hatred and division for more than 30 years. The government embarked on a process of rebuilding and transforming the country from the horrors of war and genocide, into a more stable, secure and peaceful country, with an aim of alleviating extreme poverty and considerably reducing poverty generally. Ambitious but targeted development programs aimed at transforming the country into a middle-income nation by the year 2020.

In 2000, the government of Rwanda launched Vision 2020 with an aim of transforming the country into a knowledge-based middle-income country by 2020 through poverty reduction, comprehensive reduction of health problems, and making the nation united and democratic again. The vision hinged on six interwoven pillars: good governance, an efficient state, skilled human capital, a vibrant private sector, world-class physical infrastructure, and modern agriculture and livestock; all geared towards prospering in national, regional, and global markets.

The implementation of Vision 2020 was driven by: good governance and highly accountable top leadership of the country, well-designed and implementable policies, and inclusion and poverty reduction policies, with gender inclusion becoming a top priority for the government. Today, Rwanda aspires to be a middle-income nation by 2035 and a high-income country by 2050, and this will be attained through a series of Seven Year National Strategies for Transformation (NST). Rwanda is the leading country in Africa for gender equality, with women making up 62 percent of members of Parliament and dominating in many other positions of leadership.

Despite challenges emanating from the COVID-19 pandemic which threatened to push back millions of people into poverty, pro-poor and inclusive policies with a number of home-grown solutions contribute to the country's socio-economic transformation, and poverty reduction in Rwanda is underpinned by the country's strong and accountable governance from the country's top leadership, and high accountability at all levels of both central and local government. Abbot and Mutoro (2014) argue that good governance has been the heart of the country's development strategy, with an aim of creating a sense of national unity and loyalty through an emphasis on one identity, one language, one culture, one history, and one people.

With the reforms to transform the economy and build a stable, democratic, and united Rwanda, demand for evidence-based advice by both professionals and technicians became evident in the public and private sectors and civil society institutions. The need for an independent voice in the policy space, though to a large extent shrinking in many African countries, became paramount in the need to inform the design, implementation, and evaluation of Rwandan policies. This was mainly aimed at ensuring accountability, and effective and efficient implementation of policies, by the country's top leadership.

With Rwanda's history, the chosen development path and the future aspirations by the country's leadership informed the institutional types of think tanks that have emerged over the last 20 years to inform the country's development trajectory. Some of the pioneer think tanks in Rwanda include the Institute of Policy Analysis and Research-Rwanda (IPAR-Rwanda), Never Again Rwanda, the Institute of Legal Practice and Development (ILPD) and the Legal Aid Forum (LAF).

Given the history of the genocide against the Tutsi, Rwanda's efforts to enhance reconciliation, promote peace, justice, and good governance, and heal the wounds of the people, led to think tanks such as Never Again Rwanda which was created to promote the healing of the then fractured society. To further Rwanda's objective of becoming a regional technology and business hub, think tanks such as AIMS emerged to provide intellectual input into information and communication technology (ICT) innovation objectives of the country.

The launch of Vision 2020 and its subsequent strategic implementation strategies by the government of Rwanda resulted in a need for evidence-informed decisions which led to the rise of both independent and affiliated think tank institutions, which were later to play a big role in Rwanda's socio-economic policy and strategy implementation for sustainable development. This is done through comprehensive policy analysis and research that provide evidence to decision makers. Independent think tanks, particularly IPAR-Rwanda and the Institute of Dialogue for Peace, were created to provide a second opinion to policy formulation and implementation based on evidence through research and policy analysis. Ad hoc commissions, though not usually regarded as think tanks (as per McGann, 2019), were created to solve temporary issues and often act as a bridge between the academic and policy making communities and civil society.

CATEGORIZATION OF THINK TANKS BASED ON GEOGRAPHICAL RESEARCH, POLICY ADVOCACY, IDEOLOGICAL AFFILIATIONS OR ORIENTATION

With the need to speed up national economic development, and to address the horrors of the 1994 Tutsi genocide, the government of Rwanda realizes and appreciates the need for reliable data to inform homegrown solutions that address the development challenges of disunity and reconciliation, poverty alleviation, repatriation and resettlement of refugees, Gacaca courts which aim at the promotion of good governance in the country. This has therefore led to setting up a number of affiliated and government research intuitions. Independent think tanks too were established by different stakeholders with an objective of contributing to national development.

Institute of Policy Analysis and Research, IPAR-Rwanda (2008)

The Institute of Policy Analysis and Research IPAR-Rwanda is the leading non-profit, non-governmental, independent research and policy analysis institute in Rwanda. The Institute exists to support the formulation of sound and informed evidence-based public policies through objective analysis and research, and to have maximum impact on policy formulation across the spectrum of national development priorities. It aims to provide evidence in decision making, and a forum for vibrant policy debate on policy issues in the country. IPAR-Rwanda seeks to strengthen the evidence base available to government, civil society and development partners regarding the pressing socio-economic and political issues facing Rwanda.

IPAR-Rwanda also seeks to build the capacity of professionals in policy analysis and research, and to disseminate policy ideas through workshops, panel discussions, and conferences. The Institute was created a few years after the war and genocide against the Tutsi, out of the need to provide evidence for effective policy making and subsequent economic development in Rwanda. The Institute started as early as 2002 under the Ministry of Finance and Economic Planning and was first launched in 2006, with the government of Rwanda making a sizeable funding contribution, but became fully functional in 2008 with full funding by the African Capacity Building Foundation (ACBF). Other donors such as Canada's International Development Research Center (IDRC) later came on board in 2009. Today the Institute survives on project funding and commissioned work mainly from development partners such as the IDRC, the German Development Corporation (GIZ), United Nations Food and Agriculture Organization (FOA), United Nations Population Fund (UNFPA), United Nations Development Programme (UNDP) and commissioned work from the government of Rwanda, private sector and civil society institutions.

IPAR-Rwanda was finally inaugurated in 2008 through the combined efforts of the government of Rwanda's Ministry of Finance and Economic Planning, and development partners including the World Bank, UNDP and others. Initially managed under the Ministry of Finance, IPAR-Rwanda, after securing core funding from the African Capacity Building fund and the Think Tank Initiative which was managed by the International Development Research Center (IDRC), was weaned off government funding in 2011 to become a fully independent think tank. By 2015, funding from IPAR-Rwanda's two biggest core funders, ACBF and the IDRC came to an end.

In 2019, the IDRC funding ended, implying that the think tank had to rely on commissioned research for over 90 percent of its funding. IPAR-Rwanda has stood the test of time and is currently sustainable, with over 90 percent of its project portfolio being commissioned research, while a small portion of the core funding and technical assistance is provided by institutions, project funding donors, and private organizations.

The Institute is governed by a General Assembly (GA) which is the supreme decision making body of the Institute, and the Board of Directors which oversees and monitors the utilization of resources. The Board of Directors composition represents a diversity of stakeholder interests including the government of Rwanda, tertiary institutions, research organizations, civil society, the private sector, and development partners. Day-to-day management of the

Institute is entrusted to the Executive Director, supported by a Director of Research and an Administration and Finance Manager. The Institute has close to 20 in-house researchers with PhD, master's and bachelor's degrees in different fields of specialization, including senior research fellows (SRFs), research fellows (RFs), research assistants, and administrative staff. The Institute also employs a pool of research associates with various skills required, and has a pool of more than 100 research assistants hired as and when they are needed.

The Institute's role has evolved and grown to become a credible development partner in Rwanda by providing high-quality influential and policy relevant timely research, and has developed a rigorous and useful culture of dialogue and debate on policy issues in Rwanda.

Institute of Research and Dialogue for Peace, IRDP (2001)

In the aftermath of genocide, other think tanks emerged to support different development initiatives by the government of Rwanda geared towards the socio-economic development and reconciliation of Rwandans. The Institute of Research and Dialogue for Peace (IRDP) is one of them. IRDP is the leading national non-profit and independent research institute for peace building. It was created in 2001 to support peace and reconciliation efforts after the genocide. Through its work, IRDP strives to encourage the participation and inclusion of all Rwandans in the quest for peace. It places importance on the promotion of open dialogue to create forums of exchange and debate, to generate consensus on key issues, and to create opportunities to share, and learn from, good practices coming from other peace initiatives. It is an independent and neutral space where critical and sensitive issues challenging peace are debated by all categories of Rwandans, aiming to influence positive changes in behavior at the community and national levels, and to inform policies and practice on issues of national interest.

National Council for Science and Technology, NCST (2012)

The National Council for Science and Technology was established in 2012 by the government of Rwanda to provide informed and strategic policy advice on matters pertaining to the development of science, technology, innovation, and research into national development strategies and plans. NCST advises the government on policies, legislation, and regulation in the fields of science, technology, research, and innovation; monitors the implementation of such policies and legislation; advises the government on setting national priorities; regulates science and technology innovation and research, and grants research permits; and manages the National Research and Innovation Fund. The Council also serves as a science and technology think tank for the government in the setting of priorities for the national science and technology innovation research and development agenda.

National Industrial Research and Development Agency, NIRDA (2013)

NIRDA was first established in 2013 to support the diversification of the Rwandan economy, replacing the Institute of Scientific and Technological Research. The NIRDA is a government institution established to support the diversification of the Rwandan economy. It is mandated with a mission to enable a generation of industrial innovators to become competitive through technology monitoring, acquisition, development, and transfer, and applied research.

NIRDA is a service-based institution that provides an array of support services aimed at improving the competitiveness of existing industries in order to increase their export potential, or their potential to undertake import substitution, identifying new subsectors or value chains where investment by the private sector would likely lead to export growth or import substitution.

The institution focuses on the creation, dissemination, and utilization of industrial technology research. The organization monitors the most relevant technologies and expertise nationally, regionally, and internationally to strengthen existing industries and focus on building new ones with a purpose of informing policy and strategic industry-related decision making, and providing firms with the latest reliable data, knowledge, and expertise relevant to technology, market, and scientific information.

Kigali Collaborative Research Centre, KCRC (2016)

KCRC was established on October 5, 2016 with the aim of becoming a leading research organization in Africa dedicated to establishing and facilitating high-quality and diverse research and innovations. It is committed to promoting research and innovations in Africa. Its main objectives are to facilitate research collaboration among researchers, industry, public sector, and non-governmental organizations; to establish a quality research environment following best practices; connect researchers to various research and funding networks locally and internationally; promote projects and innovative solutions through collaborative research; and finally, to impact higher education through training instructors and scholars.

Economic Policy Research Network, EPRN-Rwanda (2018)

EPRN is a forum that brings together researchers and analysts working in economic policy, poverty reduction, and related fields in Rwanda and abroad.

EPRN was established under the umbrella of IPAR-Rwanda to enhance communication and collaboration among these experts for a stronger community of policy practitioners in Rwanda. The research network was formally registered in 2018 as non-governmental organization with a mission of contributing to evidence-based economic policy making by providing high-quality research, building capacity, and creating networking opportunities.

The network supports members in research by providing mentors/supervisors; facilitating researchers to make presentations of their research findings at conferences and other events; and supporting members to publish their research findings. The network further organizes networking events such as policy dialogues on policy issues, research conferences, experts' seminars, and so on. Through events, members of the network have opportunities to meet and exchange ideas with experts from various domains, making business contacts and appointments, exchange job and consultancy-related information, details of study/scholarship opportunities, and so on. EPRN also prepares and delivers demand-driven training to respond to specific needs of institutions.

Other Organizations

Rwanda has other organizations with larger components of research such as the University of Rwanda, Rwanda Governance Board and Rwanda Agricultural Board, Never Again Rwanda, Transparency International, Legal Aid Forum (LAF), and many others with different institutional specific mandates of serving the public interests as independent voices that translate applied and basic research to understandable, reliable and accessible information for policy makers, to inform policy; but whose major objective is not only focused on research and policy analysis.

THE INFLUENCE OF THINK TANKS IN THE GOVERNANCE PROCESS: LEGISLATION, SOCIAL WELFARE PROGRAMS, AND SO ON (SELECTED SPECIFIC CASES)

Despite their operational challenges, think tanks have continued to expand their sphere of influence in Rwanda. They have enabled policy makers and the public to make informed decisions on public policy issues through their rigorous research backgrounds and disciplined analytical approaches, that provide the evidence-based arguments needed for effective decisions and implementation. They provide quality evidence and knowledge that is grounded into local reality to the changes that often happen.

Independent research organizations, including the Institute of Policy Analysis and Research (IPAR-Rwanda) and the Institute of Dialogue for Peace

(IRDP), have continually participated in and contributed to knowledge production that informs different national development strategies. Dissemination of their research results and data has been through organized workshops, panel discussions and conferences which bring together different stakeholders to discuss and analyze development strategies, assess and evaluate the implementation of different policies, and generally provide evidence on most decisions that impact wellbeing for Rwandan citizens.

IPAR-Rwanda in particular has since its establishment contributed to Rwandan policy design, policy implementation, and evaluation, under thematic areas of agriculture, social development, governance, economic growth and transformation, and environment and natural resource management. The Institute has actively engaged with the public and policy makers in examining a wide range of ideas that form the foundation of a country's policies, and has regularly produced reliable and accessible data useful to policy design and implementation. The evidence produced through research and policy analysis further links citizens with the policy makers, civil servants, development partners, civil society organizations, media, and researchers through its annual research conference, workshops, panel discussions, and deliberative forums via radio, social media publications, and monthly email updates.

Rwandan think tanks have further played an important role in informing the global continent development priorities of the SDGs (the 2030 Agenda) and the African Agenda 2063. Previously the Institute of Policy Analysis and Research—Rwanda (IPAR-Rwanda) assessed and rated Rwanda's implementation of the Millennium Development Goals (MDGs), and has also worked with the international organizations of the United States Agency for International Development (USAID), FAO, UNDP, the United Nations Economic Commission for Africa (UNECA), GIZ, UNDP, and others, with the purpose of providing local evidence to the studies that inform their work in Rwanda. A few examples of IPAR's role have been mainly to provide an independent voice and evidence through and policy analysis and evaluation of Rwandan policies based on empirical findings which inform the subsequent design and implementation of new policies. The organisation implemented a three-year project from 2020 to 2023 which aimed at providing timely evidence on business and household performance to inform policy and facilitate the socio-economic recovery from the COVID-19 pandemic in Rwanda. The project has provided up-to-date and relevant information to policy makers on the impact of COVID-19 on businesses and vulnerable households, and has generated and proposed policy solutions to the challenges faced by businesses and vulnerable households in Rwanda.

IPAR-Rwanda is in the process of evaluating the concluded Vision 2020 strategy that guided Rwanda's economic growth and development from 2000 to 2020. It provided a midterm review of the National Strategy for

Transformation (NST1). The National Strategy for Transformation (NST1) is a key document guiding the national development agenda up to 2050. The report informed planning in the Ministry of Finance and Economic Planning and other high government organs.

In 2017, IPAR-Rwanda was commissioned by the government of Rwanda to carry out an independent evaluation of the Seven-Year Government Program (7YGP 2010–2017) which was to inform the design of the National Strategy for Transformation (2017–2024). Three major pillars—good governance and justice; economic development; and social welfare—were transparently and independently evaluated, and findings were submitted to relevant and top decision makers to inform the design of the Rwanda National Strategy for Transformation NSTI (2018–2024) and Vision 2050.

Evaluation of the Rwandan Central and Local Government Performance Contracts

IPAR-Rwanda was commissioned by the Office of the Prime Minister of the Republic of Rwanda to conduct an independent evaluation of the Annual Rwandan Central and Local Government Performance Contracts, also known as the Imihigo, between 2015 and 2018. The overall objective of Imihigo is to ensure accountability, and to measure annual performance of the central and local governance entities and their contribution to national development. The findings further informed the design of the subsequent performance contracts.

Research on Strengthening Administrative Justice in Rwanda

In 2019, IPAR-Rwanda in collaboration with the University of Massachusetts Boston (UMass) conducted research on 'Strengthening Rwandan Administrative Justice (SRAJ)' with the aim to understand how administrative justice is administered in Rwanda, and the perceptions of the people. Three areas—land expropriation; public and private labor; and public procurement—were empirically studied.

Information flows in decision making: the case of Girinka and the Vision 2020 Umurenge Programme (VUP).

IPAR-Rwanda in collaboration with Palladium Ikiraro cy'Iterambere imple-mented a research project on 'Information Flows in Decision Making', from the citizens to the local authorities and vice versa. The project used Girinka, which is a Kinyarwanda word meaning 'have a cow', and the Vision 2020 Umurenge Programme (VUP), which are extreme poverty reduction strategies that the Government of Rwanda uses to drive people out of poverty. The objective of the research project was to assess channels of communication for effective citizen participation in the planning, budgeting, design, monitoring, and evaluation, feedback and reform of policy and service delivery in relation to these strategies.

Think tanks further play an important role in the dissemination of their research findings, views and opinions through publications of papers and reports, websites, social media and newspaper articles. Rwandan think tanks, however, need to strengthen their publications and communication roles to contribute to evolving socio-economic policies aimed at the economic transformation of the country. Since the inception of most of the Rwandan think tanks, a lot of work has been done and documented. There is a need for increased research uptake by the public. There are still limitations in the communication and dissemination of research findings in the media, panel discussions, and public debates, due to limited funding. Think tanks connect policy makers with relevant data analysts, experts, and scholars, which enriches and informs decisions and create a robust evidence base on which to base policy decisions that positively impact the lives of citizens.

IPAR-Rwanda in particular has played a big role in equipping the Rwandan workforce in key institutions with skills in policy analysis and research, encouraging a culture of debate and dialogue on policy issues through its annual research conference workshops, panel discussions, publications, policy briefs, press releases, advocates, and articles that attract decision makers in both public and private institutions at national and regional levels. Think tanks also provide an opportunity to researchers to participate in local, regional, and international conferences for networking and knowledge sharing purposes, but also for knowledge exchange and debates on major pressing issues affecting the continent.

IPAR-Rwanda disseminates its research findings through local, regional, and international newspapers—*New Times Rwanda*, the *East African*, the *Independent*—the CIGI website (Canada), and through monthly email updates to over 900 stakeholders, the African Research portal, and the IPAR website and its monthly newsletter that is shared to all stakeholders in the region and beyond. Rwandan think tanks have further become a 'go-to' institution for many development institutions and international think tanks, universities, and consultants visiting or based in Rwanda.

IPAR-Rwanda has worked and collaborated on project implementation with the universities of Aberdeen, Michigan, and Massachusetts, and the University of Rwanda, on a number of policy research projects that have informed policy and design, implementation, and evaluation. These contribute to stronger and more impactful decisions that usually have a positive impact on the wellbeing of Rwandan citizens.

Think tanks build strong relations, networks, and partnerships with key decision makers, parliamentarians, and key opinion leaders, civil society, and the media, both inside and outside Rwanda. IPAR has built some networks and partnerships, such as the Economic Policy Research Network (EPRN) a network started under a joint partnership of IPAR-Rwanda, the World Bank, National Institute of Statistics (NISR), Ministry of Finance and Economic Planning (MINECOFIN), and the National University of Rwanda.

IPAR's growing reputation and influence has been widening both locally and internationally. The institute is commissioned by the development partners community, USAID, the former Overseas Development Agency (ODI; now the Foreign, Commonwealth and Development Office, FCDO), International Development Centre (IDRC), the African Capacity Building Foundation (ACBF), the United Nations Children's Fund (UNICEF), FAO, the former UK Department for International Development (DfID), ActionAid, UNFPA, OXFAM, UNDP, GIZ, Trademark East Africa (TMEA), Southern Voices Network, and many others. IPAR-Rwanda, like many other think tanks, is often called upon by key government officials and development partners to participate in or lead policy discourse, and to undertake and disseminate policy research. In 2015, IPAR-Rwanda moderated a high-level workshop on accelerating growth in Rwanda between the government ministers and development partners. Previously, in 2014, IPAR-Rwanda moderated three workshops funded by DfID on urbanization in Rwanda, and was nominated to sit on the steering committee that designed the Rwandan NST1 and Vision 2050.

CHALLENGES CONFRONTING THINK TANKS AND STRATEGIES TO ADDRESS THEM

The literature has indicated that the output for many African think tanks remains on the shelves and rarely makes it into the public space, and their research uptake by policy makers remains low. According to McGann (2019), African think tanks are faced with four types of challenges: competitiveness, resource, organizational and technological challenges. Despite the continent's dire need for evidence, and the major role played by think tanks in national development, most African think tanks have remained minimally utilized as strategic partners, and their contribution to decision making has continually remained low. This is despite their contribution in responding to policy challenges in their individual countries, and at regional and global levels. Research in Rwanda is still lacking in terms of funding, capacity in terms of skills, rich experience, and quality. This therefore calls for strong support by all stakeholders in terms of financial and human resources, quality, and the organizational development and sustainability of think tanks. The Rwandan policy environment is favorable for the development of think tanks, since the country's policy makers are eager for evidence-informed policies and to hear from independent voices which support the individual accountability and quick implementation of national development policies.

The establishment of the National Council for Science and Technology in 2017, and a US$30 million National Research and Innovation Fund (NRIF) in 2018, filled significant gaps in the research system (Fosci et al., 2019). According to the report, however, its impact is yet to be felt. The report further notes that the research production in Rwanda has been limited by a lack of domestic funding and a shortage of researchers in the country. Rwandan think tanks are constrained by a lack of diversified funding sources, weak institutional capacity, inadequate capacity to influence or shape public policies, lack of capacity and funding to disseminate their findings, and lack of enough primary sources of information. Other challenges include lack of human, financial, and material resources, dependence on single donors, and lack of synergy between national and regional think tanks.

Shrinking of Foreign Funding Opportunities

Rwandan think tanks, like many others on the continent, have been affected by a lack of enough funding due to shrinking funding opportunities from multilateral, bilateral, and international funding organization. Most donors recently withdrew their grant support from think tanks and have instead focused their support on governments only. This is a major challenge not only for Rwandan think tanks but also across the African continent. In the early 1980s and 1990s, most think tanks were established with funding from the World Bank and ACBF, Canada's International Development Center (IDRC), and other philanthropies and international organizations and NGOs. Ten years later, the donor funding began to shrink, and think tanks were left to sustain themselves on their own. This was despite the rapid economic growth the continent was undergoing, and the need to put up appropriate policies and structures that were favorable for the continent's social economic transformation in the 1990s. The resource mobilization challenges therefore threaten think tanks' quality of research and institutional sustainability. Think tanks must work hard to mobilize enough resources to sustain their performance, and to remain true to their mandate of informing policy and decision making of policy makers through research and policy analysis, and to be able to fully contribute to their respective national development agendas.

The biggest funding hit for IPAR-Rwanda, like many other African think tanks, was a rapid drop in core funding by the African Capacity Building Foundation (ACBF), and later the closure of the International Development Centre (IDRC) Think Tank Initiative, both of which had been funding operations for almost a decade. This has left think tanks depending on project funding and commissioned work, with short-term and insecure funding. IPAR-Rwanda has been able to sustain its operations through project funding. Today, most other think tanks are relying on funding from their governments, which damages their total independence. Some governments are not eager to use data that is not sanctioned by the state. There has been a mushrooming of consultancy firms which disguise themselves as think tanks, and hence the need to differentiate consultancy reports and reports produced based on empirical evidence. Think tanks must remain focused on their research institutional mandate and their research agendas, if they are to remain relevant and true to their mandate of improving policies of concern to the public's wellbeing.

Weak Institutional Capacity

The need to secure sustainable funding to respond to their institutional mandate, and retain independence from hidden interests of different stakeholders becomes key in the performance of think tanks. Lack of such independence weakens the institutional, organizational, and individual capacities of think tanks to bridge the knowledge gap and produce timely quality research to inform policy. The role of research institutions has never been paid attention to. The literature has shown that donors' financial support at times shifts think tank research agendas, and leaves their work questionable in terms of the country's policy relevance. Since 2015, core funding to research was stopped; and few donors are willing to give grants for long-term strategic objectives, and few allow project funding with overhead costs. Less has been discussed in the development agenda, and contribution of think tanks, though immense, has not been well articulated within this agenda. Literature has shown that most think tanks in Africa are very capable, but at the same time insecure, and their space for rigorous research, debate, and dialogue in the policy space is shrinking. Most decision makers prefer to co-opt researchers and experts rather than to engage in public discussions.

Few Qualified Researchers

The country has very few qualified researchers: PhD holders with the experience to conduct rigorous research are still very low in number. The few that there are in the country are highly competitive, and hired by government, universities, and better-paying development partner institutions. Others opt for self-employment as individual consultancies after gaining enough experience and knowledge of the local market. This affects productivity and the organizational capacity to conduct high-quality, relevant, and timely research, and the capacity to engage and communicate. Think tanks in Rwanda are faced with an inability to recruit, retain, and build research capacity. This challenge, however, is addressed by the fact that institutions opt to hire and use research associates in the market, who are only hired on a project basis for sustainability purposes.

Limited Women's Participation

A bigger challenge of African think tanks is limited women's participation. The continent has fewer women researchers who are likely to invest in their local communities and not at policy level. Even at policy levels, the number of women researchers is still low. Africa cannot therefore fully develop, given less inclusivity of women and underrepresentation of more than half of its population in the development.

Limited Access to Credible Data

Additional challenges facing thinks tanks include limited access to credible data to inform policy making which is accentuated by funding difficulties for core research and reliance on traditional funders whose funding has been shrinking, and finally closed down in 2015 and 2017 for most African think tanks.

Balancing Core Funded Research Projects with Commissioned Projects

Think tank performance and effectiveness is also affected by lack of interest from state funding. Since ACBF and IDRC grants came to an end, the majority of affiliated think tanks now survive on state funding for continued institutional operations. This sometimes makes it hard for them to remain completely autonomous, due to lack of their own funding, and further leads to unreliable and compromised data. Independent non-governmental think tanks have continued to rely on commissioned work and short-term small project funding, as opposed to institutional contributions from their traditional donors, which limits effective implementation of their research agenda and limits their level of influence on policy. Their research uptake is further hindered by mistrust from policy makers who deem think tanks as untrustworthy.

Think tank influence on policy is further faced with limited time allocated to research. Most of think tank researchers' time is allocated to fundraising and resource mobilization through commissioned work to support their daily operations and staff salaries, and for sustainability purposes. They face increased competition from advocacy organizations, consultancy firms, law firms, and other non-governmental organizations. Decreased funding creates a more competitive environment rather than a collaborative one. Think tanks have continually been faced with increased competition from for-profit think tanks, consultancies, and law firms, which have continually acted as platforms for proactive thinkers who push for big ideas.

Government institutions and commissions, and universities too, continue to provide data and research which policy makers rely on for decision making. Effective communication among African think tanks results in limited influence in policy making and capacity building.

CONCLUSION AND RECOMMENDATIONS

Traditional think tanks must innovate if they are to survive and stay true to their mandate. Think tanks need to draw from their unique power to convene thinkers from across the pollical spectrum to deliberate on and contribute to major policy issues. They need to invest heavily in the design and implementation of systems and procedures necessary to safeguard the integrity and independence of the work they produce. Any think tank funding, whether grant, project, or commissioned funding, should be able to support think tank mandate and promote innovations with respect to policy research and analysis.

There is a need to strengthen the linkage between think tanks and policy makers through increased communication and information sharing via social media and other modern communication avenues. They should invest in the design and implementation of systems and procedures necessary to safeguard the integrity and independence of the work they produce. Think tanks should obtain enough capacity through training on policy making, and develop strategic engagement with policy makers. They need to create creative avenues to attract funds, and partner with other think tanks to produce variable data, engage with policy makers at all stages while carrying out research, and offer independent and accurate analyses to help the public understand the increasing complexity in the policy environment. Think tanks need to reaffirm their core focus on fewer ideas, and develop outreach strategies to bring their ideas to the attention of decision makers, if they are to influence policy change and impact the lives of citizens.

Governments and development partners should protect the status and the role of independent think tanks as vital pillars for national development through providing indispensable evidence for policy making ideas, to support evident decision making; and should explore a favorable environment of African think tanks to make a difference in tackling major issues facing the continent, and further explore how to develop global multidisciplinary solutions to address the think tank crisis in Africa. The world of research has traditionally been influenced by Africa's relationship with Europe. However, think tanks should encourage South–South partnerships rather than the usual model of Northern partner subcontracting African partners, to be able to provide solutions and increase the favorable environment for African think tanks to make a difference and tackle challenges facing the continent.

Concerning the challenge of think tank funding, there is need for them to organize their available resources in the most efficient and productive way, and to learn how to respond in a timely manner to the context factors that are beyond their institutional control. Forces beyond think tanks' sphere of influence include politics, the role of donors, the country level of economic development; all impact their influence. Think tanks need to transform their funding into organizational development grants that should support critical areas of research quality, and strengthen capacity at individual, organizational, and institutional levels, in order to challenge their competitors in the market including universities, consultancy firms, government commissions, and individual researchers. This should be through defining their research agenda and their products, and sticking to producing quality policy recommendations, obtained through rigorous, relevant, and quality research, that policy makers implement.

Think tanks need to be strategic in their stakeholder engagements through engagement with companies that develop highly collaborative, inclusive, and innovative engagement strategies that offer mutual benefits and help to improve sustainability performance. They should extend their target audiences beyond formal policy makers to reach other critical decision makers and agenda setters: informal leaders in the public sphere, the private sector, and the broader civil society. Think tanks need to retain their independence in order to be truly credible influencers of policy, and trusted by civil society as a channel for dialogue. They should have a clear mission and vision that is achievable. Maintaining autonomy may be challenging when donor financing is the main source of income, but it is important to move from a donor–recipient relationship to one of partnership.

Think tanks' sustainability is connected to their performance, and only think tanks that produce high-quality and relevant advice remain in demand. However, many think tanks are still in their early stages of development and will require external financial support until they can be independent. It is also important to diversify the sources of funding. Ultimately, think tanks need to take full responsibility for their funding decisions, and not to blame a funding agency for coercing their direction. If the vision of the funding agency differs from the objectives of the think tank, the think tank should have the strength to walk away from the funds.

Ensuring financial sustainability through the creation of dedicated units for resource mobilization creates innovative ways to mobilize resources and ensure financial security that is important for sustainability. These units should design projects with funding from government and international donors, introduce a sustainability account that sets aside money raised through projects, and reduce operational costs by owning their office facilities. Today, IPAR owns office facilities which it obtained by using rental to pay a mortgage facility. Think tanks should further move from narrow focus on poverty alleviation to the inclusive structural transformation agenda; should mobilize resources through offering executive training in research and policy; should create partnerships with major regional think tanks, Northern universities, and consulting firms; and reframe their research work to stay aligned with national development strategies.

Think tanks should work to ensure that their research results are applied to policy making, providing a deeper understanding of the local context over a wide range of issues. They should continually scan the environment in order to predict changes that would call for adaptation. Think tanks should effectively communicate and engage in marketing themselves; they should also resist building their organization around any one individual.

Finally, think tanks should adapt to the rapid development of technology to enhance visibility and impact and reach policy makers beyond the traditional academic culture of publishing. They should be effective at communicating research results by playing a critical role in analyzing social media information, and fostering open dialogue that enables researchers from a wide range of backgrounds, expertise, interests, and experiences to exchange knowledge and ideas with decision makers. Think tanks should strive to have intellectual autonomy in order to earn credibility; they should understand other organizations; and should be responsive to African development needs.

African think tanks should aspire to become centers of excellence by maintaining a diversity of financial sources, providing a catalytic role in policy debates, and playing a key role in setting the policy agenda for both African issues and Africa's engagement in the global economy. By placing Africa at the center of their agendas, think tanks can better position Africa to the world, offering bold ideas and an optimism about the future, and change the prevailing pessimistic impressions about the continent.

This can only be attained when think tanks do the following:

1. Understand their country's political context and policy making process (know where power really resides), understand perspectives of stakeholders with regard to issues and challenges facing individual countries.
2. Encourage face-to-face exchanges, to help build relationships.
3. Build interest in research work, and create advocates to market it.
4. Develop regular channels of communication (for example, a regular newsletter or monthly email updates); and understand perspectives of stakeholders with regard to issues and challenges facing Africa's respective countries: what is the major decision maker and the focal point which think tanks try to influence?

5. Engage with government to increase demand for evidence-based decision making; help in empowering policy makers to own evidence, and build relationships and close information gaps.

In Rwanda, it is easy to meet key decision makers informally and formally. However, think tanks should target not only policy makers, but rather the whole population, for public conversations and dialogues, and hence to strengthen dissemination of research findings at all levels through radio, television, skits, and focused discussions with citizens and policy makers. These should bring together policy makers and beneficiaries who are citizens.

REFERENCES

Abbott, P. and A. Mutoro (2014) Using Action Research to Build Capacity at the Institute for Policy Analysis and Research (IPAR), Rwanda. In M. Saleem (Ed.) *Action Research and Organizational Capacity Building: Journeys of change in Southern Think Tanks* (pp. 78–104). Lahore: Sang-e-Meel Publications.

African Capacity Building Foundation (ACBF) (2017) African Think Tanks and Industrialization in Africa—Report of the Africa Think Tank Summit. https:// www .acbfpact .org/ sites/ default/ files/ COMMUNIQUE %25202017 ,A fricaThink TankSummit.pdf&ved=2a.

African Capacity Building Foundation (ACBF) (2018) The 5th AFRICA THINK TANK SUMMIT on Tackling Africa's Youth Unemployment Challenge: Innovative Solutions from Think Tanks, https:// elibrary .acbfpact.org/ acbf/ collect/ acbf/ index/ assoc/ 5th%20Africa%20Think%20Eng.pdf

African Capacity Building Foundation (ACBF) (2019) The 6th Think Tank summit, Accra, Ghana, April 26. https:// www .acbf -pact .org/ media/ news/ 6th -africa -think -tank-summit.

Aiyede, E.R. and Muganda, B. (2023). Conclusion: Towards Excellence in Research, Learning and Teaching Public Policy. In E.R. Aiyede and B. Muganda (eds), *Public Policy and Research in Africa* (pp. 267–270). Cham: Palgrave.

Brown, E., A. Knox, C. Tolme, M.K. Gugerty, S. Kosack, and A. Fabrizo (2014) *Linking Think Tank Performance, Decisions, and Context*. Washington, DC: Results for Development Institute.

Fosci, M., L. Loffreda, A. Chamberlain and N. Naido (2019) Assessing the needs of the research system in Rwanda, Report for the SRIA programme. Report commissioned by: The UK Department for International Development. https:// assets .publishing .service .gov .uk/ media/ 5ef4a d7886650c1 295cb5ebb/ NA _report_Rwanda _ _Dec _2019_Heart_.pdf.

Ian, C. (2015) Review of Five South Africa Based Think Tanks Supported by Sida. https://cdn.sida.se/publications/files/sida61904en-review-of-five-south-africa-based -think-tanks-supported-by-sida---final-report.pdf.

Kimenyi, S.M and A. Datta (2011). *Think tanks in sub-Saharan Africa How the political landscape has influenced their origins*. London: Overseas Development Institute.

Laakso, L. (2021). The social science foundations of public policy in Africa. In G. Oyanga (ed) *Routledge Handbook of Public Policy in Africa* (pp. 23–33). London and New York: Routledge.

Malunda, D. and L. Musana (2012) Report for the African Centre for Economic Transformation (ACET). Kigali, Rwanda. https://opendocs.ids.ac.uk/opendocs/bitstream/handle/20.500.12413/7153/Rwanda%20case%20study%20on%20economic%20transformation.pdf?sequence=3&isAllowed=y (accessed February 24, 2024).

McGann, J.G. (2009) The Global Go to Think Tanks. Philadelphia, PA: University of Pennsylvania. https://repository.upenn.edu/entities/publication/391112e7-ef51-4c4f-ae21-c1dfe77d861f.

McGann, J.G. (2014) Global Go to Think Tank Index Report. Philadelphia, PA: University of Pennsylvania. https://www.ecologic.eu/sites/default/files/news/2015/2014-global-go-to-think-tank-index-22012015_1.pdf.

McGann, J.G. (2015) 2015 Africa Think Tank Summit Report: The Rise of Africa's Think Tanks: Practical Solutions to Practical Problems, https://core.ac.uk/download/pdf/76389695.pdf.

McGann, J.G. (2016) The Fifth Estate: Think Tanks, Public Policy, and Governance. Washington, D.C.: Brookings Institution Press.

McGann, J.G. (2019) 2018 Global Go To Think Tank Index Report. Philadelphia, PA: University of Pennsylvania. https://repository.upenn.edu/server/api/core/bitstreams/d9a3c231-2d8b-47ed-83d5-3fbdf868d4e4/content.

McGann, J.G. (2020) 2019 Global Go To Think Tank Index Report. Philadelphia, PA: University of Pennsylvania. https://www.bruegel.org/sites/default/files/wp-content/uploads/2020/01/2019-Global-Go-To-Think-Tank-Index-Report.pdf.

McGann, J.G. and K. Weaver (eds) (2000) *Think-Tanks and Civil Society: Catalysts for Ideas and Action*. New Brunswick, NJ: Transaction Publishers.

New African Magazine. (2019). Insight: What role do African think tanks play in development, September 22, https://newafricanmagazine.com/category/focus-unga-special-report.

Partnership for African Social and Governance Research (PASGR) (2016). Think Tank–University Relations in Sub-Saharan Africa. A Synthesis Report on 10 Country Studies. Nairobi: Partnership for African Social and Governance Research. https://www.pasgr.org/wp-content/uploads/2016/05/Synthesis-Paper_Think-Tank-University-Relations-in-Sub-Saharan-Africa.

Thorat, S., A. Dixit, and S. Verma (eds) (2018). *Strengthening Policy Research: Role of Think Tank Initiative in South Asia*. Delhi: SAGE

9. Think tanks in Senegal: working to inform and influence national (and regional) public policies

Ibrahima Hathie, Elias Ayuk and Cheikh Oumar Ba

INTRODUCTION

In the complex modern society with many actors and diverging interests, the ultimate objective of public policy is to reconcile market forces and the optimum well-being of the people. In addition, public policy aims to enhance social justice, while serving as an arbiter for the rivalry between economic, social and political actors. In the context of the Sustainable Development Goals (SDGs) Agenda 2030 that aims to 'leave no one behind', carefully designed public policies have become more relevant today than ever before. The African Union's Agenda 2063 also highlights the importance of evidence and public policies. Brand (2013) underscores the fact that public policy must be seen 'in relation to the heterogenous structures within the state itself; the heterogenous structures of society; and the functions in reproducing the state itself and society'. In sum, public policies strive to level the playing field for all actors.

There is an emerging consensus that public policies needed to improve the working of the market and ensure that societal equity is based on and/ or informed by solid evidence. Some have argued that the potential of public policy to attain its main objectives is conditioned on the availability of robust, credible, timely and relevant evidence (Phoenix et al., 2019; Goldman and Pabari, 2021a). Others (Mayne et al., 2018), posit that evidence, while necessary, may not be a sufficient condition for public policy making. Goldman and Pabari (2021b) summarize some findings which show that the use of evidence for public policy making remains a major challenge. Evidence from South Africa indicates that although 45 per cent of senior managers desired to use evidence in public policymaking, just 9 per cent were able to put this into practice (Cronin and Sadan, 2015). The major sources were informal rather than rigorous sources of evidence. Goldman et al. (2021) reported that between 40 and 50 per cent of managers in Benin, Uganda and South Africa did not use evidence frequently in their public policy making. At the international level, only about 15 per cent of results from health research is being used; during the Obama administration, only about 1 per cent of government spending was informed by evidence (Bridgeland and Orszag, 2013). In the United Kingdom, only four out of 21 government departments could provide information about the status and whereabouts of the evidence from their commissioned research (Sedley, 2016).

During the COVID-19 pandemic, there has been renewed interest in letting science speak for itself, as epitomized by the United States administration's emphasis on political gain rather than on science. Diawara (2020) shows that think tanks in Africa played a significant role in informing policies in response to the COVID-19 pandemic. There are numerous examples of research informing health policies (Naude et al., 2015; Ongolo-Zogo et al., 2014; Agyapong and Adjei, 2008; Ellen et al., 2018; Koduah et al., 2015; Liverani et al., 2013; Ridde and Yameogo, 2018; Sombie et al., 2017; Uneke et al., 2020; Vecchione and Parkhurst, 2015), and in agriculture (Zougmoré et al., 2019; Partey et al., 2018).

The broad acceptance of evidence as a key component to making policy has seen the emergence of initiatives, spearheaded by governments and development partners, aimed at generating evidence. This has led to the establishment of research centres of excellence[1] and a proliferation of think tanks. There has been increased support provided to African think tanks (HF, 2018) in recent years. Several development partners, such as the Hewlett Foundation, Bill & Melinda Gates Foundation and the Canadian International Development Research Centre (IDRC), have invested considerable resources in supporting think tanks and research institutions. Over the past three decades, IDRC has attached high importance to the policy relevance of its support. Several Secretariats that the Centre established developed strategies to strengthen the capacity of research institutions to undertake research that informed policy. In the 1990s, the Secretariat for Institutional Strengthening of Economic Research in Africa (SISERA) provided support to research institutions to carry out policy-relevant research. The Micro Impacts of Macroeconomic Adjustment Policies (MIMAP) project, the Poverty and Economic Policy Network (PEP) and recently the multi-donor Think Tank Initiative, just to name a few, all had as an anchor, capacitating researchers and research institutions in developed countries to undertake research that informed public policy making. The work undertaken within these networks helped policy makers in understanding the extent of poverty and the profile of the vulnerable groups. This information is relevant in designing social protection measures.

The landscape of think tanks in Africa engaged in generating evidence shows a remarkable diversity. Broadly speaking, these can be classified in five categories: independent (non-profit), university-affiliated policy research centre, state-affiliated, corporate-affiliated, and political party-affiliated (McGann, 2018). The extent to which a specific think tank can inform public policy making can be affected by typology. Government-affiliated thinks tanks might work directly on an issue that will immediately inform public policy. Non-government-affiliated research institutions might inform or influence policies through co-creation of research outputs with public sector actors and building coalitions with relevant stakeholders.

The generation of evidence does not necessarily mean that it will be taken up in the policy formulation process; and when taken up, there is no guarantee that the policy will be implemented as required. Two relevant and fundamental questions are whether the right evidence is being generated, and whether the people who need it are aware of it (Ayuk and Marouani, 2007). There is also the question of capacity to use evidence; do policy makers have experience with home-grown research and evaluation designed to fit their purposes (Carden, 2009)? The proof of the pudding, as they say, is in the eating, which raises another pertinent question that is the key to uptake: is there any evidence of the link between research and policy making? (Ayuk and Marouani, 2007). The answers to these questions can pinpoint the challenges of evidence use, but more importantly point to opportunities for further improving the use of evidence.

These issues have been extensively explored in the past (see Ayuk and Marouani, 2007; Carden, 2009; Parkhurst, 2017; Goldman and Pabari, 2020). While some insights have been gained from a growing body of research, including lessons from many case studies, the challenges remain. Indeed, Parkhurst (2017) points out that although there has been a proliferation of interest in the use of evidence in policy making, most studies have failed to engage with the political nature of decision making and how this influences the way evidence is used (or misused) within political areas. Furthermore, policy and political dynamics continue to evolve. For example, UNICEF (2017) points out that the emergence of China as a key development player, with less emphasis on evidence, is displacing Western donors, who had put evidence at the centre of policy making. New challenges are emerging, for example, the COVID-19 pandemic, that called for a revisiting of the question to further explore how to improve evidence generation and its uptake in policy making. Therefore, a constant revisiting of this topic is warranted, especially as resources become scarce, while expectations from citizens continue to rise. Carden (2009) notes that events happen which create opportunities for the uptake of evidence. These include moments of crisis, creating demand for evidence; and the emergence of new technologies that create new ways of exploring questions, and consequently new opportunities for the use of evidence. Seizing the moment, however, will require well-prepared researchers and a robust evidence ecosystem.

This chapter provides evidence on the contribution of think tanks in Senegal in informing and influencing public policy in the country, and in the West Africa region in general. The chapter illustrates with specific examples of public policies related to economic governance that have been informed by think tanks in Senegal. Following this introductory section, the next section examines the landscape of research institutions or think tanks involved in research to inform public policy. The chapter then presents selected case studies of examples where think tanks in Senegal have informed public policy. The challenges and opportunities for research institutions to effectively inform public policies are examined. The challenges and opportunities provided here are not unique to the think tanks in Senegal. The final section concludes the chapter and identifies further research that might be necessary for an improved understanding of the potential role of think tanks in public policy making.

THINK TANKS LANDSCAPE IN SENEGAL

Think tanks are better known in Anglo Saxon countries where they appeared, especially during the Second World War when military jargon employed the term to indicate a safe place to discuss plans and strategies. Although most independent think tanks in Senegal emerged at the beginning of 2000 (Ndiaye, 2018), as early as 1973 the Council for the Development of Social Science Research in Africa (CODESRIA) – a pan-African institute also serving Senegal – was created. The emergence of the think tanks reflected the democratic opening that allowed for the coming to power of different governments. Very quickly, think tanks developed and intellectual debates emerged. This culminated in the launch at the Institut Sénégalais de Recherche Agronomique (ISRA) – the national agricultural research institution – of the Bureau d'Analyses Macro-Economiques (BAME) Tuesdays,[2] which was a space for exchanges between political actors, researchers and civil society leaders to discuss the results generated by research, to formulate recommendations for decision makers. At the same time, civil society actors gathered around the non-governmental organization (NGO) Enda Graf Sahel to launch the Circle of Interest on Rural Development (CIDR).

The combination of these different initiatives led to the establishment in 2004 of a think tank with an interest in the outlook of agriculture and rural development, the Initiative Prospective Agricole et Rurale (IPAR). The momentum continued in 2008, thanks to a change from institutional membership to including membership of independent individuals, and the opportunity of the Think Tank Initiative (TTI) coordinated by IDRC.[3] Indeed, if at the beginning IPAR brought together the Conseil national de concertation et de coopération des ruraux / National Council for Concertation and Rural Cooperation (CNCR), ISRA, the Direction de l'analyse de la prévision et de la statistique (DAPS) and Enda Graf, with the technical support of the Swiss Cooperation, its independence really began in 2008 with the creation of the IPAR Association. The Consortium for Economic and Social Research (CRES), like IPAR, has also benefited from this context of growth of independent policy research institutions.

A mapping of think tanks in Senegal (Ndiaye, 2018) undertaken to inform the creation of a Senegalese think tanks network (SENRTT) identified three main categories. These are:

- Independent think tanks: independent from interest groups or donors and autonomous in their operations regardless of funding opportunities. IPAR, CRES and the Center for Research on Political Economy (CREPOL) fall under this category.
- University-affiliated or university think tanks: policy research centres based at the university. The Centre de recherches économiques appliquées (CREA), Consortium régional pour la recherche en économie générationnelle (CREG) and Centre de Recherche en Economie et Finance Appliquées de Thiès (CREFAT) are examples of such think tanks.
- Government-affiliated think tanks: part of government organizations and mostly financed and supported by the government. The Centre d'études de politiques pour le développement (CEPOD) at the Ministry of Finance, BAME and Bureau de Prospective Economique (BPE) are examples of a government-affiliated think tank in Senegal. The African Capacity Building Foundation (ACBF) has over the past 15 years provided substantial support to CEPOD.

Table 9.1 summarizes the types and focus areas of the work of the think tanks in Senegal. It is evident that these thematic areas are related to the country's development agenda.

The creation of the network of think tanks in Senegal (SENRTT) stemmed from the desire to contribute to the development of an evidence ecosystem to promote consultation between independent think tanks, and to better contribute to impacting upon public policies. The initiative started in 2017 from three institutions: an independent think tank (IPAR), a government-affiliated think tank (BPE) and a civil society think tank (Environnement, Développement et Action dans le Tiers Monde, ENDA TM). The cartography presented during the celebration of Think Tanks Day opened the reflection on the identity, typology, and the challenges to be taken up. These challenges include the turnover of researchers, the low level of diversification of funding, dependence

Table 9.1   *Areas of focus of selected think tanks in Senegal*

Think tank	Type	Areas of focus
BAME	Government-affiliated	Natural resources management and governance; forecasting, monitoring and evaluation; impacts of policies, projects, and technologies; functioning and dynamics of agricultural exploitations; professionalization of value chains and market regulation.
BPE	Government-affiliated	Monitoring and evaluation of public policies; forecasting.
CEPOD	Government-affiliated	Economy; development; growth; competitiveness; formulation of public policy and development strategies.
CREFAT	University-affiliated	Demographic dividend; finance and development; generational economics; social and economic policy; and digital economics.
CREA	University-affiliated	Economic policy; poverty analysis
CREG	University-affiliated	Generational economics; demographic dividend; social protection; and aging.
CREPOL	Independent non-profit	Political economy
CRES	Independent non-profit	Agriculture; education and health; poverty analysis; gender and equity; resilience to climate change; globalization, regional integration, and local development; information and innovation; and business law.
ENDA	Independent non-profit/Civil society	Diverse areas covering natural resources management and social policies.
GESTES	University-affiliated	Human rights; land tenure; food security; migration; governance; peace and security; gender-based violence; reproductive health.
LARTES	University-affiliated	Development policy analysis and governance; evaluation of projects and programmes on education, health, social protection, local languages, and training.
IPAR	Independent non-profit	Youth employment and migration, climate change, natural resources governance and land tenure, structural transformation of agriculture.

Source: Ndiaye (2018).

on donors, uptake of research results by policy makers, and the distinction between research and consultancy.

At the subregional level, several initiatives have been launched which have involved think tanks from Senegal. In 2016, with the support of IDRC, a network known as Wattnet was launched. The network consists of a consortium of think tanks established in their respective countries, mobilizing ten research and policy advocacy organizations. The constituent general assembly was held on the sidelines of the conference on 'Transforming West Africa for Inclusive Development'. The consortium consists of four Francophone institutions – Centre d'Études, de Documentation et de Recherches Économiques et Sociales (CEDRES), CRES, Centre ivoirien de recherche économique et sociale (CIRES) and IPAR – and five Anglophone institutions: the Centre for Population and Environmental Development (CPED), Centre for the Study of Economies in Africa (CSEA), African Heritage, International Distance Education Centre (IDEC) and the Institute of Economic Affairs (IEA). Wattnet aims to create a synergetic, coordinated, and concerted approach to research on policies and above all to strengthen the capacities of think tanks in the process of developing sub-regional public policies.

The network of the West African Economic and Monetary Union (WAEMU) think tanks was created in 2017 with the technical and financial support of WAEMU. It brings together more than 30 research centres from member countries to contribute to decision making through quality research on topics of community interest. Its mission is to promote collaboration between research institutions in the WAEMU space, encourage generation of policy-related knowledge products, and contribute to decision making support for WAEMU bodies.

In sum, over the past 20 years there has been a rapid growth of think tanks in Senegal that undertake research to inform public policy making. Three main categories of these have been identified, including independent think tanks, government-affiliated think tanks and university-based/affiliated think tanks.

CASE STUDIES TO INFORM NATIONAL AND REGIONAL PUBLIC POLICIES

In this section we illustrate with a few examples the work of think tanks in Senegal to inform public policy and contribute to the development process. This list is by no means exhaustive. The aim is to present a sample of how think tanks are contributing to the development process and in informing public policy making.

Reforming the Senegalese Agricultural Subsidy System

For decades, public policies have strongly supported Senegalese agriculture through subsidies. These subsidies target mainly the acquisition of seeds, fertilizers and agricultural equipment. However, the performance of the agricultural sector does not necessarily reflect the significant budgetary resources mobilized by subsidies. Agriculture's share of gross domestic product is stagnating, while input subsidies are increasing from year to year.

In 2015, IPAR conducted a study on 'Traceability and Impacts of Agricultural Subsidies', focusing on key policy directions, constraints, successes and failures noted in agricultural subsidies (IPAR, 2015a, 2015b). The study revealed important limitations in the agricultural input subsidy policy: (1) access modalities and inequitable distribution; (2) high costs; (3) lack of transparency in the system at all levels; and (4) poor quality of distributed inputs, along with trafficking to neighbouring countries.

The results of the study informed policy discussions on prospects for improving agricultural subsidy practices. The May 2016 roundtable brought together the government (various ministries and agencies involved, and parliamentarians), civil society, the private sector, research, and technical and financial partners. IPAR organized a second consultation in 2017 in Kaolack,[4] in the heart of the groundnut basin, with key stakeholders of the groundnut sector. The aim was to take stock of the implementation of the recommendations made by stakeholders at the first roundtable, particularly for the ground nut sector. At the end of the workshop, participants set up a follow-up committee chaired by the region's Governor and composed of stakeholders (producer organizations, oil producers, public support services).

There are already encouraging signs in this process of reforming the subsidy distribution system. In October 2017, the authorities recognized through the Joint Agricultural Sector Review that the e-subsidy platform created to improve the targeting of subsidy beneficiaries had not had the expected effects, due to multiple constraints (DAPSA, 2017). In 2018, as part of the definition of its intervention programme focused on social protection, the European Union Delegation decided, by mutual agreement with the Government of Senegal, to target the poorest small-scale producers to ensure them privileged access to input subsidies.[5] Finally, the Ministry of Agriculture and Rural Equipment launched an audit of the file of large producers to ensure that the subsidies granted to this category truly benefit agricultural production.

Progress is therefore tangible, although much work remains. Key stakeholders have now taken ownership of the process, basing their advocacy on the results of IPAR's research. In 2019, the plenary of the Parliament session debated the issue. As a sign of recognition, the Minister of Economy, Finance and Planning has sent a letter of congratulations and appreciation to IPAR for its research and advocacy towards an equitable and transparent agricultural subsidy system.

Senegal Rejects Economic Partnership Agreements Based on Evidence

Since 1975, the African, Caribbean and Pacific (ACP) states have benefited from preferential access to the European Union market thanks to the Lomé Convention. In 2000, the Cotonou Agreement between the European Union and the ACP countries extended the preferential access of ACP countries to the European Union until the end of 2007, and defined a strategy towards a new trade regime starting from 2008. This new regime would transform non-reciprocal ACP agreements into reciprocal EU–ACP free trade agreements.

Like other African countries, Senegal has asked many questions about the impact that this type of agreement could have on its economy. To answer these questions, the Bureau d'analyses macroéconomiques (BAME) of the Institut sénégalais de recherches agricoles (ISRA), with support from the International Food Policy Research Institute (IFPRI), conducted studies on the impact of the adoption of economic partnership agreements (EPAs) on Senegal. A macroeconomic policy research network involving the Centre d'études de politiques pour le développement (CEPOD) of the Ministry of Economy and Finance, the Direction de l'analyse de la prévision et de la statistique (DAPS) of the Ministry of Agriculture, and the Centre de recherches économiques appliquées (CREA) of Cheikh Anta Diop University in Dakar, collaborated in this initiative.

On the eve of an important summit between the European Union and the African Union on these EPAs, the Senegalese government turned to ISRA-BAME to help it better position itself on the agreements. Based on the results of the impact studies, BAME drafted a policy brief for the President of the Republic, Abdoulaye Wade. Based on the information received, the President decided not to sign the agreements, and in a memorable speech called on his African peers to follow him on this path. President Thabo Mbeki had the same attitude. Finally, the Lisbon summit held from 7 to 9 December 2007 was a relative failure: 'Most African countries do not accept the new economic partnership agreements (EPAs) proposed by the European Union and want to negotiate different agreements', President Wade announced at the end of the summit.

For Senegal, EPA reform would mean little improvement in market access for Senegalese exporters, and a significant opening of its economy to European products. In addition, the reform would imply a substantial loss of tariff revenue for Senegal. The EPAs would therefore result in little additional trade flows for Senegal, and much trade detour (Ndir and Diop, 2008; Fall et al., 2008; Berisha-Krasniqi et al., 2008).

Informing Rural Youth Employment Policy: IPAR Provides Evidence and Analysis for Rural Youth Employment Policy Development in Senegal

In Senegal, agriculture employs 70 per cent of the active population and offers many employment opportunities. Nearly 300 000 young people enter the labour market each year, 57 per cent of whom are from rural areas. Thus, agriculture represents an important lever that can have a decisive influence on the creation of decent rural jobs for young people.

Until now, integration strategies have mostly targeted urban youth, particularly unemployed graduates. In response to the knowledge gap regarding rural employment and activity structures, in 2014, IPAR launched research on 'Youth Employment and Migration in West Africa' (EJMAO), with a focus on rural youth employment and mobility in Burkina, Mali and Senegal (Hathie et al., 2015).

It is in this context that the Food and Agricultural Organization (FAO) and the National Agency for the Promotion of Youth Employment (ANPEJ) successfully organized an inclusive policy dialogue on youth employment in March 2015, in collaboration with IPAR (FAO, 2015). In addition to facilitating the dialogue around rural youth inclusion issues, IPAR provided evidence and analysis that informed the preparation and organization of the dialogue, using research findings from the EJMAO project's work.

This dialogue provided an opportunity to gather recommendations from the government, the private sector, development partners, civil society and youth representatives. A multi-stakeholder Steering Committee, chaired by the Prime Minister's Office and coordinated by ANPEJ, was formally created in 2016 by an order of the Prime Minister to support the formulation of a Policy for the Promotion of Youth Employment in Rural Areas. Following the two days of dialogue, the FAO, based on its Integrated Country Approach (ICA), accompanied ANPEJ in the development of a specific three-year project focused on the promotion of decent rural youth employment.

CRES's Steady Effort to Provide Evidence Supporting Fiscal Policy Reforms in the Tobacco Industry

Despite ratifying the Framework Convention on Tobacco Control, countries of the Economic Community of West African States (ECOWAS) have been slow to adopt laws and measures to operationalize the Framework Convention due to a lack of information on the different aspects of tobacco that can inform their decision-making. To fill this evidence gap, the think tank CRES, with funding support from the International Development Research Centre, undertook a research project on tobacco taxation in West Africa entitled 'Fiscal Solutions for Maximum Reduction of Smoking in West Africa'.[6] Research themes included country profiles on tobacco taxation, costs of smoking, effectiveness of tobacco product taxation systems, impact on the economy, and issues of smuggling.

Research results led to significant decisions in countries such as Senegal as well as at the regional level. Key decisions taken in Senegal included increases in existing tax rates in 2009 and 2014; the adoption of a law related to the manufacture, packaging, labelling, sale and use of tobacco, by the Parliament in 2014; and the promulgation of this law by the President in 2016. At the regional level, ECOWAS adopted a new Directive on the taxation of tobacco products in December 2017.[7] This Directive provides a set of measures including a mechanism for regular rate increases, a minimum rate of the *ad valorem* tax set at 50 per cent with the removal of restrictions on the maximum rate level, and a specific tax of US$0.02 per cigarette associated with it.

During these reform processes, CRES undertook targeted studies to feed information to policy makers along with recommendations for change. For the Senegal case, for instance, CRES showed a negligible contribution of the tobacco industry to the national economy (CRES, 2017a). This is reflected in a very low and declining job creation, and a low level of fiscal revenue relative to Senegal's total revenue. Additionally, costs incurred from smoking tobacco are well above the contributions of the tobacco industry. In 2017, smoking cost 123 billion FCFA to the Senegalese society, while it brought in only 24 billion FCFA. Households bore a larger share of the total costs of smoking than the government (Diagne et al., 2017).

Studies in other West African countries also highlighted an inefficient tax system in Benin and Cote d'Ivoire, or a regulatory system without strict enforcement measures such as in Nigeria (CRES, 2017b, 2017c, 2017d). This resulted in low tax revenues and a favourable environment for an increase in tobacco consumption. Consequently, CRES made recommendations that would lead to the effectiveness of tobacco taxation in West Africa. In parallel with the think tank's research efforts, civil society organizations contributed decisively to the fight against smoking by organizing sensitization campaigns on the dangers of tobacco for health, relying mostly on evidence provided by CRES. They also pressured governments, pointing to the ineffectiveness of several of their policies on tobacco control.

The above are just a small sample of how the research undertaken by think tanks in Senegal is helping the national government and other countries in the region to design public policies. These think tanks, however, face a few challenges. There are also several emerging opportunities that these think tanks can take advantage of, especially given the changing policy environment not only in the country but worldwide. The next section explores these challenges and opportunities.

CHALLENGES AND OPPORTUNITIES IN INFORMING PUBLIC POLICY

The complexity of modern society with interposing interest groups means that contributing to policies and the development process comes with several challenges. There are also emerging opportunities. This section addresses some challenges that think tanks may face, and opportunities for informing public policy making, drawing from the experiences in Senegal.

Challenges

Navigating the policy landscape with controversial issues and diverse interests

In 2015, when IPAR launched its agricultural subsidies traceability study, there was no idea of the strong polarization that this process would generate among different stakeholders. On the one hand, development partners, civil society organizations, and the Ministry of Economy and Finance wanted a thorough reform of the subsidy system, with better targeting of beneficiaries and traceability of interventions and products distributed. On the other hand, the Ministry of Agriculture and some interest groups were very reluctant to engage in dialogue on these issues, and could sometimes be aggressive towards their critics.

From the outset, IPAR formally informed the Ministry of Agriculture, to facilitate access to data. It also involved key stakeholders in the design of the research project, with interactions on objectives, methodology and expected results. This first stage went smoothly. The difficulties began at the results-sharing stage, with clashes between researchers and civil society on the one hand, and those who felt targeted by the research results on the other. A pre-recorded television programme highlighting discussions between researchers, policy makers and the private sector was censored after it was scheduled and advertised on national television.[8]

The culmination of this process was the threats of retaliation against IPAR by some policy makers. Had it not been for the intervention of its Board of Directors, IPAR's existence could have been jeopardized. Learning from this ordeal, IPAR changed its advocacy strategy, relying more on stakeholders to take charge of advocacy, based on sharing research results and strengthening their capacities. Another lesson is the recognition of the diversity of views within the group of decision makers. The government is not uniform. Individual and collective interests at stake strongly influence attitudes and support for change.

Weak institutional capacities

Our experiences based on observations and discussions with think tanks in Senegal highlight inadequate capacities to engage and partner with a wide range of stakeholders as a significant challenge for these think tanks to contribute effectively to public policy making. Organizational capacities, which include issues around leadership, governance and sustainability, are sometimes weak, and the type of skills needed may be in short supply at think tanks. Think tanks must develop good communication skills and strategies to identify relevant policy questions. Some think tanks experience high turnover of their staff, making it difficult to achieve continuity in efforts to promote the research–policy nexus.

Funding needs

As is the case with most think tanks elsewhere, especially in Africa, funding constraints hinder the potential of think tanks to cater to the needs of policy makers. In many instances think tanks will give priority to project activities, which may or may not be associated with concrete policy issues for the country.

Opportunities

Participation in inter-ministerial committees and working groups

IPAR, CRES, ISRA-BAME and CEPOD participate in inter-ministerial committees and working groups. This activity provides an opportunity for these institutions to have a better grasp of relevant policy issues which should receive their attention. It also enables them to develop good working relationships with key personnel in government ministries, and build the trust and credibility that are essential for informing policy discourse.

Evidence-informed policy making at the local level: the Podor Laboratory

The Hewlett Foundation has provided core support to IPAR aimed at contributing to strengthening the system of evidence-informed policy making in Senegal. IPAR's goal is to ensure that policy makers in Senegal use consistent, relevant data, research and evaluation findings to inform decision making in the design, implementation, monitoring and evaluation of projects, programmes and policies, as well as in resource allocation and priority choices. One of the objectives was to support local development with innovative and locally tailored systems. Improving local development involved interventions in municipalities and in departments. This represents the second layer of decentralization and regroups several municipalities. IPAR choose the department of Podor in the north of Senegal to initiate key experiments. This laboratory is a unique opportunity for IPAR to inform public policy making in Senegal.

Initially, IPAR initiated a joint review process in partnership with the departmental administration to bring together various stakeholders to reflect on the priorities set, the achievements over the year, challenges encountered and the way forward. With additional support from a United States Agency for International Development (USAID)-funded project, IPAR launched a process aiming to develop an investment facilitation ecosystem. The ambition is: (1) to build a territorial information system for investment; (2) to analyse the priority agro-sylvo-pastoral value chains and propose an action plan for their development; (3) to boost the activities of young people and women; and (4) to support multi-stakeholder dialogue. All these objectives aim to generate evidence and promote interactions between stakeholders for better decision making. The economic forum of Podor is an extension of these various interventions of IPAR in the department.

CONCLUSION

This chapter has illustrated with specific examples how selected think tanks in Senegal have contributed to the development process by undertaking research to inform public policies. Important lessons from the experience of these think tanks highlight the following:

- There is a diversity of views and interests among policy makers, thereby calling for the need to provide policy options rather than firm recommendations. Policy makers appreciate knowing the consequences of their actions and how this might affect their constituencies.
- Co-creation of research outputs with stakeholders, especially public sector actors, facilitates buy-in and enhances the chances of research informing or influencing policies. The participation of researchers in inter-ministerial committees and similar constituent bodies will enable them to have first-hand knowledge of the needs of policy and decision makers.
- Think tanks may not have a comparative advantage in undertaking advocacy themselves. Forging partnerships with institutions with the required skills and experience in outreach activities may be a better strategy.
- Research institutions and think tanks are well served when they involve a broad range of stakeholders (communicators, private and public sector actors) throughout the research process.
- Communication strategies of research results need to be diverse to appeal to the different segments of the audience. Researchers should build their capacity to be able to communicate technical issues in a way that is digestible to the public.
- Researchers at think tanks must demonstrate their independence from political influence. This requires them to build their credibility by undertaking rigorous and high-quality research.

Although think tanks in Senegal have been successful in using their research findings to inform and influence policies, they face significant challenges, as mentioned earlier. Owing to the financial constraints that they face, the whole dimension of knowledge translation or knowledge brokerage is quite limited. There is a need for improved understanding of how think tanks can improve their knowledge translation. This may require building coalitions with appropriate actors that have a comparative advantage.

Further work may also be needed to better understand the political nature of the research–applied policy nexus; that is, the political nature of decision making and how this influences how evidence is used. Many think tanks argue that the required evidence is available to inform policies, but is never used. Many insights can be gained from understanding the necessary and sufficient conditions for the use of research evidence to inform public policy making.

NOTES

1. For example, in 2014, the African Development Bank approved bilateral loans to develop five centres of excellence in biomedical sciences in East Africa. Also in 2014, the World Bank launched the 15 Africa Centres of Excellence Project in collaboration with West and Central African countries., in areas of agriculture, health, science and technology (Tijssen and Kraemer-Mbula, 2017).
2. The first conference was organized to cross-examine the strategy for agriculture in Senegal, which was being developed by the government.
3. The TTI was a multi-donor undertaking consisting of the William & Loral Hewlett Foundation, the Bill & Melinda Gates Foundation, the United Kingdom Department of International Development (DfID), IDRC and the Netherlands Directorate General for International Cooperation (DGIS). The initiative aimed to strengthen independent policy research institutions in developing countries. In Senegal, CRES and IPAR benefited from this funding support.
4. http:// ipar .sn/ Concertations -sur -les -subventions -agricoles -Les -acteurs -a -la -recherche-des.html.
5. http://projet-tiers-sud.com/index.php/about-us-style-1/.
6. https:// www .idrc .ca/ en/ project/ tax -solutions -optimal -reduction -tobacco -use -west-africa.
7. https:// untobaccocontrol .org/ impldb/ wp -content/ uploads/ sierra _leone _2018_annex-5_ECOWAS_directive_tobacco_2017.pdf.
8. http://ipar.sn/Plateau-TV-IPAR-RTS-sur-les-subventions-agricoles-au-Senegal .html.

REFERENCES

Agyapong, I.A., and Adjei, S. (2008). Public social policy development and implementation: a case study of the Ghana National Health Insurance scheme. *Health Policy and Planning* 23(2): 150–160. https://doi.org/10.1093/heapol/czn002.
Ayuk, E.T., and Marouani, M.A. (2007). *The Policy Paradox in Africa: Strengthening Links between Research and Policy Making*. Ottawa: IDRC and Africa World Press.
Berisha-Krasniqi V., Bouët, A., and Mevel, S. (2008). Les accords de partenariat économique: Quels enjeux pour le Sénégal? *Revue de l'OFCE* 4(107): 65–116.
Brand, U. (2013). The role of state and public policies in processes of transformation. In: M. Lang and D. Mokrani (eds), *Beyond Development. Alternative Visions from Latin America*, pp. 105–115. Amsterdam TNI. https://www.tni.org/files/download/ beyonddevelopment_complete.pdf.

Bridgeland, J., and Orszag, P. (July/August 2013). Can government play money ball? *The Atlantic.* https:// www .theatlantic .com/ magazine/ archive/ 2013/ 07/ can -government-play-moneyball/309389/, accessed 20 March 2020.

Carden, F. (2009). *Knowledge to Policy: Making the Most of Development Research.* New Delhi: SAGE Publications.

CRES (2017a). Senegal profile on tobacco taxation: adopt more effective taxation and better information on the prevalence of tobacco products. CRES Policy Brief. Research project on tobacco taxation in West Africa 'Fiscal Solutions for Optimal Reduction of Smoking in West Africa'. https:// idl -bnc -idrc .dspacedirect .org/bitstream/handle/10625/58914/IDL%20-%2058914.pdf.

CRES (2017b). Benin profile on tobacco taxation: adopt more effective taxation and better information on the prevalence of tobacco products'. CRES Policy Brief. Research project on tobacco taxation in West Africa 'Fiscal Solutions for Optimal Reduction of Smoking in West Africa'. https:// idl -bnc -idrc .dspacedirect .org/bitstream/handle/10625/58917/IDL%20-%2058917.pdf.

CRES (2017c). Profile of the Ivory Coast on tobacco taxation: adopt more effective taxation and better information on the prevalence of tobacco products. CRES Policy Brief. Research project on tobacco taxation in West Africa 'Fiscal Solutions for Optimal Reduction of Smoking in West Africa'. https:// idl -bnc -idrc .dspacedirect .org/bitstream/handle/10625/58918/IDL%20-%2058918.pdf.

CRES (2017d). Profile of Nigeria on tobacco taxation: Adopt more effective taxa- tion and better information on the prevalence of tobacco products. CRES Policy Brief. Research project on tobacco taxation in West Africa 'Fiscal Solutions for Optimal Reduction of Smoking in West Africa'. https:// idl -bnc -idrc .dspacedirect .org/bitstream/handle/10625/58921/IDL%20-%2058921.pdf.

Cronin, G., and Sadan, M. (2015). Use of evidence in policy making in South Africa: an exploratory study of attitudes of senior government officials. *African Evaluation Journal* 3(1): 10–20.

DAPSA (2017). Revue conjointe du secteur agricole 2017. Responsabilité mutuelle PDDAA. https:// www .dapsa .gouv .sn/ sites/ default/ files/ RCSA %202017 %20v4d %C3%A9c_0.pdf.

Diagne, A., Mane, P.Y., Fall, F.A., Amavi, K. (2017). Costs of smoking in Senegal. CRES Policy Brief. Research project on tobacco taxation in West Africa 'Fiscal Solutions for Optimal Reduction of Smoking in West Africa'. https://idl-bnc-idrc .dspacedirect.org/bitstream/handle/10625/58882/IDL%20-%2058882.pdf.

Diawara, B. (2020). *COVID-19 and African Think-Tanks: Challenges, Needs and Solutions. Think Piece in COVID-19 Initiative Survey Results.* On Think Tanks Network. https:// onthinktanks .org/ articles/ covid -19 -and -african -think -tanks -challenges-needs-and-solutions/.

Ellen, M.E., Lavis, J.N., Horowitz, E., and Berglas, R. (2018). How is the use of research evidence in health policy perceived: a comparison between the reporting by researchers and policymakers? *Health Research Policy and Systems* 16: 64. https:// doi.org/10.1186/s12961–018–0345–6.

Fall, C.S., Gueye, A., and Dial, M.L. (2008). Impact macroéconomique d'un partenariat économique sur le secteur agricole et agroalimentaire au Sénégal. *Institut Sénégalais de recherches agricoles, Réflexions et Perspectives,* 6(4): 1–30.

FAO (2015). Appui à l'élaboration de la Politique de promotion de l'emploi des jeunes en milieu rural (PPEJMR). https://www.fao.org/3/i7598f/i7598f.pdf.

Goldman, I. and Pabari, M. (eds) (2020), *Using Evidence in Policy and Practice: Lessons from Africa.* Rethinking Development Series. London: Routledge. DOI: https://doi.org/10.4324/9781003007043.

Goldman, I., and Pabari, M. (2021a). Introduction to the book. In: I. Goldman and M. Pabari (eds), *Using Evidence in Policy and Practice: Lessons from Africa.* Rethinking Development Series. London: Routledge.

Goldman, I., and Pabari, M. (2021b). An introduction to evidence-informed policy and practice in Africa. In: I. Goldman and M. Pabari (eds), *Using Evidence in Policy and Practice: Lessons from Africa.* Rethinking Development Series. London: Routledge.

Goldman I., Olaleye, W., Ntakumba, S.S., Makgaba, M., and Waller, C. (2021). Mere compliance or learning – M&E culture in the public service of Benin, Uganda, and South Africa. In: I. Goldman and M. Pabari (eds), *Using Evidence in Policy and Practice: Lessons from Africa.* Rethinking Development Series. London: Routledge. DOI: https://doi.org/10.4324/9781003007043.

Hathie, I., Wade, I., Ba, S., Niang, A., Niang, M., Sow, M.K., Ndione, Y., and Ba, C.O. (2015). Emploi des jeunes et migrations en Afrique de l'Ouest. Rapport final. https://idl-bnc-idrc.dspacedirect.org/bitstream/handle/10625/54153/IDL-54153.pdf.

HF (2018). *Evidence-Informed Policymaking Strategy.* Hewlett Foundation.

IPAR (2015a). Traçabilité et impacts des subventions agricoles. https://www.ipar.sn/IMG/pdf/rapport_final_sur_tracabilite_et_impact_des_subventions_agricoles.pdf.

IPAR (2015b). Subventions des intrants agricoles au Sénégal: controverses et réalités. Rapport annuel sur l'état de l'agriculture et du monde rural au Sénégal. https://www.ipar.sn/IMG/pdf/ipar-rapport_agriculture-2015-_p_p_.pdf.

Koduah, A., van Dijk H., and Agyepong, I.A. (2015). The role of policy actors and contextual factors in policy agenda setting and formulation: maternal fee exemption policies in Ghana over four and a half decades. *Health Research Policy and Systems* 13(1): 27. https://doi.org/10.1186/s12961-015-0016-9.

Liverani, M., Hawkins, B., and Parkhurst, J.O. (2013). Political and institutional influences on the use of evidence in public health policy: a systematic review. *PloS One*, 8(10). https://doi.org/10.1371/journal.pone.0077404.

Mayne, R., Green, D., Guijt, I.M., Walsh, M., English, R., and Cairney, P. (2018). Using evidence to influence policy: Oxfam's experience. *Palgrave Communications* 4. 10.1057/s41599-018-0176-7

McGann, J.G. (2018). 2017 Global Go TO Think Tank Index Report. TTCSP Global Go To Think Tank Index Reports. https//repository.upenn.edu/cgi/viewcontent.cgi?article=1012&content=think_tanks.

Naude, C.E., Zani, B., Ongolo-Zogo, P., Wiysonge, C.S., Dudley, L., Kredo, Garner, P., and Young, T. (2015). Research evidence and policy: qualitative study in selected provinces in South Africa and Cameroon. *Implementation Science* 10: 126.

Ndiaye, J.P. (2018). *Cartographie des Think Tanks en Activité au Sénégal.* Rapport Final. Dakar: IPAR. https://www.ipar.sn/Cartographie-des-think-tanks-en-activite-au-Senegal.html.

Ndir, B., and S.M. Diop (2008). Impact macroéconomique d'un partenariat économique sur le Sénégal. Institut Sénégalais de recherches agricoles, *Réflexions et Perspectives*, 6(3): 1–45.

Ongolo-Zogo, P., Lavis, J.N., Tomson, G., and Sewankambo, N.K. (2014). Initiatives supporting evidence-informed health system policymaking in Cameroon and Uganda: a comparative historical case study. *BMC Health Services Research* 14: 612.

Parkhurst, J. (2017). *The Politics of Evidence: From Evidence-Based Policy to the Good Governance of Evidence*. New York: Taylor & Francis.

Partey, S.T., Zougmoré, R.B., Ouédraogo, M., and Campbell, B.M. (2018). Developing climate-smart agriculture to face climate variability in West Africa: challenges and lessons learnt. *Journal of Cleaner Production* 187: 285–295.

Phoenix, J.H., Atkinson, L.G., and Baker, H. (2019). Creating and communicating social research for policymakers in government. *Palgrave Communications* 5: 98. https://doi.org/10.1057/s41599–019–0310–1.

Ridde, V., and Yameogo, P. (2018). How Burkina Faso used evidence in deciding to launch its policy of free health care for children under 5 and women in 2016. *Palgrave Communications* 4: 119. https://doi.org/10.1057/s41599–018–0173-x.

Sedley, S. (2016). *Missing Evidence: An Inquiry into the Delayed Publication of Government-Commissioned Research*. London: Sense About Science.

Sombie, I., Bouwayé, A., Mongbo, Y., Keita, N., Lokossou V., Johnson E., Assogba, L., and Crespin, X. (2017). Promoting research to improve maternal, neonatal, infant, and adolescent health in West Africa: the role of the West African Health Organisation. *Health Research and Policy System* 15(Suppl 1): 53.

Tijssen, R., and Kraemer-Mbula, E. (2017). Research excellence in Africa: policies, perceptions, and performance. *Science and Public Policy* 45(3): 392–403. https://doi.org/10.1093/scipol/scx074.

Uneke, C.J., Sombie, I., Johnson, E., Uneke, B.I., and Okolo, S. (2020). Promoting the use of evidence in health policymaking in the ECOWAS region: the development and contextualization of an evidence-based policymaking guidance. *Globalization and Health* 16: 73. https://doi.org/10.1186/s12992–020–00605-z.

UNICEF (2017). *Political Economy Analyses of Countries in Eastern and Southern Africa: Case Study – Kenya Political Economy Analysis*.

Vecchione, E., and Parkhurst, J. (2015). The use of evidence within policy evaluation in health in Ghana: implications for accountability and democratic governance. *European Policy Analysis* 1(2): 75–90. https://doi.org/10.18278/epa.1.2.6.

Zougmoré, R.B., Partey, S.T., Totin, E., Ouédraogo, M., Thornton, P. Karbo, N., Sogoba, Dieye, B., and Campbell, B.M. (2019). Science–policy interfaces for sustainable climate-smart agriculture uptake: lessons learnt from national science–policy dialogue platforms in West Africa. *International Journal of Agricultural Sustainability* 17(5): 367–382. DOI: 10.1080/14735903.2019.1670934.

10. Think tanks and governance in South Africa

Bright Nkrumah and Radhamany Soorymoorthy

INTRODUCTION

The 2017 Global Go To Think Tank Index Report states that about 8000 think tanks exist across the world (McGann, 2018). This includes Africa, where their presence continues to expand (ibid.). The role of think tanks and their evaluation has become a subject of scholarly interest in recent years (Abelson, 2018). The emergence and expansion of think tanks are attributed to certain factors. McGann (2018) finds that the information and technological revolution and the end of the monopoly of governments on information, the increasing complexities of the technical nature of policy issues, and globalisation of the growth of state and non-state actors, are among them. However, it is still a challenge to assess the impact of think tanks in influencing policy decisions. In Africa, they have their role mainly in the areas of development, peace and security, and governance. Gounden and Coning (2021) further speculate that the role of think tanks in Africa is likely to be more significant in the future, given the change in the international global order, and due to the challenges that Africa is facing today. The case for South Africa is no different.

On 8 May 2019, South Africa held its sixth democratic polls to elect a new president, as well as national and provincial legislatures (Alence and Pitcher, 2019). Although the election was marked by the African National Congress's (ANC) worst electoral support since the dawn of democracy, the party's victory has still been hailed in some quarters (Africa, 2019). To the observers, the silver lining was the election of President Cyril Ramaphosa, considering his anti-corruption agenda and strong leadership traits (Beckmann, 2019; Shubin, 2019). Despite these qualities, there is an evolving commentary underscoring one key challenge that will militate against the new leadership's efforts toward improving the quality of life for the downcast, the marginalised and the poor. The coronavirus (COVID-19) and related contagious diseases have led to dire health and socioeconomic hardships among millions of the country's population (Mbunge, 2020). At the time of writing in 2021, the ongoing debate is: how should the state fund the COVID-19 vaccine which citizens need? While the Treasury proposes a further hike in taxation, economists dispute this measure, as it might trigger extreme hardship since businesses have been locked down and many people have lost their jobs (Davis, 2021; Mackenzie, 2021).

In resolving similar stalemates, most government departments have in-house research units (IHRUs) that assess existing policies and provide sound policy advice to relevant ministers (Glied et al., 2018). However, a range of internal structures could hinder the efforts of these units to critically interrogate departmental or national policies in delivering on their mandate. Ideally, the focus of the IHRUs is informed by the directive of the director of the unit, who is ultimately answerable to the minister (a political appointee). Arguably, these civil servants aspire to generate an output that satisfies the whims and caprices of their superiors, rather than adopting a critical lens to examine existing policies and practices.

Against this backdrop, a considerable number of independent research institutes, also called think tanks, have sprung up and carved a niche in the arena of institutional research. The Global Think Tank Index Report of 2017 (McGann, 2018) estimates that there are 92 such institutions in South Africa, making it the jurisdiction with the highest number of think tanks in sub-Saharan Africa. These include some of the key think tanks in sub-Saharan Africa. In other words, their evolution in the contemporary era cannot be overlooked, whether in the realm of political or human development. They perform three key roles, namely, policy analysis, advocacy and capacity building. One area where they could make a significant contribution is in the realm of (under)development, as poor social policy continues to drive inequality and poor-quality healthcare. This concern brings about an important discourse on the extent to which research institutes influence South Africa's governance, and what barriers constrain their operations.

This chapter is structured as follows. The next section begins with a brief explanation of the notion of think tanks, and provides an illustration of some of their main mandates. It then considers the evolution of these institutions under the apartheid regime and their subsequent proliferation since the 1990s. The chapter then considers the different types of these institutes operating in their respective policy spaces, with specific reference to their ideological orientation, research and advocacy agendas. The following section examines an important aspect of think tank operations in democratic South Africa: the degree of influence in agenda setting and policy operationalisation. Here, think tanks are perceived as not merely founts of knowledge, but also as shapers and implementers of policies. The last section surveys some of the barriers they face, and concludes with recommendations.

THEORY OF THINK TANKS

The rise of think tanks continues. Think tanks may be construed as autonomous organisations that use research and advocacy to shape ideas and policy (Niblett, 2018). Given the selective themes that these organisations focus on, they may be perceived as interest groups established to supply strategic information to a growing body of policy actors. By extension, the growing proliferation of think tanks may be tied to the rapidly changing demands of citizens, and the urgency to tailor complex policies to satisfy these expectations (Mullon and Ngoepe, 2019). This niche has ultimately created a business prospect for policy experts to create research centres to satisfy the demand for contemporary information that (national and provincial) assembly members desire. While autonomy is the hallmark of think tanks, the need to stay afloat and sustain the costly operations of the organisation makes patronage of their research direction somewhat inescapable. Thus, the research focus of think tanks is not static, but increasingly diversified in response to political opportunities, or simply put, supply and demand (Krastev, 2001). This section explores the evolution and key features of think tanks within the South African context.

On a canvas of broad strokes, a nation-state may be depicted as a political organisation with three sectors: the government, the business sector and not-for-profit organisations (NPOs). Since think tanks do not fit neatly into the first two camps, they may be classified under the third sector, NPOs. Their non-profit agendas, separation from government and volunteer staff further inform their categorisation. They serve as a bridge between academia and policy. Think tanks may be construed as autonomous, non-political institutions that employ research, consultation and lobbying to influence the content of public policy and its operationalisation. They can be generally defined as public policy research, analysis and engagement institutions that are able to provide research, analysis and advice on issues (McGann, 2021). The lack of autonomy, coupled with insufficient resources and incentives, may stifle attempts towards framing innovative ideas for more concrete forms of decision-making and operationalisation.

Think tanks share four distinctive features: (1) they are privately established; (2) they enjoy some level of autonomy; (3) they are well structured; and (4) they do not pursue a commercial agenda. With a fair number of experts enlisted as staff, these institutions provide policy advice on key civil/political and social/economic issues (Niblett, 2018). Apart from serving as a fertile ground for poaching potential civil servants, these institutions contribute to democracy by playing advocacy roles, training policy-makers, and acting as watchdogs. In terms of the last of these, they hold state officials accountable for incompetence or corrupt acts.

In contemporary times, policy research institutes have assumed considerable political weight in local and national politics. They continue to evolve as key actors in the realm of people-centred community development (Mullon and Ngoepe, 2019). The notion of development, as used in this chapter, implies a process where available resources are distributed and utilised by members of the local community to improve their living conditions. This phenomenon invariably answers the needs and exigencies of citizens, such as food, healthcare, and other essentials of life. By undertaking development projects, these institutions seek to uplift communities and individuals out of poverty. This role is evident in their use of research and training to develop the capacities of marginalised communities and relevant stakeholders to pursue social development (Gonzales Hernando and Williams, 2018).

As an embodiment of intellectual innovation, think tanks may be seen as founts of ideas for shaping public policy (Fraussen and Halpin, 2017). A disproportionate percentage avidly targets (sub)national politics as they assist with the drafting, operationalisation and monitoring of government programmes. Against this backdrop, actors in the policy-making arena continue to interact with and provide some degree of support to these non-state actors. To some observers, there has been a proliferation of these institutions seeking to use policy analysis and advocacy to shape South Africa's democratisation (Mullon and Ngoepe, 2019; McGann, 2020).

Some have argued that think tanks do not necessarily foster democracy per se. To them, think tanks are arms of international capitalism or imperialistic designs forged to drive the Western neoliberal package of liberalisation, privatisation and marketisation (Scott, 1999; Krastev, 2001). Differing opinions notwithstanding, the extent to which these actors have been successful in influencing South Africa's policy discourse forms the central focus of this chapter. Nonetheless, before undertaking this form of assessment, an analysis of their evolution suffices.

THE TRAJECTORY OF THINK TANKS IN SOUTH AFRICA

The rise and subsequent growth of think tanks may be traced back to the global strategic reforms that occurred in the 20th century (McGann, 2003). Their evolution was given an impetus when article 71 of the 1945 United Nations (UN) Charter named this body as an important player with which UN bodies ought to have regular consultation in the process of coordinating socioeconomic and humanitarian interventions across the globe.

Think Tanks Under an Apartheid Regime

The recognition of think tanks at the international level trickled down to the national level. Although a few of these institutes were established in the third quarter of the 1990s, some in South Africa gained prominence in the 1980s, when the apartheid regime came under increasing global pressure to peacefully address the mass insurrections that engulfed its minority rule (Niblett, 2018). Three types of think tanks existed within this era: (1) radical or anti-apartheid research centres; (2) conservative or pro-apartheid organisations; and (3) non-aligned or socioeconomic policy foundations (Habib and Taylor, 1999).

The primary objective of the radical or anti-apartheid research centres was total democratisation and integration of all racial groups in the political process, devoid of special treatment of one race over another (Habib, 2005). Institutions in this cluster included the Institute of Race Relations (IRR), the Centre for Conflict Resolution (CCR) and the Institute for Security Studies (ISS). On the other hand, as their name suggests, the conservative institutions abhorred reforms and used their expertise and resources to support the government towards upholding the apartheid status quo. Two notable institutions that actively supported the oppressive regime were the Nederduitse Gereformeerde Kerk and the Broederbond (Habib, 2005). By acceding to a neutral ground, the third group of think tanks performed a mediatory role between the state and ordinary citizens, by researching to assist in socioeconomic interventions towards the otherwise termed 'homelands' or native reserves (Gassama, 1996).

The Think Tanks under the Immediate Post-Apartheid Regime

Following the country's negotiated transition to democracy in 1994, the ANC regime embarked on a process of decentralisation and the granting of considerable autonomy to provincial administrations by bringing basic social services to the population (Koelble and Siddle, 2014). This phenomenon somewhat enhanced greater collaboration between local administrators and think tanks, with a disproportionate percentage of the latter shifting from their previous anti- or pro-apartheid agendas. Arguably, the shift was a response to the greater autonomy that was accorded to provincial administrations to adopt specific policies to regulate their internal affairs. In seeking to promote reforms, these structures became more receptive to the policy advice and training provided by existing research centres, particularly in areas of reconciliation, reconstruction and development (Binns and Nel, 2002).

Despite this initial goodwill, there were latent forms of national government hostility towards this sector, particularly those performing oversight roles. This came to the fore when they were branded as puppets of Western power, rather than voices of the voiceless or ordinary citizens (Hearn, 2000). Thus, whereas local government collaborated with research institutes, the national administration treated some of these institutions with suspicion, thereby pursuing a centralist or closed-door approach to a government–independent think tank relationship. To some extent, the hostility might have been directed towards conservative think tanks that still clung to their apartheid orientation, thereby opposing the newly elected administration. As vehemently articulated in his 1995 parliamentary address, Nelson Mandela stressed that: '[s]ome have misread freedom to mean license, popular participation to mean the ability to impose chaos ... Let me make abundantly clear that the small minority in our midst which wears the mask of anarchy will meet its match in the government we lead' (cited in Bond, 2014: 223).

In such an environment, some institutions shifted from their antagonistic relationships with the state by paying greater attention to soft power in their advocacy and research output. In contrast to hard power that is often confrontational, soft power revolves around attaining an objective by eliciting emotions and standards to persuade public actors to make certain policy choices (Gallarotti, 2011).

Aside from the tense political engagement, the institutions were presented with two other hurdles. The first was the loss of financial support: a considerable percentage of donor support during apartheid was earmarked to dismantle minority rule (Habib, 2005). Once these efforts materialised and democracy was attained, there was no need for further funding. Donors therefore shifted their attention to support the new ANC government, in areas of democracy consolidation, administration of justice, and poverty eradication (Rogerson, 2010). This phenomenon heavily impacted upon the financial stream of some policy research centres, which forced them to become dormant or to limit their operations (Hearn, 2000). Secondly, the insufficient funding for NPOs led to a 'brain drain', as leading members of these institutions defected to government departments or operated private businesses. Put differently, leading researchers in these institutions deserted these institutions in pursuit of better prospects (Habib, 2005). For the few who remained, survival implied rebranding their aspirations to conform to emerging trends. The shift in goals and core functions of the organisations caused something of an identity crisis, as many were not well equipped to undertake action-oriented research in areas such as human rights, access to healthcare, or corruption (Heinrich, 2001).

Nonetheless, by 1997, this shift had drawn the attention of some donors, which began funding these areas of research (Wiggill, 2014). At the same time, the ANC had begun rebuilding ties with a few existing institutions. To foster their contribution to its democratic experiment, the regime adopted a string of interventions that encouraged former anti-apartheid activists and young graduates to form and/or join such institutions. The first of these was the enactment of the 1996 Constitution that professed freedom of association and speech. The

Preamble of the Constitution recognises the right of every individual to form and join research centres, as well as the right of such bodies to determine their activities and programmes. The second intervention flows from the first. Aside from regulating the activities of think tanks, the adoption of the Non-profit Organisations Act (No. 71 of 1997) granted tax exemption and subsidies for their operations.

While there is no exact data on how many research centres evolved as a result of these enabling conditions, Wyngaard (2013) argues that they some-what influenced the revival of dormant ones and the formation of new insti-tutions. McGann (2020) observes that the country currently houses 92 such institutions, making it the jurisdiction with the highest number of think tanks in sub-Saharan Africa. Yet, since he clarified that the figure is for 'registered' think tanks or policy institutes, the implication is that there may be more, as some could be operating informally. With increasing democratisation, the scope of their research has further evolved to include the contemporary issues of fair electioneering, children's rights, rule of law and government account-ability. It is worth highlighting that this enabling environment did not come without strings attached. Similar to donor funding conditionalities, research commissioned by the state was accompanied by terms of reference that dictated the objectives, scope and plan of action of recipients of these grants (Nzimakwe, 2008). These directives ultimately shrunk the autonomy of the institutes to conduct impartial scientific research.

These think tanks could only thrive in an environment that encourages engagement between civil society and civil servants, the latter being framers and implementers of policies. There is also the need for a considerable degree of academic freedom to forestall state interference in the research agendas of these institutes. The influence of think tanks in democratisation may be catego-rised into two areas: (1) direct involvement in policy formulation by providing recommendations; and (2) engaging in advocacy to bring the plight of poor communities to the attention of policy-makers.

Having situated South African think tanks in their historical contexts, the next section assesses their influence on the contemporary policy process. It is important to first classify these institutions in terms of their ideological ori-entation and research focus, with particular reference to how these ideologies have shaped their operations.

THINK TANKS IN CONTEMPORARY SOUTH AFRICA

Think tanks differ in areas of specialisation, research output, ideological ori-entation and institutional independence (Abelson, 2018). Policy research insti-tutes, for example, are catalysts of development in their proximity to realities on the ground. Consequently, they can directly transfer the concerns of community members to policy-makers through their research and consultations. These institutions are answerable to two key actors: the constituency in whose name they seek funding, and donors or agencies that fund their operations. At the local level, these policy institutes vary greatly. Their disparity is more distinctive in their ideological proclivity and thematic area. The institutional ideologies of South Africa's contemporary think tanks may be grouped under three headings: Pan-Africanism, Evangelism and Mandelaism. We briefly highlight the notable elements of each of these orientations, and identify specific institutions that conform to these ideals.

Pan-Africanism

This acknowledges that political stability on the African continent is a *sine qua non* for uplifting and unifying people of African descent (Adogamhe, 2008). As a result, institutions that were originally launched in South Africa have extended their tentacles and provided policy recommendations to other African countries. Classic illustrations of such research centres with a pan-African outlook are the Institute for Security Studies (ISS) and the African Centre for the Constructive Resolution of Disputes (ACCORD). The regional approach of these institutions may have been informed by the ethnic conflict and political instability that have continued to ravage certain parts of the continent over the last five decades (Müller-Crepon et al., 2020).

Evangelism

This group engages in the dissemination of religious doctrines to shape the conduct of certain actors. Institutes in this category are often faith-based research centres that seek to foster religious tolerance and safeguard the vulnerable population from inhumane treatment. Among this cluster of institutions are the South African Faith and Family Institute (SAFFI) and the Institute for Theology and Religion (ITR) which rely on theological perspectives to counter patriarchal traditions that undermine the rights of women and children in traditional communities. The Desmond Tutu Centre for Religion and Social Justice (DTCRSJ) advocates for equality by drawing from religious doctrines to counter systemic powers that foster oppression and discrimination against women or sexual minority rights. Despite sharing somewhat similar belief systems, certain variations are evident in the activities of institutes in this group. As an illustration, the portfolios of SAFFI and the DTCRSJ are characterised by radical activists who use workshops as tools for shaping gender and child policies, while the ITR adopts a less radical action of information dissemination and training of policy-makers.

Mandelaism

As the name suggests, the notion was inspired by the ideals of Nelson Mandela. As an African nationalist, Mandela was a strong proponent of three ideals: non-racism, anti-poverty and accountable government (Garba and Akuva, 2020). A particular feature of institutions that follow this tradition is the multi-racial composition of their board members and staff, which to a large extent reflects their mission of fostering non-racism. As a result, one of the core missions of the Institute for Justice and Reconciliation (IJR) is to mobilise the legacy of Mandela in finding sustainable solutions to racial tension and other social issues. The Institute therefore uses its research and advocacy cluster to deepen the government's effort towards inclusive societies, as well as socioeconomic justice across communities. Like other ideological think tanks described here, there has been a considerable transformation in its research focus and audience. The IJR has broadened its geographical focus to providing policy advice to other African countries in areas such as transitional justice, post-conflict reconstruction and restorative justice. In terms of poverty eradication, Mandela was more emphatic when he advocated: 'Overcoming poverty is not a gesture of charity. It is an act of justice. It is the protection of a fundamental human right, the right to dignity and a decent life. While poverty persists, there is no true freedom' (UN, 2018: para. 8).

This belief has given rise to many research institutes that undertake specific research and advocacy drives to improve living standards in *ikasi* (townships). Institutes in this category perceive skills development, job creation and education as antidotes to addressing historical disadvantages and the social conflict which is pervasive in post-apartheid South Africa. In 2004 and 2006, the Mandela Initiative and the Studies in Poverty and Inequality Institute (SPII, 2020) were established as independent research centres to provide strategic leadership and guidance toward alleviating the country's rising level of poverty and inequality. Although these institutions have to some extent fulfilled the central ideals of Mandela's aspirations, their role in promoting accountable government seems to be muted. Their insufficient advocacy is manifested in recent inter-provincial food parcels and personal protective equipment procurement scandals, where state officials allegedly siphoned off millions of dollars (Moche, 2020).

Surprisingly, this phenomenon is not limited to the government but extends to think tanks. Having been instrumental in the removal of a former president on allegations of corruption, the Nelson Mandela Foundation (NMF) has in recent times come under the spotlight after its senior management was allegedly entangled in a procurement impropriety (Shange, 2017; Fisher, 2021). It might therefore be argued that the institutes ought to be more introspective and pay greater attention to contemporary issues. Resources should be directed toward addressing tender impropriety. There is a link between misappropriation and socioeconomic deprivation, as one could impact upon the other. Regardless of their ideological inclinations, think tanks could further be categorised in terms of their affiliation and/or source of funding.

Affiliated institutes

This camp consists of think tanks that are affiliated with established and traditional institutions, such as universities. Notable examples include the South African Institute of International Affairs (SAIIA), the Centre for the Study of Violence and Reconciliation (CSVR) and the IJR. While all these institutes share topical interests in conflict resolution and justice, some university-affiliated think tanks such as the Centre for Social Development in Africa (CSDA) link their research to social justice.

Non-affiliated institutes

The second group is non-affiliated institutes. Corporations, foundations and private individuals mainly fund these bodies. These include the NMF, SPII and the Socio-Economic Rights Institute of South Africa. The common thread running through these institutes is that they seem to be adherents of Mandelaism, partnering with the government to develop and monitor the operationalisation of economic and social strategies in local communities. The third cluster is comprised of government-funded and/or sponsored institutes. Known examples include the Council for Scientific and Industrial Research (CSIR), the Human Sciences Research Council (HSRC) and the National TB Think Tank (TBTT). While this chapter might not be able to assess the contributions of all the institutes to South Africa's governance and democratic exercise, the role of the TBTT merits some consideration.

The TBTT (2022) was established in 2014 to explore the mode of transmission of the bacteria and provide policy directions regarding diagnostic tests, protective gadgets and preventive measures. Against this backdrop, the relevance of the TBTT in shaping health policies and ideas in contemporary South Africa is telling, particularly in the era of the COVID-19 pandemic. With the epidemic having a devasting effect on the country's health system, the role of an organisation whose strategic research focuses on transmission of bacteria through coughs and sneezes, which is similar to COVID-19 transmission, becomes inevitable. With COVID-19 being the most pressing issue in contemporary South Africa, and the TBTT's mandate directly linked to this crisis, the next section teases out the nuances of the organisation in the governance of the country's health sector.

THE INFLUENCE OF THINK TANKS IN THE HEALTH SECTOR: THE TBTT

Democracy does not only mean extending civil/political rights to the governed. It includes providing basic services to citizens to ensure their sustenance and well-being. This perspective resonates with Mandela's visual disposition of social/economic rights, where he mooted that a 'simple vote, without food, shelter, and healthcare is to use first-generation rights as a smokescreen to obscure the deep underlying forces which dehumanise people' (Mandela, 1991). To this end, the 1996 Constitution imposes an obligation on the government to promote second-generation rights, including access to quality healthcare delivery. As a response, policies and institutions have been established to safeguard citizens from actions that might deprive them of these rights, with the Department of Health (DoH) being one such institution.

It may be argued that COVID-19 ought to be a central focus of any research undertaken in the contemporary era. This assumption is informed by the massive death toll and the impacts of the virus on all facets of human industry and livelihoods. Like other African countries, the year 2021 witnessed a surge of the epidemic, which led to the reimposition of lockdowns on citizens, with rights such as freedom of movement and association curtailed. Whereas an analysis of a specific COVID-19 think tank in South Africa might have been prudent, there is arguably no such centre at the time of writing. In the absence of such an institution, a health concern that shares a striking similarity to COVID-19 is tuberculosis (TB). While the latter has a slower onset and longer incubation period, both COVID-19 and TB share three similarities: (1) both are infectious diseases; (2) both affect the lungs; and (3) common symptoms include fever, cough and shortness of breath.

As well as the surging number of people being infected with COVID-19, South Africa recorded a 20 per cent increase in the number of people who fell ill with TB between 2019 and 2020 (Green, 2020). As its name implies, while the National TB Control Programme (NTCP) continuously seeks to mitigate this increasing number, its efforts are often challenged by the insufficient capacity to effectively treat patients and safeguard ordinary community members from becoming infected (Wood et al., 2011). Although the World Health Organization (WHO) continues to provide universal guidance on how to contain TB, these recommendations often do not adequately capture the domestic context and unique challenges experienced by patients at the district or municipal levels. Against this backdrop, some officials from the DoH partnered with relevant academics and civil societies to form the South African TB Think Tank (TBTT) which was launched in 2014 (Hippner et al., 2019). The formation of the institute seems to have been inspired by existing health-related think tanks such as the South African Medical Research Council (SAMRC) and the African Health Research Institute (AHRI) that share a common aspiration of promoting quality healthcare through research and technology transfer.

Despite the existence of these institutions, there is a paucity of scholarship on the extent to which health-related think tanks influence government policies or foster quality healthcare. As Shaw et al. (2014) argued, think tanks need to become a concern in the field of healthcare policy. A yardstick ought to be used to measure the efficiency or the level of influence of think tanks. In the main, the section adopts a cautious approach to the treatment of influence here, as this may differ within and across policy fields. Caution should be observed regarding misleading information in the media, understating or overstating an institute's hegemony in governance processes.

Under the present discussion, the influence might be perceived as: (1) the close ties with relevant policy actors; (2) the timely publication of research output; and (3) the generation of credible data. Flowing from this benchmark, the TBTT equally seeks to enhance the operations of the NTCP collating and evaluating reliable data (Caelers, 2017). Therefore, it has a representative on the South African National AIDS Council (SANAC) that oversees the management of HIV/AIDS patient information and distribution of antiretroviral drugs. Its membership may be seen as an important avenue to access useful data to influence the content and structures of interventions geared towards TB and AIDS patients, and provide useful guidance to their households.

One of the maiden activities of the TBTT was a 2014 childhood screening where the institute compiled a policy brief, advising the DoH that primary and secondary education systems were not fertile grounds for spreading TB (White et al., 2018). Being amenable to this conclusion, the department shifted its focus and surveyed the rate of infection among infants, mainly in pre-schools (Reuter and Furin, 2018). Also, in 2014, the institute's impact on modelling formed the framing of an R70 million (US$4 million) United Kingdom–South African Medical Research Council call for proposals on operational research (White et al., 2018: 609). The following year it was instrumental in framing the concept note, and subsequently organised a series of engagements that led to the launch of the National TB Research Plan (NRP). As a collaborative project with the WHO, the NRP relies on epidemiology and mathematical modelling to quantify TB risks and its economic burden among subpopulations (DoH and SANAC, 2016). The main target of the assessment was a population that is the primary driver of the pandemic, and what specific interventions ought to be fashioned to contain their related economic hardships. An extra layer of the plan was an assessment of the extent to which the proposed intervention might mitigate the spread of the epidemic.

The operationalisation of the NRP further resulted in the launch of an investment drive in 2015. Termed the 'Investment Case for HIV and TB', to ensure the sustainability of the national response to TB and HIV the programme sought to raise sufficient capital and identify cost-effective means of combating the spread of HIV/TB infections among vulnerable populations (Meyer-Rath et al., 2019). The campaign ultimately contributed to an increased budget allocation for TB/HIV in the subsequent year, from R25.81 billion in 2015/16 to R28.814 billion in 2016/17 (Guthrie et al., 2018: xii).

Additionally, the TBTT has contributed to the DoH's effort of using research and innovation to leverage the country's action toward mitigating the national TB crisis. Through the data submitted by the think tank, the state increased government funding for the pandemic by up to R500 million, and specifically launched a conditional grant for research into the health condition in 2016 (Meyer-Rath et al., 2019: 609). Within the same year, the recommendation of the think tanks influenced the decision of the DoH to switch from its use of six months of Isoniazid preventive therapy to 3HP as a treatment for TB (Caelers, 2017). The latter consists of two antibiotics (rifapentine and isoniazid), which are taken once a week for 12 weeks by persons with HIV and their households (Unitaid, 2019). To some observers, this form of treatment eliminates previous challenges faced by health workers in the administration of TB treatment, as it provides options for self-administration of the antibiotics, as well as a shorter treatment time-frame (CDC, 2018).

One important role played by the think tank in recent times was its instrumental role in the framing of the DoH's National Tuberculosis Programme Strategic Plan 2017–2021 (GovZA, 2017). In brief, by assessing the existing literature, conducting colloquiums and compiling the first draft of the strategy, the institute became a key player in shaping the government's TB response for over four years. Despite these positive contributions to national health response, some challenges exist which militate against the TBTT's effective role in this regard. It is these constraints that are briefly highlighted in the next section.

CHALLENGES CONFRONTING THE TBTT

In the African context, think tanks face several challenges. These vary from the fragmented interpretation of policies by political parties, ownership and privacy of the free flow of big data, insufficient funding, and the scarcity of experts (Acquah, 2021). The situation of think tanks in Africa is more serious than the world situation (Okeke-Uzodike, 2021). Some of these challenges are also relevant to South Africa. In an empirical study of think tanks in South Africa, Chikozho and Saruchera (2015) argue that the size of the challenges faced by South African society requires a collaborative approach to enable more knowledge to transform ideas into better policies and practices.

In recent times, some scholarships have underscored the importance of the participation of think tanks in consolidating democracy and basic rights. The success of any think tank is often based on two elements: (1) intellectual freedom or complete independence to research without occasional political interference; and (2) the ability of experts to fully commit their time to research and provide advice as required by policy-makers. Yet there is a likelihood that formidable barriers could hinder the effective operationalisation and influence in the policy arena. In applying the two thresholds to the TBTT, there is little indication that the institute experienced any political interference in the conduct of its research and advocacy roles. Nonetheless, four constraints are particularly revealing.

Firstly, as discussed above, the cardinal aspiration of the institute is to respond to TB through two channels: (1) undertaking independent research; and (2) conducting research commissioned by the DoH. Nonetheless, half a decade since its establishment, it seems to have developed a proclivity for the latter, with most of its activities tailored towards developing policy briefs and serving as a point of reference for the department. Under this condition, the institute could be viewed as an extension of the government department, without much focus on proactively undertaking independent research like its contemporaries. While this approach might have the merits of directly influencing the content of health interventions, it somewhat compromises the neutrality and independence of the institute, as the research focus might be dictated by its funder, the state. Thus, to sustain continuous support from the state, the institute might be compelled to generate reports and propose recommendations that appeal to its benefactor.

Secondly, considering that a disproportionate percentage of the institute's researchers are volunteers from the DoH, there is a challenge in terms of the amount of time dedicated to the operations of the institute, particularly in instances where official leave or authorisation to undertake external research has not been secured. In such cases, an individual may be compelled to divide their working hours between official duties and think tank deadlines. The divided attention might ultimately compromise the quality of the research output. This setback is linked to the neutrality and/or (im)partiality of the institute's reports and research outputs. With some experts still operating in the public sector, there is the possibility that the agenda of the institute may be influenced by external partners, particularly the DoH, which will use its participating staff to shape the content of the institute's research and advocacy agenda.

The third constraint is linked to the DoH's short-term funding of the TBTT's programmes. The absence of long-term financial instruments may disincentivise the institute from conducting overarching research, for fear of running out of resources. This holds for external experts who are constrained as the institute's insufficient grant often limits the amount of time they could dedicate to collating and analysing data. As an illustration, data collection and analysis can be burdensome and time-consuming, which may deplete the institute's already stretched budget. Thus, the ability of the institute to conduct large-scale research may be limited by financial constraints, as some studies may take up to three years, thereby exceeding the time-frame of available grants.

Finally, there is the institute's lack of visibility and poor dissemination of research to the media and the general public. With this setback, the institute's overall contribution of informing and limiting the spread of the pandemic is swallowed up in its annual report, which the majority of the general public might not have access to, or they might be unable to grasp the import of the report, particularly its technical content.

To ensure the sustainability and continuous utility of the institute, three recommendations come to the fore. Firstly, despite the setbacks illustrated above, there is a glimmer of hope, as there is political will on the part of state agencies to partner with this institute in mitigating the spread and adverse effects of TB. Yet, for the DoH to continue tapping into the knowledge base of the institute, it ought to allocate additional funding towards non-commissioned projects, to originate new ideas and innovation. Through this approach, new funding could be instrumental in providing new policy directions and interventions for containing the pandemic.

Secondly, there is an urgency for the TBTT to maintain some degree of autonomy. Evolving as an autonomous body requires the ability to attract long-term financial support from private and non-state actors, such as foundations, transnational corporations and United Nations bodies. With sustained (external) financial support, the institute could hire and retain experts as permanent staff, which will give the latter job security and motivation to break new ground in their research. In the absence of sufficient financial incentives, as is the case under the present circumstances, the contributions of researchers need to be acknowledged. Acknowledgment could take the form of being cited as co-authors of reports or publications, giving visibility to their work on the institute's website, or sponsorship for conference travel. These gestures could motivate researchers to make meaningful contributions towards achieving the mission of the institute.

Thirdly, it appears that the institute does not have a broader partnership with other think tanks in the sector. To enhance its influence and visibility, it must strengthen the existing relationships with relevant policy research institutes, while forging new alliances with established institutions. Broader partnership with non-health think tanks – including ACCORD, ISS and the Institute for Justice and Reconciliation (ICJ) – is paramount. Their long existence may be accompanied by extensive experience which could be harvested for improving relations with the government, securing external funding through endowments, contracts and grants, improving the quality of research, dissemination of research outputs to broader consumers, and breaking new ground in research.

CONCLUSION

Since South Africa transitioned to democracy in 1994, there has been a surge in the number of think tanks seeking to influence state policies on issues of democratisation, development, human rights and quality healthcare. As a group of intellectual and non-partisan entities, they exercise considerable autonomy over their research focus and public advocacy. Through their research, policy advice and capacity building, they foster accountable government and the well-being of marginalised communities. Some are consulted by the government in policy formulation and operationalisation in light of their evolving role in people-oriented development. In supporting policy development, some are active in conducting systematic reviews, dialogues and verbal briefings. One important aspect of democratisation where these institutions have thrived is in health.

The TBTT was identified as one think tank which has made a considerable contribution by partnering with the state to develop strategies for tackling one of the country's health threats. With strong ties to relevant policy actors, yet with a considerable degree of autonomy from government interference, the institute has made enormous contributions to the country's attempts to contain the spread of TB amongst vulnerable groups. This effort was evident in the provision of relevant scientific data to inform the actions of the DoH in addressing TB and related epidemics such as HIV/AIDS. Yet the institute faces the perennial problem of inadequate specialised staff, as it lacks long-term funding to hire and retain experts. As a result, a considerable proportion of the operations of the institute are carried out by officials of the DoH, which somewhat compromises the autonomy and neutrality of its research output, findings and recommendations. There was also the concern of overdependence on government support that might compromise its autonomy and position in the policy arena. There is a need for the institute to strengthen ties with existing think tanks and source external funding to enhance its autonomy and the capacity of its researchers.

REFERENCES

Abelson, D.E. (2018). *Do Think Tanks Matter? Assessing the Impact of Public Policy Institutes* (3rd edn). Montreal and Kingston: McGill-Queen's University Press.

Acquah, E. (2021). The future of African think tanks. In J. McGann (ed.), *The Future of Think Tanks and Policy Advice Around the World* (pp. 27–32). Cham: Palgrave Macmillan.

Adogamhe, P.G. (2008). Pan-Africanism revisited: vision and reality of African unity and development. *African Review of Integration*, 2, 1–34.

Africa, C. (2019). Do election campaigns matter in South Africa? An examination of fluctuations in support for the ANC, DA, IFP and NNP 1994–2019. *Politikon*, 46, 371–389.

Alence, R., and Pitcher, A. (2019). Resisting state capture in South Africa. *Journal of Democracy*, 30, 5–19.

Beckmann, J. (2019). Thuma Mina and education: volunteerism, possibilities, and challenges. *South African Journal of Education*, 39, S1–S8.

Binns, T., and Nel, E. (2002). Devolving development: integrated development planning and developmental local government in post-apartheid South Africa. *Regional Studies*, 36, 921–932.

Bond, P. (2014). *Elite Transition: From Apartheid to Neoliberalism in South*. London: Pluto Press.

Caelers, D. (2017). SA's TB Think Tank puts the country's brightest minds at helm of its TB response. *Mail and Guardian*. https://mg.co.za/article/2017–03–24–00-sas -tb-think-tank-putsthe-countrys-brightest-minds-at-helm-of-its-tb-response/#:~:text =The%20country's%20TB%20Think%20Tank,and%20women's%20and%20child %20health. Accessed 26 January 2021.

CDC (Centers for Disease Control and Prevention). (2018). 3HP for latent TB infection treatment media summary. https://www.cdc.gov/nchhstp/newsroom/2018/3HP -media-summary.html. Accessed 26 January 2021.

Chikozho, C., and Saruchera, D. (2015). Universities and think-tanks as partners in the African knowledge economy: Insights from South Africa. *African Journal of Science, Technology, Innovation and Development*, 7, 286–300.

Davis, G. (2021). Economists warn govt against further tax hikes to pay for COVID-19 vaccines. *Eyewitness News*. https://ewn.co.za/2021/01/19/economists-warn-govt -againstfurther-tax-hikes-to-pay-for-covid-vaccines. Accessed 27 January 2021.

DoH (Department of Health) and SANAC (South African National AIDS Council) (2016). South African HIV and TB Investment Case – Summary Report: Phase 1. http://www.heroza.org/wp-content/uploads/2016/03/SA-HIV_TB-Investment-Case -Full-Report-Low-Res.pdf Accessed 29 January 2021.

Fisher, S. (2021). Mandela Foundation says allegations against CEO, COO taken very seriously. *Eyewitness News*. https://ewn.co.za/2021/01/20/mandela-foundation-says -allegations-against-ceo-coo-taken-very-seriously. Accessed 27 January 2021.

Fraussen, B., and Halpin, D. (2017). Think tanks and strategic policy-making: the contribution of think tanks to policy advisory systems. *Policy Sciences*, 50, 105–124.

Gallarotti, G.M. (2011). Soft power: what it is, why it's important, and the conditions for its effective use. *Journal of Political Power*, 4, 25–47.

Garba, D., and Akuva, I.I. (2020). The leadership styles of Nelson Mandela as a pattern for African leaders. *Covenant University Journal of Politics and International Affairs*, 8, 49–64.

Gassama, I.J. (1996). Reaffirming faith in the dignity of each human being: the United Nations, NGOs, and apartheid. *Fordham International Law Journal*, 19, 1464–1541.

Glied, S., Wittenberg, R., and Israeli, A. (2018). Research in government and academia: the case of health policy. *Israel Journal of Health Policy Research*, 7, 1–8.

Gounden, V., and Coning, C. de (2021). The future of think tanks in Africa. In J. McGann (ed.), *The Future of Think Tanks and Policy Advice Around the World* (pp. 21–26). Cham: Palgrave Macmillan.

GovZA (Government of South Africa). (2017). South Africa's National Strategic Plan for HIV, TB and STIs 2017–2022. https://www.gov.za/sites/default/files/gcis_document/201705/nsp-hiv-tb-stia.pdf. Accessed 26 January 2021.

Green, A. (2020). What is behind SA's higher TB numbers? *City Press*. https://www.spotlightnsp.co.za/2020/10/21/what-is-behind-sas-higher-tb-numbers/ October 21, 2020. Accessed 27 January 2021.

Guthrie, T., Chaitkin, M., Khoza, N., Zulu, N., Madisha, V., Ndlovu, N., ... Ghai, K. (2018). *Consolidated Spending on HIV and TB in South Africa (2014/15–2016/17)*. Pretoria: National Department of Health; Washington, DC: Health Finance and Governance Project, Results for Development Institute.

Habib, A. (2005). State–civil society relations in post-apartheid South Africa. *Social Research*, 72, 671–692.

Habib, A., and Taylor, R. (1999). South Africa: anti-apartheid NGOs in transition. *Voluntas: International Journal of Voluntary and Nonprofit Organizations*, 10, 73–82.

Hearn, J. (2000). Aiding democracy? Donors and civil society in South Africa. *Third World Quarterly*, 21, 815–830.

Heinrich, V.F. (2001). The role of NGOs in strengthening the foundations of South African democracy. *Voluntas: International Journal of Voluntary and Nonprofit Organizations*, 12, 1–15.

Gonzalez Hernando, Marcos, and Williams, Kate (2018). Examining the link between funding and intellectual interventions across universities and think tanks: a theoretical framework. *International Journal of Politics, Culture, and Society*, 31, 193-206.

Hippner, P., Sumner, T., Houben, R.M.G.J., Cardenas, V., Vassall, A., ... White, R.G. (2019). Application of provincial data in mathematical modeling to inform sub-national tuberculosis program decision-making in South Africa. *PLoS ONE*, 14, 1–11.

Koelble, T.A., and Siddle, A. (2014). Decentralization in post-apartheid South Africa. *Regional and Federal Studies*, 24, 607–623.

Krastev, I. (2001) Think tanks: making and faking influence. *Southeast European and Black Sea Studies*, 1, 17–38.

Mackenzie, J. (2021). South Africa treasury considers tax hike to fund vaccine. *Daily Maverick*. https://www.dailymaverick.co.za/article/2021-01-18-south-africa-treasury-considers-tax-hike-to-fund-vaccines-business-day/. Accessed 26 January 2021.

Mandela, N. (1991). Address: On the occasion of the ANC's Bill of Rights conference. In *A Bill of Rights for a Democratic South Africa: Papers and Report of a Conference Convened by the ANC Constitutional Committee, May 1991*, 9–14.

Mbunge, E. (2020). Effects of COVID-19 in South African health system and society: an explanatory study. *Diabetes and Metabolic Syndrome: Clinical Research and Reviews*, 14, 1809–1814.

McGann, J.G. (2003). Think tanks and the transnationalisation of foreign policy. *Connections*, 2, 85–90.

McGann, J.G. (2018). 2017 Global Go To Think Tank Index Report. Pennsylvania, PA: The Lauder Institute University of Pennsylvania.

McGann, J.G. (2020). 2019 Global Go To Think Tank Index Report. TTCSP Global Go To Think Tank Index Reports. 17. https://repository.upenn.edu/think_tanks/17. Accessed 19 September 2020.

McGann, J. (2021). Introduction and background. In J. McGann (ed.), *The Future of Think Tanks and Policy Advice Around the World* (pp. 1–20). Cham: Palgrave Macmillan.

Meyer-Rath, G., van Rensburg, C., Chiu, C., Leuner, R., Jamieson, L., and Cohen, S. (2019). The per-patient costs of HIV services in South Africa: systematic review and application in the South African HIV Investment Case. *PloS One*, 14, 1–15.

Moche, T. (2020). Timeline: COVID-19 food parcels, PPE corruption timeline. *SABC News* https://www.sabcnews.com/sabcnews/timeline-covid-19-food-parcels-ppe-corruption-timeline. Accessed 27 January 2021.

Müller-Crepon, C., Hunziker, P., and Cederman, L.E. (2020). Roads to rule, roads to rebel: relational state capacity and conflict in Africa. *Journal of Conflict*, 65, 563–590.

Mullon, P.A., and Ngoepe, M. (2019). An integrated framework to elevate information governance to a national level in South Africa. *Records Management Journal*, 29, 103–116.

Niblett, R. (2018). Rediscovering a sense of purpose: the challenge for western think-tanks. *International Affairs*, 94, 1409–1430.

Nzimakwe, T.I. (2008). South Africa's NGOs and the quest for development. *International NGO Journal*, 3, 90–97.

Okeke-Uzodike, U. (2021). The future of think tanks and policy advice: an African perspective. In J. McGann (ed.), *The Future of Think Tanks and Policy Advice Around the World* (pp. 33–40). Cham: Palgrave Macmillan.

Reuter, A., and Furin, J. (2018). Bedaquiline use in South Africa reveals a policy in action. *The Lancet Respiratory Medicine*, 6, 653–655.

Rogerson, C.M. (2010). Local economic development in South Africa: strategic challenges. *Development Southern Africa*, 27, 481–495.

Scott, J.M. (1999). Transnationalizing democracy promotion: the role of Western political foundations and think-tanks. *Democratization*, 6, 146–170.

Shange, N. (2017). All 'tentacles' of corruption need to be cut out from government, says the Nelson Mandela Foundation. *Times Live*. https://www.timeslive.co.za/politics/2017–05–31-all-tentacles-of-corruption-need-to-be-cut-out-from-government-says-the-nelson-mandela-foundation/. Accessed 27 January 2021.

Shaw, S.E., Russell, J., Greenhalgh, T., and Korica, M. (2014). Thinking about think tanks in health care: a call for a new research agenda. *Sociology of Health and Illness*, 36, 447–461.

Shubin, V. (2019). South Africa: A new dawn?' *Brazilian Journal of African Studies*, 4, 33–48.

SPII (Studies in Poverty and Inequality Institute) (2020). Annual Report. http://spii.org.za/wp-content/uploads/2021/12/SPII11-ANNUAL-REPORT-2020-FINAL.pdf.

TBTT (TB Think Tank). 2022. TB Think Tank. https://tbthinktank.org (accessed March 17, 2023).

UN (United Nations) (2018). Quoting Nelson Mandela on his centenary, Secretary-General says overcoming poverty 'is not an act of charity, it is an act of justice'. SG/SM/19138-OBV/1806. https://www.un.org/press/en/2018/sgsm19138.doc.htm #: ~: text = To %20quote %20Nelson %20Mandela %3A %20 %E2 %80 %9COvercoming,there%20is%20no%20true%20freedom.%E2%80%9D. Accessed 26 January 2021.

Unitaid (2019). Catalyzing Pediatric Tuberculosis Innovations (CaP TB). https://unitaid .org/ assets/ Catalyzing -Pediatric -Tuberculosis -Innovations -CaP -TB .pdf. Accessed 26 January 2021.

White, R.G., Charalambous, S., Cardenas, V., Hippner, P., Sumner, T., Bozzani, F., ... Churchyard, G. (2018). Evidence-informed policymaking at country level: lessons learned from the South African Tuberculosis Think Tank. *International Journal of Tuberculosis and Lung Disease*, 2, 606–613.

Wiggill, M.N. (2014). Donor relationship management practices in the South African non-profit sector. *Public Relations Review*, 40, 278–285.

Wood, R., Lawn, S.D., Johnstone-Robertson, S.J., and Bekker, L. (2011). Tuberculosis control has failed in South Africa – time to reappraise strategy. *South African Medical Journal*, 101, 111–114.

Wyngaard, R.G. (2013). The South African NPO crisis: time to join hands. *International Journal of Not-for-Profit Law*, 15, 5–12.

11. Conclusion to *Think Tanks, Governance, and Development in Africa*

Joseph R.A. Ayee and Frank L.K. Ohemeng

INTRODUCTION

This chapter summarizes the findings on institutionalism, think tanks, and the case studies and their implications for the theoretical, comparative and empirical literature. It provides an agenda for future research in light of the developmental challenges which face Africa, the threats and opportunities offered particularly in the post-COVID-19 period, and the Fourth Industrial Revolution, specifically artificial intelligence (AI), and how think tanks can leverage the context in partnership with other stakeholders such as governments, regional organizations and the private sector in order to deepen governance and development. Africa is on the cusp of development due to its abundance of human and natural resources. Yet, how to manage these resources continues to be problematic. Hence the role of civil society groups, and especially think tanks, in this developmental trajectory is of the utmost importance, as discussed throughout this book.

SUMMARY OF FINDINGS FROM THE CHAPTERS

This book set out to address the following questions:

1. What accounts for the proliferation of thinks tanks in sub-Saharan Africa since the 1990s and what institutional forms do they take?
2. How and why do thinks tanks influence governance, policy formulation and implementation?
3. How are think tanks funded, and what are the implications for their operations?
4. What has been the contribution of think tanks, if any, to politics and the development process?
5. What challenges do think tanks face, and how have they been addressed?

6.   What lessons can be learned from think tanks, and what are the implications for the literature on politics, public policy and administration and civil society?

These questions have been addressed by the chapters in a number of ways. First, each chapter tried as much as possible to deal with the issues within the context of its specific case study area. The common underlying themes of the chapters are the role of think tanks as policy progenitors and entrepreneurs, influence in governance and development through advocacy, dissemination of information, and the contextual variables such as human and financial resources, legal and institutional framework of the country, that have contributed positively or negatively in the pursuit of their mandates. The chapters reinforce the view that think tanks are new organizational actors that continue to flourish generally in Africa, and more specifically in the case study countries of Botswana, Cameroon, Ghana, Kenya, Nigeria, Rwanda, Senegal and South Africa. Seen as part of the wider civil society groups, they have performed ideational and discursive functions with the aim to shape the public's perceptions of what constitutes the public good through the generation and dissemination of, as well as mobilization around, ideas and ideologies (Åberg et al., 2019).

Second, to understand this role, the chapters draw on institutional theory, to understand the rapid development of think tanks in Africa. Institutional theory is one of the oldest theories to understand and explain organizational development, and the processes by which structures become established and shape social behaviour. Thus, as a theory to understand and explain social behaviour, it helps to appreciate the actors which shape these organisations and the processes promoting ideas to alter and institutionalise new behaviours, including values and norms in the society (Arshed, 2017). From this theoretical perspective, the findings of the chapters have helped us to chart new ways for understanding and appreciating think tanks as a unique group in the larger civil society literature, and their contributions to national development, as well as challenges facing them. Furthermore, they have enabled us to understand the nature of the policy context – whether it is enabling, obstructing or vulnerable – and how it is an important contributing factor with respect to the level of effectiveness of these institutions in the governance and developmental process.

Third, since the 'third wave' of democratization hit sub-Saharan Africa in the 1990s, there has been a steady proliferation of think tanks in the governance, development and policy environment, leading to what may be described as the mushrooming of think tanks. The chapters have shown that, irrespective of the context of the countries, think tanks have played significant roles both in the political and policy processes, as well as in the education of the general masses on their rights and obligations under current democratic regimes. They have contributed to an understanding of what they stand for, what they do, and how they do it, that is, the mechanisms used to achieve their stated objectives, which are not well known or articulated to the general populace, politicians, scholars and the donor community. This has led to the dispelling of some of the unfair criticisms levelled against them in the past. In addition, the chapters have emphasized that think tanks have come to stay, and their potential in influencing public policies and programmes and thereby becoming policy progenitors and entrepreneurs cannot be understated. They have therefore filled the lacunae on think tanks from both comparative and empirical perspectives.

Fourth, the chapters approached their analyses from two main methodological imperatives. One is the comparative historical analysis, which deals with 'a sustained focus on a well-defined set of national cases, a concern with a substantial time frame and with the unfolding of causal processes over time and the use of systematic comparison to generate and/or evaluate explanations of outcomes at the level of national politics' (Collier, 1998: 1–2). This approach helped us as the editors to draw on common underlying themes from the various chapters in the concluding chapter. The second is the qualitative approach which addressed the 'what' and 'how' questions, in understanding the mandates and activities of think tanks as policy progenitors and entrepreneurs. In employing the qualitative approach, the authors of the chapters, with the exception of those for Botswana and Cameroon (who used both fieldwork and documentary sources), used the documentary and secondary techniques in data collection. These techniques have no doubt yielded a rich resource of information not only from think tanks, but more so from policy makers in these countries.

LESSONS

The findings highlight a number of lessons worth considering. First, even though there has been a proliferation of think tanks in Africa, their contribution to agenda setting, policy design, implementation, governance and development, including peacebuilding, remains modest due to structural challenges such as resources and organizational deficits, as well as ineffective country-specific legal and institutional frameworks. In some countries such as Botswana and Cameroon with relatively less liberal legal and institutional frameworks, the growth and activities of think tanks are retarded due to the shrinking policy space.

Second, funding remains the Achilles heel of all the think tanks in the countries and this has to a large extent affected their advocacy and policy dissemination roles, especially in a highly digital communication world. This therefore calls for regular sources of funding, a situation which has prompted some people to advocate for public funding for think tanks, which in itself is problematic given the tendency for co-optation by the governments, as well as launching endowment funds and appealing to the private sector.

Third, think tanks have been linked to the realization of some of the international development blueprints such as the Sustainable Development Goals (Agenda 2030) and the African Union's (AU) The Africa We Want (Agenda 2063). As already pointed out in Chapter 1, this has led the AU to launch in February 2023 the African Network of Think Tanks for Peace (NeTT4Peace) with the objective of driving the partnership between the African research community and the AU Department of Political Affairs Peace and Security (DPAPS) on governance, peace and security to address the limited collaboration between the AU and think tanks.

Fourth, even though there are 54 countries in Africa, the book covers only eight, namely Botswana, Cameroon, Ghana, Kenya, Nigeria, Rwanda, Senegal and South Africa. Conspicuously missing are the Lusophone and Arab-speaking countries. Even though the choice of the eight countries in itself is not poor, there is the likelihood of the sample size being seen as non-representative, in spite of efforts made without success by the editors to include the Lusophone and Arab-speaking countries.

Fifth, think tanks as institutions have developed an organizational culture with vision, mission and core values and norms that have withstood the test of time in a highly competitive environment. This culture enables one to understand what they stand for, what they do, and how they do it, and gives them a sense of identity. Despite having an organizational culture, there seems to be no succession plan in place in most of the think tanks, as the founding chief executive officers as owners stay long-term without any intention of handing over the baton of office, or grooming or mentoring staff to take over. This has undermined the growth of some of the think tanks on the continent.

Finally, there is the perception that think tanks are fighting for recognition, being underutilized in Africa by most governments because of the perception that they cannot be trusted, or they are working for someone else or an agent, who might turn out to be the enemy of the government in power. This mistrust between some governments and think tanks will have to be ironed out by both parties if they are to see their respective roles as complementary to governance and development.

IMPLICATIONS OF THE FINDINGS AND LESSONS FROM THE THEORETICAL, COMPARATIVE AND EMPIRICAL PERSPECTIVES

The findings and lessons have reinforced the point that think tanks are here to stay as policy progenitors and entrepreneurs, thereby influencing governance and development in Africa. The AU's think tanks partnership launch in 2023 is a testament to the contribution of think tanks to democratic development and governance. This notwithstanding, there is more room for improvement in the pursuit of their mandates, which will require self-introspection.

At the theoretical level, think tanks as institutions need to develop lasting values, norms and culture which will set them apart and be recognized as such in the pursuit of their mandates. In this connection, think tanks must continue to exhibit their independence and impartiality, and bring out ideas and provide advocacy to promote governance and development. Of course, their independence and impartiality largely depend on their funding robustness, the lack of which has become their bane.

At the comparative level, the liberal context within which think tanks operate is crucial to their effectiveness and survival. The Francophone countries seem to have less liberal legal and institutional frameworks, which have more or less stunted the growth and operations of think tanks. There is therefore the need for legal and institutional framework reforms which will support the operations of think tanks, perhaps not only limited to the Francophone countries, but across the whole of Africa.

At the empirical level, the relevance of think tanks is key in responding to the demands for good governance and sustainable development in the post-COVID-19 period, and the opportunities and challenges of digital technology or AI, usually referred to as the Fourth Industrial Revolution. This can only be done if think tanks are well resourced to leverage the opportunities offered by the Fourth Industrial Revolution in order to deal with the threats and challenges (Puplampu et al., 2023). The post-COVID-19 period also offers an opportunity for think tanks to take stock and restrategize to see how best to contribute more meaningfully to governance and development, especially when most of them had contributed in one way or the other in combating COVID-19.

AN AGENDA FOR FUTURE RESEARCH

The key agenda for future research is to produce a book which will include countries in the four linguistic zones of Africa, namely Anglophone, Francophone, Lusophone and Arabic-speaking countries, with their diversity in terms of politics, history, geography, economy and culture. This is necessary since Africa is not a homogenous continent, as assumed by many, but a diverse one with different histories and trajectories of development (Cooper, 2002; Lwasa, 2019; Young, 2012). In this sense, different cultures exist, and they affect governance and development differently. For example, the Arab Spring in 2010 only occurred in North Africa, and had a tremendous impact on those countries' governance and development, rather than on those in sub-Saharan Africa, although it continues to have enduring effects on other Arab nations outside the continent (Ahmad, 2020; Joseph, 2013). Therefore, looking at such differences can help researchers to move away from the one-size-fits-all approach that has characterized African studies.

Thus, the comparative element in such a book will be an added advantage. The contribution of think tanks to governance and development seems broad, rather than being specific to themes such as policy entrepreneurship, agenda setting, democracy, poverty reduction, service delivery, natural resource management and the Fourth Industrial Revolution, which are supposed to promote governance and development anyway.

We have also seen what has been described as democratic backsliding in Africa, with the recent military takeovers from democratically elected governments in Mali, Niger, Burkina Faso and Gabon, and the fear that this may have a ripple effect on governance and development. The backsliding seems to be occurring in the face of democratically elected governments showing disdain for democratic governance, and changing the institutional frameworks that brought them to power, as well as destroying democratic institutions (Arriola et al., 2022; Gyimah-Boadi, 2015; Lewis, 2019). Even states considered to have consolidated their democracies have backslided (Oduro et al., 2022), thus making a mockery of what President Obama said in his first visit to the continent, that 'Africa needs strong institutions and not strong men' (Baker, 2009).

Future research may look at how think tanks can continue to play more meaningful roles in governance and development, especially how they can be part of the fourth estate to check the various autocratic tendencies of democratically elected elites, to enhance development and promote good enough governance. Many think tanks are also taking up advocacy roles and helping to develop the capacity of local indigenes. Future research can look at this role too in enhancing democratic governance, since economic development and democratic consolidation are seen as bedfellows. This agenda for future research, however, is not to detract from the enormous academic contribution of this book in filling the lacunae on think tanks, governance and development in Africa.

REFERENCES

Åberg, P., S. Einarsson and M. Reuter (2019) 'Think tanks: New organizational actors in a changing Swedish civil society', *Voluntas*, 32(3), 634–648. DOI.org/10.1007/s11266-019-00174-9.

Ahmad, T. (2020) 'The enduring "Arab Spring"', *Indian Foreign Affairs Journal*, 15(2), 91–107.

Arriola, L.R., L. Rakner and N. van de Walle (2022) 'Democratic backsliding in Africa? Autocratization, resilience, and contention', in Leonardo R. Arriola, L. Rakner and N. van de Walle (eds), *Democratic Backsliding in Africa? Autocratization, Resilience, and Contention* (1–36), Oxford: Oxford University Press.

Arshed, N. (2017) 'The origins of policy ideas: The importance of think tanks in the enterprise policy process in the UK', *Journal of Business Research*, 71, 74–83.

Baker, P. (2009) *Obama Delivers Call for Change to a Rapt Africa*. https://www.nytimes.com/2009/07/12/world/africa/12prexy.html.

Collier, D. (1998) 'Comparative historical analysis: Where do we stand?' *APSA-CP. Newsletter of the APSA Organized Section in Comparative Politics*, 9(2), 1–2, 4–5.

Cooper, F. (2002) *Africa Since 1940: The Past and the Present*, Cambridge: Cambridge University Press.

Gyimah-Boadi, E.E. (2015) 'Africa's waning democratic commitment', *Journal of Democracy*, 26(1), 101–113.

Joseph, R. (2013) 'Democracy at bay: The Arab Spring and Sub-Saharan Africa', AFRICAPLUS. https://africaplus.wordpress.com/2013/09/03/democracy-at-bay-the-arab-spring-and-sub-saharan-africa/#more-541.

Lewis, P.M. (2019) 'Aspirations and realities in Africa: Five reflections', *Journal of Democracy*, 30(3): 76–85.

Lwasa, S. (2019) 'Appreciating the heterogeneity in the unity of Africa: A socio-ecological perspective on Africa's geographies', *Canadian Geographer*, 63(4), 594–602.

Oduro, F., L-M. Selvik and K. Dupuy (2022) 'Ghana: A stagnated democratic trajectory', in Leonardo R. Arriola, L. Rakner and N. van de Walle (eds), *Democratic Backsliding in Africa? Autocratization, Resilience, and Contention* (112–136), Oxford: Oxford University Press.

Puplampu, K.P, K.T. Hanson and P. Arthur (eds) (2023) *Sustainable Development, Digitalization, and the Green Economy in Africa Post-COVID-19*, Cham: Springer.

Young, C. (2012) *The Postcolonial State in Africa: Fifty Years of Independence, 1960–2010*, Madison, WI: University of Wisconsin Press.

Index